Praise for
The Truths That Free Us

"I see dozens of women who are walking a straight line to frustration and bitterness. *The Truths That Free Us* really could bring them freedom. Ruth Haley Barton offers a straight line—a narrow but liberating way—to joy in the Spirit."

—DR. LARRY CRABB, author of *Shattered Dreams* and *The Pressure's Off*

"With courageous honesty and depth of insight, Ruth Barton challenges us to think clearly and biblically about how we see ourselves as Christian women. *The Truths That Free Us* calls us to boldly live out God's purposes as we fully embrace the Truth that sets us free."

—LESLIE VERNICK, author of *How to Act Right When Your Spouse Acts Wrong*

"*The Truths That Free Us* is empowering, insightful, liberating, challenging, thought provoking, fearless, balanced, compassionate, practical and revolutionary! Barton dispels myths concerning women in marriage, motherhood, society, sexual matters, and much more. This book gives a voice to what I've always felt but could not express, shining light on dark places and deep longings in my soul."

—DA'DRA CRAWFORD GREATHOUSE,
songwriter and Dove–award winning recording artist with Anointed

"With an honest voice, Ruth Barton helps women move away from small ideas of what we should be, think, and do, and instead embrace the enormity of our calling in Christ. This book is an invitation to drink in the rich truths that free us to live as his disciples in the whole of our life—in marriage, motherhood, friendships, and in service to the church and the world."

—ANDI ASHWORTH, author of *Real Love for Real Life: The Art and Work of Caring*

"This book is a substantive, gut-level, practical, and well-researched piece of writing that deals with real life issues from a vibrantly biblical perspective. To women and men who are confused by the welter of conflicting definitions of their own gender, roles, and sexuality that is currently thrown at them, the author offers excellent, biblically grounded guidance for the development of authentic Christian womanhood. I predict that this work will become a classic textbook for Christians in quest of wholesome, God-honoring, biblically accurate answers to some of the most urgent personal issues of the day."

—DR. GILBERT BILEZIKIAN, professor emeritus of biblical studies,
Wheaton College and author of *Beyond Sex Roles*

"This is a book filled with wisdom, truth-telling, encouragement, and practical help for today's Christian woman struggling with issues of marriage and parenting, identity and work as she seeks to know and follow Jesus. I found it enjoyable reading as well as challenging."

—REV. DR. ROBERTA HESTENES, minister-at-large with World Vision International
and founder of the Hestenes Center for Christian Women in Leadership

"I have often wished that women would tell each other the truth—that we would not stand idly by and watch our sisters scrounge around in the dirt of trial and error searching for answers. I am deeply grateful to Ruth Haley Barton for being brave, honest, and loving enough to share *The Truths That Free Us* with all who seek to know a God who gives us the courage to be our best selves."

—REV. BRENDA SALTER MCNEIL, president of Overflow Ministries, Inc.

THE TRUTHS
that FREE US

THE TRUTHS
that FREE US

A WOMAN'S CALLING *to* SPIRITUAL TRANSFORMATION

RUTH
HALEY BARTON

SHAW BOOKS

an imprint of WATERBROOK PRESS

The Truths That Free Us
A SHAW BOOK
PUBLISHED BY WATERBROOK PRESS
2375 Telstar Drive, Suite 160
Colorado Springs, Colorado 80920
A division of Random House, Inc.

All Scripture quotations, unless otherwise indicated, are taken from the *New Revised Standard Version of the Bible,* copyright © 1989 by the Division of Christian Education of the National Council of the Churches of Christ in the USA. Used by permission. All rights reserved. Scripture quotations marked (NIV) are taken from the *Holy Bible, New International Version®.* NIV®. Copyright © 1973, 1978, 1984 by International Bible Society. Used by permission of Zondervan Publishing House. All rights reserved. Scripture quotations marked (NASB) taken from the *New American Standard Bible®* (NASB). © Copyright The Lockman Foundation 1960, 1962, 1963, 1968, 1971, 1972 1973, 1975, 1977, 1995. Used by permission. (www.Lockman.org). Scripture quotations marked (Phillips) are taken from *The New Testament in Modern English, Revised Edition* © 1972 by J. B. Phillips. Scripture quotations marked (MSG) are taken from *The Message.* Copyright © by Eugene H. Peterson 1993, 1994, 1995. Used by permission of NavPress Publishing Group.

ISBN 0-87788-069-7

Copyright © 2002 by Ruth Haley Barton

This book incorporates content that originally appeared in *Becoming a Woman of Strength,* copyright © 1994, 1999 by Ruth Haley Barton, published by Harold Shaw Publishers.

Printed in the United States of America
2002—First Edition

10 9 8 7 6 5 4 3 2 1

To My Daughters:
Charity Ruth
Bethany Joy
Haley Hope

*It is one of the greatest privileges of my life
to walk in truth and freedom with you.*

CONTENTS

FOREWORD

I am reading the manuscript of *The Truths That Free Us* on a train en route from Dublin to Belfast. I have just visited with a dear Irish friend, a woman preparing—as I am—to enter the decade of her fifties. Last evening, as we sat under a full moon in the garden of a quaint hotel in County Wicklow, we compared notes on the busy, domestic years of our twenties and thirties when our lives revolved around the needs of our children and our husbands. Then we talked about the transitional challenges of our forties, when suddenly it seemed we received the long-desired gift of discretionary time but then had no clue what to do with it. Finally, we shared with each other our dreams of the future, shadowy at this point, but offering us just enough definition to allow us to begin taking active, preparatory steps.

This morning, as I sit here reading Ruth's manuscript, I can't help but think how much my Irish friend and I would have benefited from this book twenty-five years ago when we were young women making choices about our future. And as the train rumbles along, I find myself wishing that I had about two hundred copies of the completed book stashed away in my suitcase. I would love to be able to stack them on the book table at the conference in Belfast where I am scheduled to speak in the coming days. In fact, I would probably be tempted to say, "Hey, don't bother to sit through my talk. Just buy Ruth's book!"

I should not be surprised that this book compellingly reinforces—and pushes to greater depth—the same themes that I seek to embrace more fully in my own life and to communicate to other women. The ongoing friendship and dialogue that Ruth and I have enjoyed in recent years has shown us to be kindred spirits in many ways. We are of one mind, from our shared belief that silence can lead us into the heart of God to our shared conviction that women—strong in the strength God has given us—have the potential to change the world.

The spiritual exercises at the end of each chapter confirm truths that I have found strength in over the years. I have learned that there is great power in personal prayer and reflective journaling. I've also experienced the equal power of prayerful listening and discussion in a small community of women who are earnestly seeking the guidance of God. I'm glad that Ruth leads us into both.

As I was reading this manuscript I circled many paragraphs, scribbled down many quotes, and scattered hundreds of exclamation points in the margins—but I keep going back to one line in particular: "It is time," writes Ruth, " to stand for what you believe and never look back." I spent many years of my adult life plagued by fear and by a litany of falsehoods. In the future I want to stand strongly and firmly on the side of courage, on the side of truth, on the side of goodness, on the side of the revolutionary gospel of Jesus. *The Truths That Free Us* challenges, encourages, motivates, and empowers me toward that end. Thank you, Ruth.

—Lynne Hybels, coauthor (with Bill Hybels) of
Making Life Work and *Fit to Be Tied*

A CALL TO FREEDOM

One can never wrestle enough with God if one does so out of pure regard for truth. Christ likes us to prefer truth to him, because before being Christ, he is truth. If one turns aside from him to go toward the truth, one will not go far before falling into his arms.

—SIMONE WEIL, *Waiting for God*

Early on in my spiritual journey, I wrote and spoke as one who was delighted to have been called to the wonders of spiritual transformation, someone thrilled to have walked a little of that road but still a bit dazed by the rigors of the journey. I recalled a growing awareness of the places in my life where I was in bondage and the questions that such awareness raised for me—questions about what it meant to be a woman, what it meant to be a *Christian* woman, and what it meant to be surprised by a strength and passion within me that didn't seem to fit my existing categories. I remembered the necessity of allowing those questions to lead me beyond dogma to truth. I remembered how, when the initial euphoria wore off and the journey began to take me to unknown places, it all seemed so risky. The only thing that kept me going was my desire for freedom and my growing conviction that we cannot refuse to seek truth and still remain faithful to the God of all truth, to Christ who is Truth personified, and to the Holy Spirit, who was given to lead us in truth—right here, right now.

Today, having had time and space to reflect on the ways in which God

has called and continues to call me into spiritual transformation, I am convinced that the calling to spiritual transformation is a call to freedom—the
freedom to be completely given over to God and to others in love in any
given moment. It is the freedom to live from an inner security that leads us
beyond self-interest, self-consciousness, and self-protection. It is the freedom to live beyond the expectations and limitations placed on us by others. It is the freedom to live *beyond* our vulnerability and woundedness
while at the same time being willing to live *from* our vulnerability and
woundedness in this world. It is the freedom to bring the fullest expression
of our most authentic selves in love to others.

The road to this kind of freedom is paved with truth—the truth about
where we are now, the truth about where we want to go, and the truth
about what it's going to take to walk out of our bondage and into our
freedom. When the children of Israel embarked on their journey into the
freedom of the Promised Land, they first had to experience the truth about
their bondage with a greater level of realism. The Scriptures indicate that
for a period of time when they lived as slaves in Egypt, they were unaware
of the extent of their bondage. They might have even thought that living
under someone else's rule was the only option they had. But eventually they
could not avoid the pain and discomfort of their lack of freedom as their
taskmasters became more harsh and demanding. They needed someone to
help them envision a place where they could live in greater freedom, a place
where they were free to worship and live together according to the truths
of their own relationship with God. While the conditions of their bondage
were familiar and secure, the call to freedom would involve risk and unknown territory. They needed to believe in the possibility of freedom and
to desire it enough to risk walking away from the known into the unknown.
This is the journey for us as well.

The road to freedom always seems to lead us through the wilderness—
that solitary place where the chaos in our souls starts to settle, where it gets

so quiet that we can finally hear the still small voice with remarkable clarity. Here we are invited to lay aside those parts of ourselves that seem so significant to us but really only get in the way of what God wants to do in and through us. I realize now that this book is largely an offering of discoveries claimed in the wilderness as my own chaos settled, as I began to hear God more clearly in answer to my deepest questions, and as I let God strip away those pieces of myself that were not conducive to the life he had for me. And while my journey is intensely personal, it is also true that what is most personal is most universal.

But the call to spiritual transformation involves more than just reading a book. The kind of metamorphosis that Paul writes about in Romans 12:2 involves engaging in spiritual practices that open us to the mystery of the work that only God can do in our lives. It is no coincidence that just as I was beginning to grapple with some of the truths expressed in this book and to move into greater levels of freedom, I was also being guided into new (for me) spiritual practices—solitude and silence, spiritual reading, spiritual direction, and spiritual friendship. Establishing a rhythm of spiritual practices gave God access to the deeper places of my soul. These practices sustained me and continue to sustain me in the wilderness places of my journey and beyond.

I would like to invite you into a rhythm of spiritual practices similar to the rhythm that anchored me during this time of intense learning. I invite you to commit yourself to the disciplines of solitude and silence, spiritual reading, prayer and journaling, and spiritual friendship.

At the end of each chapter you will find spiritual exercises guiding you into these disciplines. I will give an overview of those types of exercises here, a framework for you as you begin reading the chapters. (Note: If you are someone who can't put a book down once you've started it, go ahead and read the book through as an overview. But then make the commitment to go back and read it a second time, but more slowly, engaging in the spiritual practices and allowing God to speak deeply into your life. You will also find questions in appendix C that reflect a more structured approach to reading this book. Those questions can be answered individually or in a group setting, in conjunction with the spiritual exercises or in their place.)

In Solitude

Solitude is the time we set apart to give God our undivided attention. (I write about this more fully in chapter 1.) I invite you to establish a regular time of solitude—a half-hour to one hour would be optimal—and to read *The Truths That Free Us* in the context of your solitude times. Here are some thoughts on how you might do this:

Begin with silence. Before you begin reading the book, spend ten minutes in silence for the purpose of quieting yourself, becoming consciously aware of God's presence with you, and experiencing your own desire and willingness to hear from God in these moments. You might want to repeat the prayer from 1 Samuel 3:9: "Speak, LORD, for your servant is listening."

Spiritual reading. Spiritual reading refers to the nature and intent of our reading—our intent not merely to gain information but our intent to deepen our relationship with God by allowing him to speak to us directly through what we are reading. As you read *The Truths That Free Us,* listen for God's word to you in the moment. Be willing to notice your own inner dynamics in response to what you hear. In spiritual reading it is helpful to pay particular attention to your experiences of *resonance* (those places where you resonate with what is being said through a strong, gut-level sense that something is deeply true and speaks directly to your life) and *resistance* (those places where you disagree, have an uncomfortable emotional reaction, or want to argue or resist the message of the text). You might even want to use two different highlighters as you read—one color to highlight places of resonance and one to highlight places of resistance so that you can go back at the end of your time of reading and reflect on your reactions and response.

You can also allow your reading of *The Truths That Free Us* to guide you into dwelling on pertinent scriptures as another way of receiving God's communication to you. Every chapter contains references to scripture verses and biblical narratives. As God uses different scriptures and stories in your life, live in those for as long as God is speaking to you through them—a day, a week, a month. Spiritual transformation cannot be hurried.

Silence. After reading each chapter, you will be invited to be silent for the purpose of deeper reflection on what you have read. I offer several questions pertaining to the chapter that might be helpful to reflect on as you sit in silence. You may find that one particular question stands out as an item for deeper reflection during those moments. Or at the end of some chapters you may decide that it would be best not to think about a particular question at all but to just sit in silence and allow your mind to become still.

Prayer and journaling. Read slowly enough and in small enough portions that you have time to reflect on what you have read and to write your reflections in a journal or notebook. Use your journal to record feelings, thoughts, and questions raised by the text. Especially note those places where it seemed God was speaking to you and what it is that you would like to say to him in response. Allow your journal to become a record of your prayers.

You will find several questions relevant to the text under this section of the spiritual exercises as well. Again, don't feel that you need to answer every question. Read through the questions in the same way you read the text, looking for moments of resonance or resistance. Listening to your gut-level reactions to the questions may help you discern which ones to focus on. You may find that just one or two questions spark something in you or lead you to something you would like to journal or pray about.

Invitations. At the end of each chapter (or at the end of each day's reading) ask, Is there anything that God seems to be inviting me to do as a result of what I have read today?

How will I respond to this invitation? You will find a brief prayer written in this section of the spiritual exercises. You may want to use that prayer to begin your own time of prayer and response.

Do not feel that every reading has to have a major invitation. Just make it a point to ask, giving God the opportunity to speak to you in that way if he wishes. Sometimes his invitation might be as simple as "Just keep trusting me" or "Just stay with the process. You're doing great."

IN SPIRITUAL FRIENDSHIP

The spiritual journey is not meant to be taken alone. Spiritual friendship is a relationship devoted to paying attention to the invitations of God in our lives and supporting one another in making a faithful response. Spiritual friends also check in with each other about our spiritual practices to see if we are engaging in them in a way that meets our heart's deepest desire for God.

As a part of your answer to God's call to spiritual transformation, identify one or more individuals with whom you can share the experiences of God's activity and initiative in your life, praying for one another and calling for one another to respond with courage as God calls you to deeper levels of transformation. Prayerfully consider who might be willing to share this leg of the journey by reading *Truths* along with you and meeting together regularly to share your experiences of hearing God and responding to him in the midst of your spiritual practices. This can be one other friend or a group of friends committed to one another. Each chapter will include guidance for sharing among spiritual friends.

It is a long-acknowledged truth that teachers teach the lessons they most need to learn and writers write about the very things that they are most in need of understanding. The truths presented here are truths that are at the heart of the freedom that God is leading me and other women into. Even though the process of being freed by the truth is a challenging one, I remain convinced that it is worth the cost—even when the cost seems exorbitant. It is my prayer that you will find here a safe place for opening up more deeply to truth—within yourself, in your relationship with God, and in the human relationships that matter most to you. You shall know the truth, you shall speak the truth, you shall live in the truth, and the truth shall set you free.

—Ruth Haley Barton, 2002

THE FREEDOM TO MAKE
LIFE-GIVING CHOICES

*The freedom question, then, is not whether we can do whatever
we want but whether we can do what we most deeply want.*

—GERALD MAY, *The Awakened Heart*

It used to be that a woman's choices were fairly simple: she went to school, got married, stayed married to the same man—for better or worse—and raised children. Standards of conduct and morality were widely accepted so that we knew what was expected.

This is no longer the case. An article in the *Chicago Tribune Magazine* points out that we have reached a time in our society when "choice, rather than freeing the individual, has become so complex, difficult, and costly that it has become over-choice."[1]

As contemporary women we have been deeply affected by this endless array of choices, and many of us experience at least some ambiguity about it all. Today, "a woman can do anything. She can be traditionally feminine and that's all right; she can work, she can stay at home; she can be any way she wants with a man. But whenever there are the kinds of choices there are today, unless you have some solid base, life can be frightening."[2]

Social scientists point out that "choices do not necessarily make life easier—they often make life more difficult because they produce guilt, self-doubt and stress."[3] Why? Because with increased options comes an increased awareness of the possibility for making mistakes, and this awareness can produce real anxiety. On the other hand, more choices also yield increased opportunities for *good* options—options for spending our time, energy, and resources in ways that are life-giving for us and our world. These new possibilities touch our longing to make a difference and to know that our presence on this planet matters.

These "choice points" include but go far beyond issues such as dating, career, marriage, children, and money. Underlying these glaring concerns are the more subtle choices regarding our values, moral and ethical standards, life calling, and belief systems. We look for role models who have successfully negotiated the twists, turns, and pitfalls of the road, yet we're not sure whose wisdom and insight to trust. Today many "voices" sound so intelligent and reasonable that they can be very persuasive. Celebrities on their second and third marriages are anxious to tell us how to have a happy marriage. We might listen in as sports figures and successful business people share their secrets of success only to find out later that their personal lives are fraught with immorality or addictions. Psychologists and other "experts" give advice on every issue from morality to child raising. Add to these the plethora of friends, family, and religious influences—all of which offer their own ideas about who women ought to be and what they ought to do—and things can become so confusing that it is tempting to give up and take the path of least resistance.

Of course, some of these sources do have valuable advice to offer; however, on some level we realize that even the best advice does not necessarily represent that which is most deeply called for in our own life. We have no cookie-cutter approaches when it comes to living out our own deeply held values and carefully discerned calling. The calling to spiritual transformation often takes us on "the road less traveled"—a road that, in the short run, might not make sense to those around us. To make matters more complicated, young women today have had the chance to observe the previous generation's choices and are finding the results to be decidedly mixed.

THE CHOICES WE FACE

When we are honest with ourselves and with each other it seems that many of us experience similar feelings of ambivalence about the choices we have made. We have witnessed and, in some cases experienced, the power of choice. In the '60s women burned their bras and fought for equal rights. In the '70s and early '80s women experienced the initial euphoria of having the opportunity to get out there and prove what we could do. But as the late '80s wore on into the '90s, the euphoria wore off, and we began to experience a new realism about choices we had made. Reluctantly we began to admit to a new set of questions and concerns. Now in this new millennium we recognize some of the discoveries we've made:

1. *Most of us have learned the hard way that there's no such thing as "Superwoman."* The physical exhaustion that many of us have experienced from managing a home and career has helped us to see our limitations. One woman who is chief financial officer of a Fortune 500 company put it this way: "I used to think I could work and raise a family. I realize now that it's hard just to do my job well."[4]

2. *Many of us have experienced guilt and sadness as a result of our choices.* One woman says, "I've cried on my way to work many times" after her two year old sobs, clings to her, and asks why she has to have a job. Another woman comments, "I have lots of mixed feelings about myself and what I'm doing.... I couldn't really be there for people when they needed me because my career and schooling always had to come first. So while I feel

3

proud of my accomplishments, I don't feel good about myself as a friend."[5]

3. *Our choices have brought a sense of disillusionment.* In her article "The Failure of Feminism," Kay Ebeling observes, "In general, feminism gave men all the financial and personal advantages over women. What's worse, we asked for it. The reality of feminism is a lot of frenzied and overworked women dropping kids off at day-care centers."[6] Another woman, Judith, is disillusioned in another way, "I feel split down the middle. Society is telling me to get a job and make something of my life; my mother is telling me to stay home with my children; my husband is saying he needs me to work so we can pay the bills. I have no freedom to do what is right."[7]

4. *We've realized that choosing one thing means saying no to something else.* An executive vice president of another Fortune 500 company recognizes the price she has paid to get where she has gotten. "I don't take care of the house. I don't cook. I don't market. I don't take my children to the malls and museums. And I don't have close friends. I am frequently too tired to tell my husband about my day...or to play with the children."[8]

Some of us have lived these realities while others have only observed them, but perhaps all of us can relate to comedienne Lily Tomlin's comment, "If I had known what it was like to have it all, I might have settled for less!" It is this sentiment that seems to be causing many women to weigh whether they are willing to pay such a hefty price to "have it all" by someone else's standards.

Peggy Orenstein describes our situation at the beginning of a new century as "a state of flux. Old patterns and expectations have broken down, but new ideas seem fragmentary, unrealistic, and often contradictory.... Beneath [young women's] boundless optimism lies a sneaking suspicion that the rhetoric of choice is in part a con game, disguising impossible dilemmas as matters of personal preference. They see 'choices' threatening to morph into cruel trade-offs."[9]

CHOICE IS A GOD-GIVEN FREEDOM

Contemporary women are not the only ones to be presented with choices that are confusing and fraught with significant consequences. At the very beginning of time, Adam and Eve discovered that God built into his perfect world the opportunity to choose. In Genesis we read, "The LORD God commanded the man, saying, 'From any tree of the garden you may eat freely; but from the tree of the knowledge of good and evil you shall not eat, for in the day that you eat from it you will surely die' " (Genesis 2:16-17, NASB).

Here was an opportunity for the first human beings to exercise their moral and spiritual muscles and choose who they would listen to and follow when faced with another alternative. Although the choice they eventually made was a poor one that carried dire consequences for the human race, the process that Eve went through in making her choice is instructional for us today.

We don't know how Eve was informed of God's instruction regarding the tree of knowledge. It is possible that God himself spoke with Eve about this command, or perhaps Adam relayed the information to her. Whichever the case, Eve had an accurate understanding of God's instruction (Genesis 3:2-3), and the stage was set for the first man and first woman to make their first choice.

Eve's ultimate choice to take specific action and eat from the forbidden tree resulted from a series of smaller and less tangible choices that became the foundation for a decision that had very concrete and far-reaching results. First, she *listened* to the serpent's voice of temptation. Then she

5

chose to *believe* the voice that contradicted God's instruction ("You will not surely die," verse 4, NIV) and that cast doubt on God's intentions toward her ("For God knows that when you eat of it your eyes will be opened," verse 5, NIV). Eve lost touch, at least momentarily, with God's heart of love toward her, which put her in a very vulnerable position indeed.

To Eve's credit, she started out strong by stating clearly and accurately what God had said. But eventually she began to contemplate Satan's questions and to wonder if what he said could be true. Could this be a cruel hoax perpetrated by a God who wanted her to believe that he was good while he was actually withholding what was best? Was she missing out on something wonderful? The more she allowed her doubts to take hold in her heart, the more confused she became. Knowing God's love and the beauty of all that he had created for her, Eve still chose to believe the voice of temptation, even though it contradicted the deeper knowing that came from her intimacy with God. And with that choice, she lost much more than she gained.

Paying Attention to the Questions

I was in my early thirties when my own questions about life choices got loud enough that I knew I needed to start paying attention in a different way. I longed to make choices that would allow me to live in the freedom that was available to me without sacrificing what was most precious. I wanted to live beyond regret, confident that my choices were consistent with my heart's truest desires. I was tired of being sidetracked by others' expectations and agendas; I strained to hear and respond to the One True Voice amidst the plethora of other voices that always seemed to be clamoring for attention.

My longings and questions led me to begin opening my life regularly to a spiritual director. I was noticing that in the midst of the outward busyness of my life—much like what the women quoted above described—an inner chaos was more disconcerting than my hectic external life. Not knowing exactly what I needed but knowing I needed something, I turned to someone who was more well versed in the ways of the soul than I am.

At first I talked about it all: the hectic nature of life with three kids, a husband, and a home to care for, the demands of professional life and graduate school, the issues that kept me stirred up emotionally—everything in my life that seemed so out of control. But eventually this wise woman said, "Ruth, you are like a jar of river water all shaken up. What you need is stillness and silence so that the sediment can settle and the water can become clear."

Well, I couldn't even imagine what it would be like to sit still long enough so that anything could settle. I couldn't conceive of not having an agenda or a prayer list or a study plan. I couldn't imagine being silent and not using words. Even though I could not yet envision what this silence and settling would actually mean, I knew that what my spiritual advisor had said was true. I was all shaken up inside with the swirling sediment of busy-ness and the emotions, thoughts, and inner wrestlings that I had not been able to control by any of the other means I had tried. The image of calm, clear water called to me with the hope of peace and clarity and deeper certainty.

This simple yet powerful metaphor was an invitation to *be still and know*—beyond my addiction to words and to activity. It was a hard invitation to accept because I am a word person. As an author and speaker, my whole life revolves around being able to make sense of things by using words. If something can't be put into words or processed with words or solved with words, what good can it possibly be? But fortunately my spiritual advisor had let me talk just long enough for me to realize that the answer did not lie in more talking. I had to at least be open to the possibility that the answer might come in the silence, and so I decided to try. What sounded like a lovely idea when I was sitting in my spiritual director's office was very difficult for this Type-A personality who had been moving so fast for so long!

For the first year all I did was struggle to simply sit still even for ten minutes, all the while noticing the inner chaos, the resistance, and the distractions that made it so hard to get to that ten-minute mark. However, with my friend's support, I stuck with it, and the most amazing thing began to happen. Amidst the struggling, I began to notice that I was starting to calm down. There was a quiet center that was beginning to be formed in me—a place of stillness within which I could see things more clearly, know God's love on a deep experiential level, and sense his moving in my life. I found that the choices I made from that place of silence—whether they pertained to my spiritual life, my relationships, or my vocation—were somehow truer and more deeply satisfying than anything I had experienced up until that time.

Learning to Listen

I understand now that my friend was encouraging the use of two classic spiritual practices that have been used through the ages by Christians seeking to experience, listen to, and know God more deeply. These practices are often referred to as *solitude* and *silence*.

In solitude, we withdraw from interpersonal interactions and from the noise, busy-ness, and constant stimulation associated with life in our culture. We do this for the purpose of freeing ourselves to give full attention to God for that period of time. Jesus did this regularly during his life here on this earth. A time of solitude preceded his choosing the twelve disciples (see Luke 6:12-13). Silence is closely associated with solitude because it is one way of structuring part of that time when we unplug from the constant external stimulation of life.

There are many ways we can use times of solitude, such as prayer with words, reading Scripture or other spiritual writings, meditation, journaling, and so forth. However, in silence we withdraw not only from the influence of other people but also from our addiction to noise, sounds, and words in order to listen for the still small voice of God himself.

Yet, what we as women need more than anything in the face of such complexity is the capacity *to listen deeply to God* and in that listening to discern what is true and best among all the other voices we hear.

Facing the Chaos

Silence yields powerful results that do not come to us in any other way. When God first started leading me into the quiet, I had to finally face the reality that though I had been walking with God for many years, chaos and unrest was at the core of my being.

In the silence my deepest questions reverberated throughout my soul: Am I really worth anything if I'm not constantly out there proving myself? Why is it so hard for me to stop the frantic pace of my life? What am I really afraid of? These were tough questions for they led me to understand that a lot of my activity—even my ministry activity—had been motivated by a certain amount of performance-oriented drivenness rather than a true sense of calling.

I was often sorely tempted to distract myself by getting up to do laundry, make a phone call, or pursue work projects. But I realized that if I didn't let it get quiet enough on the inside to hear the questions and issues that I had been avoiding, I would never give God the opportunity to minister to me and lead me into a place of quietness and strength from which the very best choices could flow.

All of us experience the sediment of fear, longings, questions, old thought patterns, and even addictions that keep us from seeing and hearing with clarity. The practice of silence gives us the opportunity to face our deepest fears and questions, with the express purpose of opening these up to God so he can meet us and lead us into healing. As one writer observes,

> Solitude eventually offers a quiet gift of grace, a gift that comes
> whenever we are able to face ourselves honestly: the gift of compassion

for who we are, as we are. As we allow ourselves to be known in
solitude, we discover that we are known by love. Beyond the pain of
self-discovery there is a love that does not condemn but calls us to
itself. This love receives us as we are.[10]

Silence also gives us the chance to habitually release our own agendas and our need to control everything—including God, if we're honest.
When we let go, we can open up to what he wants to give. One of the
greatest gifts that comes to us in the silence is that we come to understand that we are loved beyond anything we could ever *do* for God or for
anyone else. As we begin to grasp the reality of God's loving presence in
moments of silence, we begin to live and to choose from a centered
place, a bedrock of settledness that is worth any price we have to pay to
find it.[11]

Hearing the True Voice

The Scriptures show us that the True Voice does not usually scream or
loudly assert itself. In fact, we see just the opposite from the prophet Eli-
jah's encounter with God in the wilderness:

> There was a great wind…but the LORD was not in the wind; and
> after the wind an earthquake, but the LORD was not in the earth-
> quake; and after the earthquake a fire, but the LORD was not in the
> fire; and after the fire a sound of sheer silence. When Elijah heard it,
> he…went out and stood at the entrance of the cave. Then there
> came a voice to him. (1 Kings 19:11-13)

Our willingness to listen in silence opens up a quiet space in which we
can hear the Voice that longs to speak and offer us guidance amidst the

complexity of our lives. We can also begin to notice the major influences on our lives by asking ourselves the following questions:

- How much time do I spend allowing myself to be influenced by television and movies, music and reading material that does not support the spiritual desires of my heart?

- How much time do I spend listening for God's voice, reading and reflecting on his Word, and responding to him in prayer? Am I at a point in my relationship with him where I can recognize his truth and his voice?

- Do I spend time with people who are influencing me to seek those things that are consistent with God's purposes for my life? What is the direction or outcome of their lives, and is that what I want for myself?

- Whose advice do I solicit and take most seriously as I make my choices? Do I go to someone who will automatically agree with me or someone who will help me listen to God?

This kind of honest questioning enables us to be more intentional about what we will allow to influence us and what we will choose to dismiss as inconsistent with God's voice.

Free to Live from Our Deepest Values

There is no way to successfully negotiate the decision-making process without a clear idea of what we want to accomplish with our lives and what matters most to us. A well-defined value system can help us be aware of what is most important to us in any given situation and then choose to live out of that awareness.

For example, several years ago during an intense season of writing, I walked away from the computer one morning for just a moment. My youngest daughter, then two years old, spied the lovely red on-off switch and decided to push it. My heart sank as I realized that I had probably lost all of my work on the book that was in progress. So, how did my value system help me in choosing my response?

After my initial yelp (which was enough to scare her anyway), I remembered that in my saner moments I had decided that people are more important than things—even my writing. (If you know anything about writers, you know that's saying a lot!) So I was able to wrap my arms around my daughter and say, "Haley, I'm sorry for scaring you. You are much more important to me than my book. But you are never supposed to touch that button without asking Mommy first. Understand?" Believe me, I am not always that controlled; I do my share of "loud talking." But the process of clarifying and verbalizing my values has given me the opportunity to make choices that are consistent with those values.

Similarly, a sense of purpose can help us make powerful choices to use our lives for God rather than wandering aimlessly through life, allowing people and circumstances to pull us this way and that. As a young mother I served as director of women's ministry at a young and thriving church, a position that combined several of my deepest ministry passions and for which my spiritual gifts seemed particularly well suited. For a year I poured my heart into building this ministry from scratch and loved every minute of it. The only problem was, I had a newborn baby, a five year old, a seven year old, and a husband, who were all wishing I would pour more of my heart into them.

Toward the end of that first year I began to realize some things. Though I often *said* that I believed my responsibility to my family was one of God's significant purposes for me, I wasn't doing a very good job of making choices that were consistent with that purpose. I also faced the realities of my humanness and had to admit that I couldn't squeeze any more energy out of this body. There was no more time, no more emotional stamina, no more of *me* to go around. No matter how much I wanted to be able to do it all and do it right now, I was limited—like everyone else— by twenty-four-hour days and a very finite body and mind.

So I cried and raged and tried to finagle things. But I knew it was time to say, "Not now, maybe later" to work and ministry that required too much of me during that particular season of my life. That choice resulted in a reconfiguring of my life around freelance writing and speaking in a way that made it possible for me to evaluate each opportunity in light of my family responsibilities.

In the years since then, I have adjusted and reworked my commitments to my own spiritual development, family, and vocation in several different ways, learning more and more how to be responsive to the truest needs and invitations of that particular time and season. Although as a family we still sometimes wrestle with scheduling and priorities, we have worked more consciously toward a configuration in our family life that supports the calling of each one of us. We've learned not to assume that it is always Mom who needs to make the sacrifices for the family, but I have also grown in my willingness to accept the fact that there are times when only a mother will do—and preferably a mother who has physical, emotional, and spiritual energy to bring to the situation. It has been good for our daughters to understand and observe their mother as a woman who not only is committed to them but, at the same time, is also called to contribute in the larger community of faith and the world. I am glad that they have seen several models of what's possible for them as women, should they also be called to combine motherhood with other life callings.

WHEN YOUR OPTIONS SEEM LIMITED

Even as we talk about all the options women have today, many times we feel that our own personal choices are limited. In fact, at times in all of our lives we feel downright stuck. We don't have all the choices we would like to have, such as choices about income level, how we are treated by our husbands, educational opportunities, the size of our home, our looks or body shape, whether or not we have children. Mothers of young children go through periods when the most basic choices—when to eat, sleep, or go to the bathroom—are determined by someone else's schedule and needs! Single women who may long to be at home raising children find themselves climbing a corporate ladder they would rather leave behind.

Most of us must deal at some point with situations that narrow our range of options, such as a dead-end job, a difficult marriage, demanding toddlers, or singleness. We cannot always choose our circumstances, but *we can always choose our response to our circumstances.* Even when it seems as if some of our most basic choices are being made for us, we can choose to obey God in our attitudes and actions. These inner choices are perhaps the most powerful choices we will ever make, and no one can take that power away. And over a lifetime, these choices speak eloquently about who we are and what the outcome of our life will be.

Learning to make choices according to our values and our sense of purpose is never simple. It is part of the lifelong process of growing up and maturing as a person. It takes time to search out our own values and purpose, and then learn to use them as a springboard from which to make our choices. But the more we make these intentional choices, the more natural it becomes and the more we are freed from uncertainty and guilt.

SPIRITUAL EXERCISES

Each chapter will conclude with several spiritual exercises. If you have not already done so, you may want to turn to the preface of the book for some background on these sections.

Alone with God

Silence. As you come to the end of this chapter, take a few moments to sit with God in the silence of your own heart. In the silence, reflect on these questions. Don't feel like you have to do anything. Just sit with the questions and with whatever comes.

- In what area of your life right now are you facing a choice point?
- In what way do you sense the need to be able to distinguish the One True Voice from all the other voices that clamor for your attention?
- What is your deepest question relative to this area of your life? What is your deepest desire?

Prayer and journaling. Review the chapter that you have just read, noticing the places of resonance and resistance that you highlighted. In your journal, tell God about your thoughts, feelings, and questions, and then listen for his response.

- Where do the emotions and concerns expressed by other women mirror your own?
- Where did you find yourself saying "That's exactly how I feel!"? (resonance)
- Where did you sense your own longing and frustration (resistance)?
- What does God seem to be saying to you in the midst of your questions and desires regarding the choice that you're facing?

Invitations. *God, what are you saying to me through this reading? Are you inviting me to respond in some way?*

With Your Spiritual Friend(s)

Begin your time together with a moment of silence and a simple prayer of invitation for God to join you. Remember that your time together in spiritual friendship is not meant for problem solving, advice giving, or catching up on the details of life. This is a time to pay attention to the invitations of God in each other's lives and to support one another through listening and loving as you pray that God would enable each of you to respond faithfully to the calling to spiritual transformation.

Listening. Take turns giving each other your undivided attention. Share with each other a brief summary of what has happened between you and God this week in the context of your spiritual practices and your reading of this chapter.

- What did God say to you in your times of solitude and silence?
- What were your experiences of resonance and resistance as you read this chapter? How did you process those with God in your journal?
- What is the choice point that you are facing in your life right now?
- Was there anything in your reading and reflection that seemed to offer guidance for you?
- Does God seem to be inviting you to do anything as a result of where you have been with him this week?

Prayer. At the end of your time together, ask "How would you like me to pray for you?" and then take time to pray for one another. It is much easier to talk about prayer than to actually do it, so try to be disciplined about including prayer as a part of your spiritual companionship.

TWO

THE FREEDOM OF FINDING
OUR IDENTITY IN CHRIST

*Woman must come of age by herself—she must find her true center
alone.*

—ANNE MORROW LINDBERG, *Gift from the Sea*

When I was in my late twenties, both of my grandfathers died within a few
months of each other, each leaving behind a wife of more than fifty years.
As a young wife and mother, I watched my grandmothers approach the
caskets to gaze at their husbands' beloved bodies one last time. There was
something oddly comforting about having those bodies present with us in
the room for a little while longer, for they had housed precious souls,
enabling them to be touched and known and loved in this life. Just before
the casket was closed in that final parting of the ways, my Grandma Haley
turned to my dad, her eldest son, and asked the poignant question, "How
do you say good-bye?"

That is a good question, isn't it? As I watched my grandmothers struggling to say good-bye, I faced a reality that I had not yet been willing to
face: the reality of our ultimate separateness from one another as human
beings in this life, even those human beings that we love the most. In that
moment the truth struck me: In one sense *we are all single!* Married or not,

we all stand alone before God, accountable to him and to him alone for the expenditure of our life and love and spiritual service. Even those of us who do get married at some point in our lives are single before marriage, after marriage, or between marriages. And if the statistics hold true (on average, women live fifteen years longer than men do), most of us will find ourselves approaching the casket one day, struggling to say our own good-byes.

These moments at my grandfathers' funerals were not moments of morbid fatalism; rather, they were moments of clarity about the beauty and the limits of human relationship. No matter how greatly we have loved or how deeply we have committed ourselves, partings of the way will come— sometimes due to death but at other times due to change, human frailty, or betrayal. If our ability to survive in this world or if our sense of identity, self-worth, purpose, and value are derived from the person whose body is in the casket or from the person who could walk out the door or who is limited in terms of what they can give, then the limits of human relationships seem all the more devastating.

Against this backdrop of life and death, change and humanness, Jesus' offer to be the primary and permanent source that fills our deepest needs becomes all the more precious. He offers to be the one who brings love and meaning to our lives as we walk the road from our most open-hearted hellos to our most difficult good-byes with everything that comes in between. The reality of our "singleness" points us to a deeper truth: *None of us—regardless of our marital status—can afford to invest our human relationships and endeavors with the meaning that only a relationship with God can provide.*

As a young woman, Anne Morrow Lindberg captured this learning in her own words when she said, "I want first of all to be at peace with myself. I want a singleness of eye, a purity of intention, a central core to my life to help me carry out these activities and obligations as well as I can. I want, in fact, to live 'in grace' as much of the time as possible. By grace I mean an inner harmony, essentially spiritual, which can be translated into outward harmony. I would like to achieve a state of inner spiritual grace from which I could function and give as I was meant to in the eyes of God."[1]

As a result of her husband's death in 1975, Anne faced in a fresh way what she called "woman's recurring lesson…'woman must come of age by herself—she must find her true center alone.' The lesson seems to need relearning about every twenty years in a woman's life."[2]

So how is it that we as women—married or single—can find all we need in Christ so that our human relationships as God gives them are sources of joy in our lives but do not become *the* source of all that our hearts need? How do we live in the grace of an inner harmony that comes from God throughout all of the vicissitudes of life and relationship? How do we learn to receive from God what only God can ultimately give?

LOOKING FOR LOVE IN ALL THE RIGHT PLACES

The truth is that women, for a variety of reasons and in a variety of ways, tend to look for love and a sense of self in many of the wrong places. Some of this has to do with fallen human nature, some with the ways in which women are socialized in our culture, and some with our own psychological response to these experiences. Our willingness to see these tendencies for what they are gives us the opportunity to move beyond them to the place where our relationship with Christ becomes the bedrock of our self-esteem.

Learning to find all we need in Christ begins with understanding how much he loves and values us. For some of us this is easier said than done. A report by the American Psychological Association revealed that for one in every four women, the experience of being female in contemporary culture is cause for severe depression.[3]

> Studies of women have repeatedly shown disturbing patterns: lack
> of self-esteem, an inability to feel powerful or in control of one's life,

a vulnerability to depression, a tendency to see oneself as less talented, less able than one really is. The myriad of studies that have been done over the years give the distinct impression of constriction, a crippling, a sense of being somehow not quite as good, not quite as able, not quite as bright, not quite as valuable as men…. Certainly there are many women who have escaped this blight, who have lived full and happy lives, but when you leaf through the studies you can sense, floating in the air, ghosts of unborn dreams, unrealized hopes, undiscovered talents. The tragedies are the "might have beens," and they are the most poignant.[4]

While it is true that women and men alike share basic human needs for identity and self-worth, there is much evidence that for women these commodities, which are so crucial to living a full and functional life, can be very hard to come by. Unless a woman has been extraordinarily sheltered, her experiences in the family, the church, educational institutions, the business world, government, the medical profession, even the general public, systematically rob her of the essentials of self-esteem.

Once a girl develops an understanding of language, it is definitely communicated to her that she is less significant than boys. A girl may have learned this simply by the absence of strong, autonomous, competent female figures in the male-dominated culture that she gradually discovers during her unfolding childhood. Within her family she may have learned she was insignificant by the way her family listened more attentively during dinner conversation to males than females, or the way her brothers were encouraged to take their ideas and career plans seriously while girls were told it didn't really matter what they did.[5]

Consider some other common female experiences:

- A woman applies for admission to a Ph.D. program in computer science at a major university. Her qualifications (such as Graduate Record Exam score and GPA) are far superior to those of the two men who applied at the same time. But they are admitted and she is not. The professors tell her they do not want to waste their time on a woman because she is likely to "get married and have children." (This really did happen—in 1992!)

- A single woman who is vice president in charge of finance and accounting in her professional life finds that instead of being included in a broad range of social and ministry opportunities in her church, she is relegated to "singles activities" reminiscent of the high-school youth group. Meanwhile, her male counterparts are recruited for all manner of teaching and leadership roles. She wonders if she will ever be viewed as a full-fledged adult this side of marriage.

- A young mother spends all of her waking hours knee-deep in diapers and dishes, wondering if she has any capacity left for intelligent thinking or adult conversation. On occasion she does accompany her husband to a business function, where her worst fears are confirmed. Once her husband's associates find out she is an at-home mom, they lose interest and focus almost exclusively on her husband.

- Many women attend church year after year and never hear significant teaching or messages given by other women. More than a few begin to wonder, "Don't women have anything to say that would be valuable to the congregation?"

- A woman works for her company for twelve years in a secretarial-type position that pays $18,000 a year. Despite her repeated requests to move into a sales position that would pay considerably more, her boss (who makes $150,000 a year) tells her, "No, we need you where you are now."

- A woman who has been thin all her life finds that she cannot lose the weight she gained during pregnancy. She avoids mirrors most of the time but when she does happen to see herself, she can't help comparing herself unfavorably with images of the perfect women she sees in magazines and on television. To make matters worse, her husband often comments about the attractiveness of the women he sees and muses out loud, "I wonder how she keeps herself in such good shape?"

- A woman who has chosen to stay at home to raise her children rather than working outside the home finds that she cannot get a credit card, apply for a mortgage, or buy a car without her husband's signature. When her husband dies she realizes how dependent and vulnerable she has become.

- Over the years, a woman puts her husband through graduate school, works beside him to start his own business, manages the home and raises the children, accompanies him to business functions and gives numerous dinner parties. She looks forward to a time in the future when she and her husband can spend time relaxing, traveling together, and enjoying the fruit of their labors. Instead, just as the youngest child is preparing to leave for college, her husband leaves her for a younger woman. Rather than enjoying some long-awaited companionship in her middle years, she finds herself shattered and alone.

- A forty-three-year-old single woman sees single men her age celebrated as "eligible bachelors" while she is considered an "old maid."

These are *not* isolated incidents. Each one is a real-life experience relived over and over again by real women. In other countries the situation for women is even worse. A 1994 cover article in *U.S. News and World Report* titled "The War Against Women" documents how women are being used and abused in country after country around the world. The author boldly states that according to the 1993 United Nations Human Development Report, "there is still no country that treats its women as well as its men."[6] She then validates her statement with painful descriptions of the hiring and firing of women on the basis of their sex appeal, the aborting and poisoning of girl babies, genital mutilation of young girls, the punishment of rape *victims,* domestic "accidents" and murders that take place when a young wife doesn't please her husband, and across-the-board discrimination regarding jobs and compensation.[7]

FACING OUR OLDEST ENEMY

How are we to interpret the meaning of these realities? What is the impact on a woman's self-esteem when she takes an honest look at these facts?

For starters, we can begin to understand that the problem women have with knowing who we are and what we are worth is rooted in systems much older and larger than ourselves. Beliefs about ourselves have been shaped by ideas, principles, rules, and procedures that have governed the world in which we live. Significant—and seemingly insignificant—events whisper to us day in and day out, "See, you are not quite as good as... You don't matter quite as much." We are not untouched by the demeaning experiences of women struggling for the essentials of self-esteem and worth here and in other countries. The pain of being "put down" and having to fight for basic human rights as a population group is a part of our "collective consciousness" as women. We may find that we are shocked by articles such as the one from *U.S. News and World Report,* but the fact is, we are so used to being seen and treated as "less than" that many times we hardly distinguish the discrimination from other hard realities in life.

Whether the abuse and disrespect of women is overt or more subtle, the universality of the female experience of being "less than" is astounding. As I have delved more deeply into the experiences of women across barriers of race and time, I have become convinced that women's extraordinary struggle for dignity, equality, and worth is not only systemic in nature but *is a direct result of the enmity that came between Satan and the woman in the Garden of Eden so long ago* (Genesis 3:15). Ever since that day, women have been particular targets of Satan for all manner of discrimination, abuse, and inhumane treatment, from Bible times to the present. The introduction of shame, blame, and domination into human relationships as a result of sin became a perfect tool of Satan to destroy the human family by causing one grouping of people to set themselves up as better than another grouping—men over women, one ethnic group over another, one religious group over another.

The fight to gain equality and a sense of worth is not a new struggle for women born out of the feminist movement or some "liberal" theology. It is a battle that has been raging throughout human history. When we seek to restore to women (or anyone else who has been discriminated against) the dignity and equality that God intended when he created us, we are, in a very real sense, engaged in battle against Satan himself, who is still active in human affairs. We echo Old and New Testament prophets alike when we recognize and denounce the invisible systems that govern our world. "Our struggle is not against enemies of blood and flesh, but against the rulers, against the authorities, against the cosmic powers of this present darkness, against the spiritual forces of evil in the heavenly places" (Ephesians 6:12).

THE HIGH COST OF LOW SELF-ESTEEM

Addressing the subject of self-esteem, authors Sanford and Donovan write, "Our level of self-esteem affects virtually everything we think, say and do.... If a woman has an insufficient amount of self-esteem, she will not be able to act in her own best interest. And if a woman has no self-esteem at all, she will eventually become overwhelmed, immobile and eventually will give up."[8]

Kari, a woman who grew up as a missionary kid in China, knows the ramifications of low self-esteem in her own life. When Kari moved to the United States from China, she made herself sick trying to fit in with popular Western ideas about what a woman could and should be. Although Kari had a strong and effective witness to students on the secular college campus where she was teaching, some of her associates in the Christian organization with which she was affiliated thought she should give up her teaching post when it came time for her to get married. Not wishing to be divisive, Kari did just that. But her heartbreak at having left her teaching post and the deep friendships she had with her students caused tension during the early years of her marriage.

> I was beginning to listen to the common teaching that a woman's chief role is to be a support to her husband in his ministry, be a homemaker and raise children to follow the Lord. I was a woman at war with myself. While I tried to agree with my conscious mind to a view that limited a woman's contribution to the kingdom, my subconscious revolted within me....
>
> Overcome with grief over the ministry I had left and trying to fit into the role of a submissive homemaker, I felt myself losing my identity. Who was I? For the first time in my life, I developed the "I'm just a woman" syndrome. When I could no longer look at myself as a precious disciple and disciplemaker, a friend of Jesus Christ, I became sick. Many months were spent in bed with an undiagnosed fever. After the fever subsided, I went into a deep depression. Guilt feelings about having left my first love (Christ) swept over me—some from God and some based on false regret.[9]

Many women today do not move through life with the strength that comes from a sense of well-being, purpose, and competence. Several key truths are important to recognizing and healing our wounded self-esteem.

Know How Much You Are Worth

Jesus' conversation with the woman of Samaria in John 4 demonstrates that all of the elements of personhood that make for wholeness and abundant life are things that Christ brings to the sisters as well as the brothers in the family of God. First of all, he wants us to know how much we are worth. In the words of psychologist Larry Crabb, "each of us fervently wishes for someone to see us exactly as we are, warts and all, and still accept us. The thought that someone can remain warmly committed to us even with all our faults exposed is utterly inconceivable—yet we long for that experience."[10]

As we have already described, female children face a greater risk than male children of growing up with uncertainty and mixed messages about their worth. The Samaritan woman of John 4—we'll call her Samara since her name is not given—had additional reasons to believe that she wasn't worth much, that no one could possibly love her. Not only was she of the lesser sex, she was also of a lesser race,[11] and she was a woman known for her blatant immorality. She had had five husbands, and at the time she met Christ, she was living with a man to whom she was not married.

It is not hard to imagine the disillusionment that Samara must have carried with her as she came to Jacob's well on the day when her path crossed that of Christ himself. She must have experienced a range and intensity of emotion: anger, sadness, and disillusionment, feelings of being used and misunderstood. The fact that she chose to draw water in the heat of the day rather than in the cool of the morning suggests that she was so depressed and ostracized that she avoided contact with those who might demean her. She was aware of how people viewed her, so much so that she expressed surprise that Jesus would even initiate conversation with her: "How is it that you, a Jew, ask a drink of me, a woman of Samaria?" (John 4:9).

But Christ demonstrated that there was no damaging favoritism with him. Just by beginning an intelligent conversation with her and treating her as an equal, Jesus communicated her significance. Most men would not have been willing to risk their reputation by being found in conversation with a woman such as this (in Jewish custom it was considered inappropriate for a man to talk with his own wife in public, let alone a "loose" woman). Christ, with a surprising lack of concern about appearances, chose to walk right into Samaria that day and initiate a conversation with a woman who was "less than" in every way that mattered to the people of that day.

Even so, Christ did not treat Samara as though she were beneath him or as someone who needed to be pulled out of the sewer and saved. Instead, he treated her as someone he could talk to on an equal level. In the course of the conversation Jesus affirmed her intelligence and ability to understand spiritual truth by discussing theology with her. He revealed new truth that was (as far as we can tell), unknown to anyone else—including the disciples![12] When the disciples came to offer him lunch, he made it clear that talking with Samara was the most important thing he could be doing at the moment. The value that Christ placed on Samara was unaffected by the fact that he knew her deepest, darkest secrets. What an amazing first this must have been for her, and how life-changing it was!

Know Who You Are as an Individual and as Part of a Community

Another key to a woman's self-esteem is knowledge of herself as an individual who is unique and separate from others, balanced by a sense of how she fits into her community. Many women lack self-esteem precisely because they know so little about themselves. In their research on self-esteem, Sanford and Donovan discovered that there are real reasons that women have so little sense of themselves as fully developed individuals in the midst of a larger whole.

> Women have historically been denied the opportunities for self-discovery that many men take for granted. As a result, many women we interviewed had great difficulty describing themselves at all. "Shot full of holes," "full of gaps," "blank—not much self there," are just some of the phrases these women used to describe themselves. A woman who sees herself as a blank has virtually no chance of experiencing self-esteem.[13]

Many women move through life doing so much to please other people that they are out of touch with their own desires or needs. A married woman may feel that her purpose in life is only to support her husband in the purposes of his life or to help her children find their niche—rather than finding one of her own. She may be lulled into a false sense of security because she has a man to take care of her, naively believing that she has no need of any other skills besides those associated with housekeeping and children. Or a woman may be accustomed to accepting the values of her parents or pastor without ever asking her own hard questions and searching out God's answers for herself.

This sense of "blankness," of lost identity, perhaps is seen most clearly when we let ourselves be defined by whether or not we have a man. For instance, a single woman may feel she can't have a full identity without a husband, so she waits to pursue her interests and develop her gifts until she is married and "real life" begins. Samara is a striking example of this; it is safe to say that she had very little sense of herself apart from her continued attempts to find the right man.

In one provocative book titled *Why Do I Think I Am Nothing Without a Man?* the author makes this statement:

Women, for all their gains in the working world, still tend to get their refuge, self-esteem and pride more from the home, the family, the man they landed. Thinking you are nothing without a man is a problem women share regardless of marital status—and also regardless of age, nationality, income, upbringing, professional standing, religion, personal appearance. You don't have to live alone to think you are nothing without a man. You don't have to be divorced, widowed or never married. You can be living with a man or married and think that without this man you would be lonely, socially inhibited, emotionally and sexually barren.[14]

My experiences of working with girls and women in many different settings corroborate the truth of these words. I have known women who have dropped out of school to follow a man around, women who have rushed into marriage with the wrong man just so they wouldn't be alone, women who have given in to sexual pressure out of fear of losing a man, women who are so tied to the home and to their man's schedule that they are not even free to go out for lunch with a friend, women who live their lives so completely for their man that they wouldn't consider inconveniencing him by taking a class or a part-time job that would keep them challenged and growing.

I have known women who spend a lifetime adapting to their husband's life and calling—enduring financial hardship so he can go to school, holding down the fort at home while he travels, managing the household while he spends long hours working, studying, or ministering, being tolerant of the stress all of this places on a marriage and family—never thinking of asking for the same opportunities for themselves. Somehow they feel that the privilege of having that kind of support in life goes with being male, not female.

How has this happened? Why do we think we are worth so little that we allow our identities to be overshadowed by others? Mary Stewart Van Leeuwen draws our attention to God's warning in Genesis 3:16 that men and women, in their own unique ways, would have a tendency to misuse the dominion and "one-fleshness" that was built into humanity at creation. Just as men have a tendency to twist responsible dominion into wrongful domination, the peculiarly female sin is to preserve relationships at all costs—even if the cost is her own lack of responsible action in the world.

> The woman's temptation is to avoid taking risks that might upset relationships. It is the temptation to let creational sociability become fallen "social enmeshment." [Thus] one of the main problems of today's counseling psychologists is accounting for women's constant tendency to avoid developing personal self-sufficiency for the sake of preserving even pathological relationships with the opposite sex.[15]

Yes, men and women were created to be together and flourish in loving relationships. However, even though we may be looking forward to or are presently enjoying a relationship with a man, *we cannot let our love and desire for a man overshadow our love and commitment to serving God as fully developed human beings.* If I live my life for my husband and adapt to him in such a way that I do not live for God my Creator and Jesus my Savior and Lord, I am committing the sin of idolatry—I am putting something else as a higher priority than God.

We also have misdirected priorities when we allow others to define us rather than finding our identity in Christ. We often identify ourselves by our career, sex appeal, or the roles we play (such as "mom," or "the single daughter"). All of these forms of identity have been society's way, at one time or another, of defining us as women. The problem is that *these aspects of life are changeable and temporary.* Any woman who has lost a job, who has gone through the aging process, or whose marital status has changed would attest to that. As important as these parts of life are at different times, they are inadequate as a way of defining ourselves.

The sure foundation of self-esteem is knowing that before, during, and after life with a husband, children, career, or even a youthful and physically able body, we are created to reflect God's character, to love him and have honest, intimate communication with him. God's purposes for our lives include our roles as wives, daughters, mothers, and career women, but go beyond those identities as well. Our identity is rooted in God's unconditional love for us. He has given us gifts and resources to make a unique contribution to our world for his glory. We work in partnership with him as we receive with a grateful heart the gifts he has given us, develop them, and use them to contribute positively to this world. We honor him as we become all he created us to be, reaching out in love and service to our physical families, our spiritual families and communities, and the larger human family to which we belong.

When Samara met Christ he made it clear that it was not her relationship with a man that defined her. He encouraged a realistic assessment of herself when he gave her the opportunity to face her sin and her failure to relate in a healthy fashion with men (John 4:16-17). But Christ was quick to point out the true source of her identity: "It's who you are and the way you live that count before God. Your worship must engage your spirit in the pursuit of truth. That's the kind of people the Father is out looking for: those who are simply and honestly *themselves* before him in their worship" (John 4:23, MSG).

No longer would Samara be defined by gender, race, marital status, or desirability to men. Once she placed her faith in Jesus, realizing that he was the Messiah for whom she had been waiting (John 4:29), she received a spiritual identity that transcended all other roles and relationships. She, along with all of us who have put our faith in Christ, "are the ones chosen by God, chosen for the high calling of priestly work, chosen to be a holy people, God's instruments to do his work and speak out for him, to tell others of the night-and-day difference he made for you—from nothing to something, from rejected to accepted" (1 Peter 2:9-10, MSG).

These and many other scriptures define Christian women and men first and foremost in terms of their priestly function. We dare not lay down our true identity for any human being or system that would seek to define us as anything less than full-fledged priests and disciples. If we do, we will be very empty indeed. The challenge for women today is to take responsibility for the adult task of defining ourselves, not in relation to gender roles, careers, or sex appeal but in relation to the identity, worth, purpose, and enabling that come from God himself. (For further discussion of this subject, see chapter 4.)

Understand God's Purposes for Your Life

In relating with Samara, Christ provided her with yet another essential of self-esteem: the opportunity to live purposefully and have an impact. When the disciples returned from town with lunch, "they were astonished that [Jesus] was speaking with a woman" (John 4:27). Rather than expressing their shock out loud, they stood there gaping until Samara hurried away—probably, in part, to escape their curious stares. Knowing their thoughts, Jesus began to point out that they were sitting right in the middle of a community that was ripe for responding to the message of the true Messiah. Indeed, while they were sitting there talking about the possibilities, Samara was already out there getting the job done. With great urgency she left her water pot and went back to the city to tell everyone she knew, "Come and see a man who told me everything I have ever done! He cannot be the Messiah, can he?" (John 4:29).

And the people came! Because of Samara's witness, many of the Samaritans in that place believed in Christ. They asked him to stay a little longer, so Jesus stayed two more days, giving many more people a chance to hear him speak and to entrust their lives to him. By the time he left they were able to say to Samara, "It is no longer because of what you said that we believe, for we have heard for ourselves, and we know that this is truly the Savior of the world" (John 4:42). She had instigated a major evangelistic campaign because she had been called and enabled by God himself.

This part of Samara's story is thrilling because it answers our own deep longings to accomplish something meaningful and lasting with our lives. "We have been made with a capacity to move purposefully in a direction, to join God in his purposes. We are far more than senseless parts of a pre-ordered system that fatalistically moves us along. Therefore, in our inner-most being, we thirst to be a part of the eternal plan, to make a lasting difference in our world. *We long for impact.*"[16]

Christ knew that Samara needed more meaning for her life than "women's work" and chasing after men. And so that is what he brought her. He didn't wait for Samara to work out the right marital status, to be discipled, to join a church, or to get an education. He walked into Samaria that day and chose a woman right where she was in life to bring a whole community to himself. How refreshing!

Samara's story has motivated me over the years to open myself to the possibilities of purposeful living—even those purposes that, to others, seem inappropriate or out of the ordinary. (The process of learning to live according to God's purposes is so rewarding, so meaningful, and so crucial that I have devoted the next chapter to discussing its practical implications.)

Develop Skills for Functioning in the Real World

Closely connected with the need to know that our lives have purpose is the concept of competence—having the skills necessary to survive, thrive, and accomplish God's purposes. The need for competence presents another very real challenge for women in our society.

Women have been encouraged to become competent in very limited activities centering around home and family, putting women in what might be called a no-win situation. She has become competent in a skill that is socially devalued. (The idea that any idiot can stay home and raise kids is patently untrue, but it comes close to what our achievement-oriented society really believes about being a wife and mother.) She is being programmed for planned obsolescence. By the time a woman is forty, her child-rearing skills will be of little use, her children will be grown, and she still has nearly forty years or so to live.[17]

This is not to say that women should abandon competency in areas of home and family. Men and women alike need to take seriously the responsibility of developing skills and competencies pertaining to maintaining a home. However, women in our society have not always been encouraged to achieve outside the home or to be independent. This is another detriment to healthy self-esteem. All women need to develop the confidence that comes from knowing that their skills are valuable in society and that they have the ability and know-how to provide the sole care for themselves and their children, should they be called upon to do so.

Often a woman becomes aware of gaps in her self-esteem and personal identity around the time she begins thinking about what she is going to do once her children are in school, off at college, or married. At this time in a family's life, more income may be needed because of college bills, weddings, and other expenses, so it is decided that the woman will go back to work. (The need to be able to generate income comes even sooner for a woman whose circumstances change due to divorce, her husband's death, or her husband's unemployment—eventualities to which none of us are immune.) If a woman has not finished her education or has let her credentials and marketable experience lapse, she may find that her options are limited to low-paying jobs outside her fields of interest and abilities. Thus, she lacks the sense of self-worth that comes from spending her best energies in work that is meaningful and challenging. In many cases, she faces this situation while her husband is enjoying the satisfaction and challenge of a well-established career in his chosen field.

A single woman may confront similar challenges if she chooses not to invest in her career or further develop her skills because she assumes that when she gets married her husband will support her. In reality, she may or may not get married, and if she does, her husband may or may not be able to care for her financially. A woman who has not married may experience a sense of hopelessness about herself and her future even though she has many gifts and great potential for developing those gifts.

Given the reality of high divorce rates and women's tendency to significantly outlive their husbands, the truth is that *the American woman who cannot support herself is either an actual or potential victim of financial stress and poverty.* Thus, whether she is married or single, a woman's need to broaden her range of skills so that she can support herself with meaningful work is crucial—not only for her self-esteem but also for the provision of physical necessities.

Men can work with women to ensure that they receive the same kind of support that they themselves expect for their career and ministry goals. This does not mean that family priorities have to fly out the window, as I will discuss more fully in chapter 9. Particularly if she has the support of a loving husband, a woman can remain committed to her family and still carve out some time for further schooling, job experiences that keep her skills current and her foot in the door of a meaningful career or ministry, or volunteer work that will contribute to a well-rounded résumé.

For myself, working out a balance between being available to my family and continuing to develop vocationally has been crucial to self-esteem. There is a feeling of well-being that comes from knowing that I am doing what is right for my family and that I haven't missed out on being an integral part of their lives. *But I also need to know that in addition to that connectedness with family, the part of me that stands before God alone and fits into his larger plan is continuing to develop and grow.* I also need to have the confidence that comes from knowing that I am generating income our family needs but doing it in ways that I enjoy and that reflect God's calling on my life. Because of the commitment my husband, Chris, and I share to continue investing in these aspects of my life, I do not have inordinate fears about future possibilities—something happening to Chris or his job, or our children leaving the nest. Rather, I feel confidence and enthusiasm about the future, knowing that God's purposes for me will always remain and that I have been prepared for them. Women who value themselves—and the men who value them—will insist upon this essential element of self-esteem, recognizing that self-esteem is not just a feeling, it is a result of practical actions.

Gain Realistic Information About How the World Works

We as women also need to understand how the world outside our homes functions. The world is made up of different systems—your own family system (or way of doing things), the legal system, welfare, educational, and religious systems, and others. Each system has its own processes, communication patterns, relational webs, and ways of getting things done as well as its own vulnerabilities and dysfunctions. People who know how to work within these systems will be better off in them.

The problem is that women are often naive, uninformed, or inexperienced regarding how to "work" systems, and this leaves us very vulnerable within those systems. We lack information about how to protect ourselves from someone taking advantage of us, how to use the legal system, how to buy and take care of a car, how to invest money and plan for a financial future, how to understand the fine print on documents we sign—and the list goes on. Learning about the systems we participate in and rely on for our practical needs is another very important way of increasing our sense of well-being and confidence in the world.[18]

There is a fine line, however, between participating in a system in ways that are healthy and for the good of all and "working the system" in dishonest, selfish, or manipulative ways. This is where we rely on ethics and values. A clear sense of what is right and wrong and what matters most in life will determine how we use the information and skills we have. A person who has a strong moral ethic will work within the system in ways that are honest. She will be complimentary when she honestly has something good to say but will refuse to fall into the trap of flattery for the sake of getting ahead. To the best of her ability she will tell the truth even when the truth is unpopular, but she will know how to pick her time and place. A woman who values all people will use her knowledge of how the world works not only for her own good but also for the good of others. The Bible calls this being "as shrewd as snakes and as innocent as doves" (Matthew 10:16, NIV).

At times a woman may realize that a system in which she has been participating stands for something that goes against her ethics or values. She may begin to see that in a particular system, women or people of color are discriminated against, dishonesty is required in order to get ahead, or people are manipulated and used. In this case her ethics and values will guide her to take a stand or to leave the system altogether.

A certain confidence comes from knowing that we are increasing our understanding of the world in which we live, that we are not depending on someone else to do "the hard stuff" for us, and that even in the difficult and sometimes confusing dilemmas we face, we are hammering out a set of ethics and values that are grounded in God's Word. Without these abilities, without this foundation of ethics and values to guide us, we will tend to live our lives timidly, full of uncertainty, afraid to make a move.

THE LESSON OF A LIFETIME

Samara found herself loved in brand new ways the day she met Christ at the well. But the ultimate expression of his love—his willingness to lay down his life in payment for our sin—was still in the future. We have seen Christ's love for us in ways that Samara did not have the opportunity to see. We know that if any one of us had been the *only* one needing salvation from sin, Jesus still would have given his all. But that is only the beginning.

Each of us needs to cultivate our relationship with Christ as if it were only the two of us because, chances are, a time will come when this is the case. That is why exploring this love relationship is so important—so that we can begin to see ourselves as God sees us and root our self-esteem in the bedrock of his love.

One woman has written down brief statements that reflect what she has learned about God's view of her, and she repeats them to herself daily:

- I am complete in Christ.
- I am a worthwhile person just as I am.
- I stand alone before God as a whole person.
- I have talents and abilities that God gives because he expresses himself through me.
- I can love others and give good things to them because God's love is poured out in my heart.
- I have self-esteem and integrity on my own because I am just as God intended me to be.[19]

You might want to record your our own discoveries about God's love for you as you ponder the Scriptures (his love letter to you) and listen attentively to his voice as he speaks love to you in the midst of your ordinary days. Many experiences in society can drag us into the pit of feeling "less than" if we don't have truth with which to respond.

In addition, past messages about our worth (or the lack of it) inform the way we view ourselves today. Family and religious systems that were characterized by shame, sexism, abuse of women and children, conditional love based on performance, or an inability to express love contribute significantly to a woman's feeling of powerlessness and worthlessness. Christ, through the presence of the Holy Spirit (the Helper or Counselor as he is called in John 14–16), will walk with us as we sort through these early messages. It is important to remember that we do not confront the past for the purpose of blaming others or making excuses for ourselves; we do so to uncover the lies that are misleading us and to enter more fully into the truth. It is only then that we can be free from sinful self-absorption and self-deprecation and give to God and others from the fullness he intends.

Of course, we do not learn these lessons once and for all. There have been and continue to be times when I must come back to the most basic of life's lessons as I did at my grandfathers' funerals. On such occasions we face the reality that even though we might be married or in other ways close to another human being, life is still a solitary journey. In these moments of awareness, I need to hear God say, "I will never leave you or forsake you" (Hebrews 13:5). In times when people or circumstances seem limiting, I need to learn to come back to God and ask, "Who are you calling me to be? What do you want me to do?" When I fail and feel that my usefulness to God is over, I need to listen to him speak into that moment saying, "My love for you and your usefulness to me are not conditional upon your performance. I didn't wait for perfection from Samara before I gave love and the chance to make a difference, and I'm not waiting for perfection from you."

Learning to find all we need in Christ is truly the lesson of a lifetime. It is tempting to oversimplify and overspiritualize the problem many of us have with self-esteem, thinking that if we just tell ourselves over and over again how much God loves us, pretty soon we will be convinced. As foundational as this knowledge is, some of the essentials of self-esteem are very practical in nature, as we have seen in this chapter. God knows about these practical needs as well as the spiritual ones, and we can ask him to provide these things. He can be trusted to lead us in acquiring what is essential at the right time and in the right way as we are open and responsive to his leading.

SPIRITUAL EXERCISES

Alone with God

Silence. As you come to the end of this chapter, take a few moments to sit with God in the silence of your own heart. In the silence, reflect on the following questions. Don't feel like you have to do anything. Just sit with the questions and with whatever comes up in you as you listen in silence.

- During what moments do you experience the reality of your "singleness"—your ultimate separateness from other human beings?
- How do you feel in these moments?
- What questions does this raise for you?
- What do you tend to do during these times?

Prayer and journaling. Review the chapter that you have just read, noticing the places of resonance and resistance that you highlighted. In your journal, write and tell God about the thoughts, feelings, desires, and questions that this chapter raised for you. Notice the places where you experienced deep emotion or grief about the ways in which you are depending on others for what only God can give. Or perhaps there are places where you want to argue or express anger about the realities that women face and the ways in which those realities affect you. In your journal, go ahead and express your feelings as well as your arguments and places of disagreement.

- What does your reaction indicate about what is going on in the deeper places of your soul?
- What does God seem to be saying to you in the midst of your emotions and questions?

Invitations. *God, how are you inviting me to respond to what you are saying to me through this reading?*

With Your Spiritual Friend(s)

Begin your time together with a moment of silence and a simple prayer of invitation for God to join you.

Listening. Take turns giving each other your undivided attention. Share with each other a brief summary of what has happened between you and God this week in the context of your spiritual practices and your reading of this chapter.

- What did God say to you in your times of solitude and silence?
- What were your experiences of resonance and resistance as you read this chapter? How did you process those with God in your journal?
- In what area of self-esteem do you find yourself weak or deficient?
- How do you notice yourself looking to others to fill this gap?
- Is there anything in your reading and reflection that offers you guidance about how to allow Christ to become all that you need in this area?
- Does God seem to be inviting you to do anything as a result of where you have been with him this week?

Prayer. Ask, "How would you like me to pray for you?" and take time to pray for one another.

THREE

THE FREEDOM TO SAY YES
TO GOD'S PURPOSES

I believe that what a woman resents is not so much giving her-self in pieces as giving herself purposelessly.... Purposeful giving is not as apt to deplete one's resources; it belongs to that natural order of giving that seems to renew itself even in the act of deple-tion. The more one gives, the more one has to give—like milk in the breast.

—ANNE MORROW LINDBERG, *Gift from the Sea*

"The hardest thing about being a homemaker," I have wailed on many occasions, "is the repetitiveness of the tasks! Almost everything I do in life has to be done over again within hours or days. It all seems so pointless!"

My own personal symbol of futility is the kitchen floor. It is a white floor (I picked it out myself!) that is just beautiful when it is clean. But the problem, of course, is that no sooner have I cleaned it (usually on my hands and knees after having planned my whole day around it) than someone spills on it. I know that *never* is a very big word, but this never fails.

The inevitability of it all has made this a family joke, and on my good days I can laugh along. However, on my bad days I begin to babble inco-herently about the futility of my life; what does life matter when you spend your days doing things that have been undone by the time your husband gets home? What do I have to show for the exhaustion I feel at the end of the day? Why do I bother? It can go on and on. For sanity purposes, I have been known to wash the floor in the late afternoon and then insist that we all go out for dinner so that the floor stays clean for at least several hours. Anything for a sense of accomplishment!

Let's face it: With all the options open to women today, our lives are still often filled with the mundane, the ridiculous, the difficult, even the tragic. Sometimes it is hard to feel that life has purpose when you spend most of your days scraping Play-Doh off the floor, cleaning the bathroom, or working for a boss who doesn't recognize your potential.

And yet all of us, deep down inside, harbor a very human desire for meaning in life. We want our lives to count for something, something that will last longer than a few hours or a few days. As one poet put it: "Life without meaning is the torture of restlessness and vague desire. It is a boat longing for the sea and yet afraid."[1] It is this longing and restlessness that God wants to fill with his purposes.

ESTHER: A WOMAN TRANSFORMED BY PURPOSE

Esther was a woman for whom the mundane and tragic aspects of life took on new meaning—as she saw them in the context of God's purposes. As a result of this new understanding, she was utterly transformed from a frightened and somewhat passive woman into one of strength, courage, and action.

Esther's story takes place in Persia (present-day Iran) during the reign of King Xerxes. The opening scene, described in Esther 1, reveals Xerxes treating all of his officials, noblemen, and armies to a lavish banquet that was the culmination of a six-month period in which he had displayed the wealth and splendor of his kingdom. The royal wine flowed freely and the men drank without restraint. At the same time his wife, Queen Vashti, gave a separate banquet for the women in another part of the palace.

At the end of this seven-day banquet when Xerxes was "merry with wine" (in other words, he was drunk), Xerxes called Queen Vashti to come and display her beauty to his drunken guests. One can only imagine the state that the king and his male guests were in after drinking and partying for seven days straight. Some historians believe that the king was commanding Vashti to appear naked except for her crown, and most agree it was not a respectful request but a demeaning one. Certainly this was not the kind of situation in which any self-respecting woman would willingly place herself.[2]

When Vashti refused to display herself as the king had commanded, the king's men convinced him that the queen's behavior was a threat not only to the king's honor but also to male supremacy in general. He decided to make a public example of her by banishing her from his presence and giving her position to one who was more worthy. Women had few rights during this time period; women were expendable and at the mercy of the men in their lives. It was into this setting that Esther came.

A Beauty Pageant with a Twist

When the king's anger subsided, he began to miss Vashti. His attendants, who didn't want to risk losing all the progress they had made for mankind, came up with the idea of distracting Xerxes from what he was feeling by staging a beauty pageant! So they gathered all the beautiful young virgins in the kingdom into a harem for the king so that he could choose a replacement for Vashti.

Esther, an orphaned Jewish girl in the care of her cousin Mordecai, was one of the young virgins who was captured for the harem. We don't know if she was shopping in the outdoor market, laughing with friends, or working around her home when the king's men rode through town seizing beautiful girls. It is not hard to imagine her panic and fright as she was torn from her only family and taken against her will to the king's palace. Who knows if she even realized, as she was being dragged away, that she would spend the next full year getting ready for one night of sex with a heathen king. Esther 2:12-14 tells us that there was considerably more involved in the Miss Persia beauty pageant than in the pageants to which we are accustomed. After the young lady was brought into the harem, she spent twelve months getting ready—six months of beauty treatments with oil and myrrh and six months with herbs and cosmetics. When her turn came, she would spend the night with the king and then return to the second harem of the concubines. She was then considered used merchandise, the equivalent of a slave kept for the purposes of sex, childbearing, and housekeeping. She could never approach the king again unless he called her by name. Some beauty pageant!

If Esther was like most Jewish girls, she had dreamed all her life of marrying and bearing children; perhaps she had even imagined that she would be the one chosen to be the mother of the Messiah. But now her prospects of a normal marriage and family life were ruined, for she would become forever the property of the king. Here was the trauma of kidnapping and rape, the loneliness of being torn from family, the disappointment of a difficult marriage, and the loss of her hopes and dreams—all wrapped up in one life-changing event. Mordecai couldn't do much beyond advising her not to tell anyone she was a Jew. (Maybe he thought she would receive better treatment if no one knew she belonged to the race that had once been held captive in that country.) But certainly his presence as he walked back and forth in front of the harem every day must have been a comfort and a strength to his young cousin.

Hope in the Midst of Tragedy

As dismal as Esther's situation was, God was there—in the harem, in the palace, and in the king's bedroom—working in all of his sovereignty and power to bring about his good purposes. As Esther spent the next year preparing to go to the king, she found favor with everyone who knew her. And when her turn came, "the king loved Esther more than all the other women; of all the virgins she won his favor and devotion, so that he set the royal crown on her head and made her queen instead of Vashti" (Esther 2:17). Although she was not yet aware of it, the king's love would become the key to the accomplishment of God's great purpose in that place.

After Esther was settled in her new position as queen, King Xerxes promoted a proud and evil man named Haman to a position above all the other palace officials. The king then commanded that everyone should bow down to Haman. Mordecai, consistent with his Jewish faith and practice, refused. This refusal caused quite a stir.

> When Haman saw that Mordecai did not bow down or do obeisance to him, Haman was infuriated. But he thought it beneath him to lay hands on Mordecai alone. So, having been told who Mordecai's people were, Haman plotted to destroy all the Jews, the people of Mordecai, throughout the whole kingdom of Ahasuerus [Xerxes]. (3:5-6)

Haman cleverly convinced the king that the Jews scattered throughout the country were a threat to his supremacy. So the king gave permission for Haman to send out this edict: On the thirteenth day of the twelfth month, the king's soldiers would be sent out into all the king's provinces to "destroy, to kill, and to annihilate all Jews, young and old, women and children, in one day...and to plunder their goods" (3:13).

When Mordecai first got wind of Haman's genocide plot against the Jews, he realized immediately the significance of Esther's position. He sent her a message urging her to "go to the king to make supplication to him and entreat him for her people" (4:8). At first Esther was hesitant to get involved, and with very good reason. She reminded Mordecai that "if any man or woman goes to the king inside the inner court without being called, there is but one law—all alike are to be put to death. Only if the king holds out the golden scepter to someone, may that person live. I myself have not been called to come in to the king for thirty days" (4:11).

It was at this point that Mordecai, who must have been very wise, made an interesting suggestion. After expressing complete confidence in God's ability to deliver the Jews, he said to Esther, "Who knows? Perhaps you have come to royal dignity for just such a time as this." (4:14). He didn't presume to tell her what God was calling her to do; he merely heightened her awareness with his insightful question. Perhaps he realized that God's call on our lives is very personal and he alone must speak it to our souls.

As a result of Mordecai's comment, the light began to dawn for Esther on all that had happened to her. The trauma, the loneliness, the unusualness of her situation began to make sense. As she became conscious of what she had come to the kingdom for, a sense of purpose—not personal safety, probabilities, social norms, or convenience—began to inform her decision-making process. The knowledge that God had brought her to this time and place for a specific purpose transformed her from a frightened, hesitant woman making excuses in Esther 4:11 to the courageous woman who sent this message to Mordecai: "Go, gather all the Jews…and hold a fast on my behalf.… I and my maids will also fast as you do. After that I will go to the king, though it is against the law; and if I perish, I perish" (4:16).

Following Through

After asking the Jews to fast and pray for her, Esther took several days to think of a plan and prepare her heart. Then she swung into action. First, she made herself beautiful, the mundane task of getting dressed taking on a new significance that day. Can't you just see her standing in front of her closet, trying to choose the royal robe that would please the king and cause his heart to be open toward her? I'm sure her heart beat fast and her fingers shook as she applied her makeup. Maybe she rehearsed what she would say to the king if she did get the chance to speak. Certainly she thought of Queen Vashti in those moments, questioning whether she too would be banished for standing up for her convictions. She had spoken bravely three days earlier but now the moment of truth had come. Would she have the courage to follow through?

But Esther did follow through. She used everything she had at her disposal—her brains, her beauty, her position, the king's love for her—and risked it all to accomplish the purpose for which God had brought her to that time and place. She went and stood in the inner court of the king's palace, positioning herself so that the king could see her. She didn't have to wait long, for "as soon as the king saw Queen Esther standing in the court, she won his favor and he held out to her the golden scepter that was in his hand. Then Esther approached [the king].... [He] said to her, 'What is it, Queen Esther? What is your request? It shall be given you, even to the half of my kingdom'" (5:2-3).

From there Esther implemented a wildly successful plan that resulted in Haman being hanged on the gallows he had built for Mordecai and the Jews being delivered from annihilation. Mordecai was promoted to a position of authority second only to the king himself and used his position for the good of his people, while Esther continued to enjoy the love of the king and the privileges and responsibilities of queenship. To this day the Jews still celebrate the feast of Purim "as the days on which the Jews gained relief from their enemies, and as the month that had been turned for them from sorrow into gladness and from mourning into a holiday" (9:22). What a thrilling story of the mighty way God used a woman who had been uniquely prepared for his great purposes.

SEEING OURSELVES AS WOMEN OF PURPOSE

It's clear that the sovereignty of God permeates the book of Esther. It was such an unlikely situation in human terms. But even so, Esther needed to consider the suggestion Mordecai raised for her that day. She had not yet begun to realize that God had been carefully orchestrating her life to bring her to that place at that time and for that purpose. He had put together a package in her life—beauty, intelligence, nationality, position, love—and now the time had come for her to put it to use.

The sovereignty of God permeates our lives as well, although we don't always see it. *God is putting together a package in each of our lives, preparing us to make a unique contribution to his kingdom.* We need to ask ourselves, "What have I come to the kingdom for? Why has God brought me to this particular time and place?"

Approaching life situations in this way represents a radical shift in thinking for some of us. We are more accustomed to thinking, *But I'm so limited. God could never use me!* Many factors cause us to feel limited or inadequate: a lack of formal education, a late start in the Christian life, our marital status, financial limitations, young children or rebellious teens in the home, a lack of self-confidence, and so on. But these are only perceived limitations. So often, what we see as limitations are God's training ground for unique usefulness to him.

Joni Eareckson Tada is one who has discovered that her limitations were inextricably interwoven with God's purposes for her life. As a young girl of seventeen, she was paralyzed from the neck down in a diving accident. Facing the rest of her life as a quadriplegic confined to a wheelchair, she raged against God and wished to take her own life. But as she allowed God to deal with her at her point of deepest pain, she found that the limitations of her disabled body propelled her into ministry to others who are disabled. She found that they listened to her in a way that they wouldn't listen to someone whose body was whole. Now she has an international ministry to a group of people who, up to this point, had been largely unreached for Christ. God brought her to a time and a place in a disabled body for a purpose.

No matter what our circumstances, then, we still need to ask ourselves, "What have I come to the kingdom for?" Generally speaking, we have all come to this time and place as servants of Jesus Christ, as investors of what he has given us. But we need to go beyond the general, get down to specifics, and ask ourselves: "What unique gifts, experiences, opportunities, and burdens is God blending together in my life to make me of special use to him?"

IDENTIFYING GOD'S PURPOSES

In *The Seven Habits of Highly Effective People,* Stephen Covey points out that when you begin with the end in mind,

> Each part of your life—today's behavior, tomorrow's behavior, next month's behavior—can be examined in the context of the whole, in the context of what really matters most to you. By keeping that end clearly in mind, you can make sure...that each day of your life contributes in a meaningful way to the vision you have of your life as a whole.[3]

Paul said the same thing in different words: "Live life, then, with a due sense of responsibility, not as [those] who do not know the meaning of life but as *those who do.* Make the best use of your time, despite all the evils of these days. Don't be vague but grasp firmly what you know to be the will of the Lord" (Ephesians 5:15-17, Phillips). Let's look at four areas that will help us do that.

Purpose. A life purpose answers our larger questions about the meaning of life and the reasons for our existence. It reflects the overall vision God has given us for what he wants to do in and through our lives. Formulating a life purpose statement is not something that can be rushed, because it is forged as we search the Scriptures and listen to the Lord speak to us in a very personal way. It reflects the essence and uniqueness of who we are as created beings. Our deepest life purpose or calling will probably stay basically the same throughout the span of our lives although we may spend much time clarifying and deepening our understanding of that purpose so that we can live into it with greater joy and freedom.

Priorities. Since a life purpose statement is, by nature, rather general, it is also important to identify the specific priority areas through which these purposes will be accomplished: spiritual life, personal growth, family life, work, service in the church and the world. Then within these priority areas we can develop more specific purpose statements. If one of my larger purposes in life is to know God, I need to be more specific about what I am aiming for in this area. Do I need to learn to be quiet and just be in his presence? Do I want to develop a deeper prayer life? What character issues do I need to work on? In regard to my family, what exactly do I want my husband and children to receive from me and from our home life? As far as my contribution to my church and community is concerned, what gifts has God given me that need to be developed? How do those fit with the things I'm burdened about? And what about friendships, intellectual challenges, and healthy living?

This is the place to dream the dreams that God is whispering to our hearts—even the ones that seem so far-fetched we're almost afraid to put them into words.

Planning. The process of identifying purposes and priorities doesn't guarantee that in reality we will spend our time and energy on those priorities. It is very easy to say "I want to be more responsive to my husband sexually" or "I want to be a writer" or "I want to be more involved in my children's education." But it is quite another thing to take steps to make it so.

Goals help us plan our priorities into the minutes and hours of our days; they are the steps that will take us to the end result. An effective goal is reachable, measurable, and realistic, taking into consideration our season of life and other factors that might affect our plans, such as health, transportation, finances, husband's schedule, and so forth. If our goals are unrealistic, we set ourselves up for failure and discouragement.

For instance, one of the main purposes of my life is to serve God with my gifts. Since I understand that one of the ways I am to accomplish this is through writing, writing has become a priority. When the opportunity came along to write my first Bible studyguide, I said yes because I could see how it fit into God's purposes for my life, but I needed a realistic plan that would take into account my busy season of life. Since I had two young daughters, the only writing time I had was in the early mornings and in the afternoons while my older daughter was in preschool and my younger daughter was napping. So, my goal for accomplishing this writing project was to write early in the morning five mornings a week and during naptime three afternoons a week. It would be easy to tell if I was accomplishing my goals from day to day. And I felt confident that working at that pace, I would finish the project in a year.

Discipline. It was a great plan, but there was one problem. Quite often when I took my older daughter to preschool, I would run into a friend who was fun to be with and enjoyed shopping, as I do. If either one of us mentioned anything about shopping, we would throw responsibility to the wind and go. As you can imagine, this greatly hindered my work on the writing project (not to mention how hard it was on our budget!). I had not yet come to grips with the fact that saying yes to the goals and plans that would take me step by step toward God's purposes would also require saying no to things that interfered. I finally realized that if I wanted the long-term satisfaction of seeing my work in print, I would have to give up the short-term pleasure of those spur-of-the-moment shopping trips. Every preschool day, I faced the choice between short-term pleasure and "making the best use of my time." Sometimes I succumbed to temptation, but I grew more consistent in sticking to my plan and eventually got the job done.

Delaying self-gratification is one habit necessary to saying no, but it's a difficult one to develop! And in saying no we sometimes risk the disappointment of others. They may even think we are wrong for not being available for the activities and projects they think are important. Many women have been conditioned to be "people pleasers" and, as such, find it very hard to hold on to their own priorities in the face of this kind of pressure. But we must remember that others don't necessarily know the purposes to which God has called us or the commitments we are juggling. When we give in to pressure (that comes from ourselves or from others), we are fitting into others' purposes rather than God's. Each one of us is responsible to God for what we do with the time and energy he has given us. People who are spiritually wise will trust him to move us to do what he is calling us to.

In *A Time for Risking*, Miriam Adeney comments that, "Only those who turn down standard activities will have time and energy for priority affairs."[4] She offers this challenge:

> For you, kingdom priorities might mean saying no to talking on the
> telephone so much. Or saying no to well-established committees in
> order to serve on more needy committees. Saying no to certain
> kinds of reading in order to do other, more crucial reading. Saying
> no to thinking so much about how you feel or about the way you
> look—saying no to your "pity parties." Kingdom priorities might
> mean monitoring your imagination and bringing every thought cap-
> tive to Christ (2 Corinthians 10:5). It might mean limiting the time
> you spend thinking about fashion, shopping, romance, eating out,

backpacking, gardening, skiing, soap operas, novels, gossip, or whatever catches your imagination, in order consciously to focus a certain amount of your thoughts on people's need for Jesus, on world hunger, on nuclear weapon dangers, on teenage mothers. Kingdom priorities may mean saying no to spending so much time with certain friends in order to spend time with friends who need you more. Or limiting your mindless conversations, in order consciously to make your conversations channels of grace.[5]

This is not to say that there should be no time for fun and relaxation; we need some of that or we will burn out quickly. But in the context of purposeful living, relaxation is even more delicious because we give it to ourselves intentionally. This too is part of our conscious choice to live our lives in the balanced and fruitful way that God intended.

Another helpful discipline is actually to chart out our purposes, priorities, and plans. Many tools on the market are designed to help with this process, but I have found that creating my own chart helps me solidify my thoughts and commitments. In addition to a written life purpose statement, I use a separate sheet of paper for each priority area (spiritual life, personal development, family, church, work, etc.) and then divide the paper into three columns. The first column contains my purpose statements (what I'm aiming for) in that area. The second contains my plan (specific goals and scheduling), and the third contains any disciplines involved (things I will need to say no to in order to say yes to what really matters).[6]

SAYING YES TO GOD

Have you ever imagined what would have happened if some of the women in the Bible had said no to the purposes of God in their lives? What if Esther had said, "But Lord, I have myself set up pretty well here. Just look at me! I'm the queen and the king loves me. Why would I want to mess that up?" Or what if Deborah, when called to be a prophet, judge, and military leader in Israel, had responded like this: "But Lord, don't you know that women aren't supposed to do those sorts of things?" And what about Mary, the mother of Jesus? "But God, this is extremely inconvenient: couldn't you wait until after I get married? This is going to ruin my reputation and besides, I had a few things I wanted to do before I had kids!"

In any of these cases, history could have turned out quite differently. But these women did not allow themselves to be limited by the voices of cultural norms, personal convenience, or fear. Rather, they allowed God to put a package together in their lives, and they responded when he called them to use it.

We may not be called to be Deborahs or Esthers, leading armies or thwarting great political schemes (although I wouldn't rule that out!). God may be putting our package together in such a way that we are uniquely prepared to confront injustice and immorality in our community, to mold a young life, to care unselfishly for aging parents, to serve Jesus by opening our home, or to speak with discernment to the church. Knowing that God is in control of preparing us for his purposes adds value to many aspects of life that would otherwise be mundane. The young mother who is scraping Play-Doh off the floor can see it in the context of purpose—she has provided her child with an important tactile experience! A woman working in a job that isn't exactly a dream come true can take advantage of the character-building opportunities that are a part of the spiritual growth for which she is aiming. We can even clean the bathroom with an awareness that we are creating the atmosphere in our home that is important to us.

Of course, other opportunities will require more courage: speaking out publicly about something important, home schooling our kids, running for public office, sharing Christ with a neighbor, or moving into the inner city in order to make a difference there.

Our challenge then is to say yes to the most important things, the things for which God has brought us to this time and place. In so doing, we make room in our lives for meaning and value, and we will feel God's pleasure upon us. Rather than the "torture of restlessness and vague desire," the wind of the Spirit will fill our sails and move us into the high sea of purposeful living. Will it be frightening? At times, yes. Will it be risky? More so than staying in a quiet harbor. Will it be exhilarating? You bet! Will it be fulfilling? Well, let's put it this way: It's the only way to live.

SPIRITUAL EXERCISES

Alone with God

Silence. As you come to the end of this chapter, take a few moments to sit with God in the silence of your own heart. Ask God to help you actually "see" the package that he is putting together in your life. Think about what gifts, experiences, opportunities, burdens, and passions make up the person you are. Allow enough time for the reality of this "package" to take on full detail and color in your mind and heart. Sit with whatever emotions come—joy, gratitude, awe, and so on. You might experience some "negative" emotions such as sadness (that it's taken so long for you to see the package God is putting together in your life) or frustration (that you or others in your life can't quite see it yet). Don't censor yourself at all. Just "be with" the truth of your experience in the presence of God.

Read Psalm 139:13-18 and, to the extent that you are able, let the truth of this passage be true for you.

Prayer and journaling. Review the chapter that you have just read, noticing the places where you said, "I really want that!" (resonance) or "I'm not sure I'm ready for that" (resistance). In your journal, tell God about the thoughts, feelings, desires, hesitations, and questions that this chapter raised for you.

- What does your reaction indicate about what is going on in the deeper places of your soul?
- In what way might God be saying "I have brought you to the kingdom for just such a time as this?"

Invitations. *God, how do you want me to hear you through this reading? Are you inviting me to respond to you in some way?*

With Your Spiritual Friend(s)

Begin your time together with a moment of silence and a simple prayer of invitation for God to join you.

Listening. Take turns giving each other your undivided attention. Share with each other a brief summary of what has happened between you and God this week in the context of your spiritual practices and your reading of this chapter.

- What did God say to you in your times of solitude and silence about the package that he is putting together in your life?
- What were your experiences of resonance and resistance as you read this chapter? How did you process those with God in your journal?
- What element of purposeful living is missing in your life right now?
- How is God inviting you to a deeper level of freedom in saying yes to his purposes?
- Does God seem to be inviting you to do anything as a result of where you have been with him this week?

Prayer. Pray for one another.

THE FREEDOM TO SERVE GOD IN THE WAY THAT HE CALLS

Dear God, Are boys better than girls? I know you are one, but please try to be fair.

—FROM *Children's Letters to God*

We still laugh about the time our oldest daughter, Charity, at two and a half years old, traipsed into church during a worship service wearing a diaper on her head. She was trailing behind us as we slipped into our front-row seats a few minutes late, so we didn't realize that she was making this fashion statement until she had already caused a bit of a stir.

This was more than childhood silliness. Early in her young life she had observed that the women in our church (including her mother) wore head coverings, usually veils of some sort. To her, putting something on her head was part of what it meant to be a woman.

Since I had grown up in a church setting that emphasized submission to men's authority as one of the central elements of mature womanhood, being a woman meant wearing a head covering to symbolize this submission—and much more. It meant not being allowed to speak in church gatherings. It meant knowing that even though I was supposed to be a priest (according to 1 Peter 2:5,9), men were the only ones allowed to perform the priestly functions of teaching, leading worship, serving communion, or offering an audible prayer when the church gathered. It meant hearing letters from women missionaries read in church services but finding that when they were home on furlough they could not get up in these same gatherings and give a report. It meant listening as the men were exhorted to step forward and accept their God-given responsibility of teaching and leading, and watching as the godly women I respected had to sit in numb silence.

All of these rules, spoken and unspoken, sent a powerful message to a young, spiritually sensitive girl who was trying to figure out what it meant to be female and be Christian. The message that I and the women around me internalized was not a very positive one.

A GROWING AWARENESS

A small Christian liberal arts college in the Midwest gave me the opportunity to experience, for the first time, an environment in which gender wasn't such a big issue. Women could speak and pray in chapel, serve as leaders in student government, and receive equal encouragement from their professors. At the same time, I found that my love for the church was growing and I served there in any way I could. I realized that there was nothing I wanted more than to spend my life serving God among his people. So, in addition to certifying to teach, I also took Bible, Greek, and Christian education courses with a view to "plugging in" to the church with greater effectiveness.

I emerged from college with great eagerness but soon discovered that, while my male peers were groomed to serve as preachers, teachers, and elders in my home church, women were relegated to a much more narrow sphere of ministry. When young men demonstrated desire or ability to teach and lead the congregation, it was cause for celebration; when a young woman shared these same desires, she was viewed as rebellious. I began to wonder if God had made a mistake in entrusting a woman with my particular gifts and desires for ministry.

It was even more disturbing to see that women did not have much voice in church life at all. It was painful when the men would retreat to another room to discuss important spiritual matters, leaving the women to tend to the kitchen and the children. The belief that women (by nature of their female-ness) functioned best behind the scenes and men (by virtue of their male-ness) were best suited for up-front leadership didn't fit with my understanding of spiritual gifts and personality types. I couldn't help wondering, *Is the female perspective so devoid of value that Christian congregations can live without it?*

For many years I hid my struggle from other people's view, alternating between self-blame (Was it my own character flaws that kept me from being content with the traditional role carved out for women?) and anger at those who perpetrated such a discriminatory system. At the same time I kept serving in whatever capacity I was allowed: working with youth, teaching girls' Sunday school and women's Bible studies, directing vacation Bible school and women's ministries, playing piano, singing in the choir. While I enjoyed each of these ministry opportunities, I continued to experience a great deal of turmoil over women's lack of freedom to participate fully in all aspects of church life.

It was becoming a crisis of faith for me. After all, the church is God's church. Was this an accurate reflection of him? Was he really a chauvinistic father who allowed his sons to speak and participate in family decisions while barring his daughters from the same privileges? Was Eve's sin so much greater and more unforgivable than Adam's that the entire female gender must forever be treated with suspicion and controlling measures?

These were not the questions of a theologian; they were questions wrung from the heart of a daughter to her heavenly Father. I did not want to believe the conclusions at which some women were arriving, and yet their conclusions didn't surprise me. As one woman said, "I have read the Bible. The Christian slate is there for all to read and it cannot be wiped clean…for Christianity is a male religion, written by men, for men, with a male god."[1]

As irreverent as it seemed to question God on these matters, that was never the attitude that was in my heart. These questions were getting in the way of the most important relationship in my life, and I needed to ask them. Fortunately, I knew God well enough to be confident that he was big enough and loving enough to help me find the answers.

A TIME TO STUDY

Finally, the time came for me to quit stewing and start studying. An invitation to develop Bible study materials for the women in my church gave me the opportunity to pore over the Scriptures from beginning to end, studying anything and everything that had to do with women. My heart was stirred by women in the Bible such as Abigail, Deborah, Huldah, Esther, and Priscilla,[2] who made an impact for God's kingdom in courageous ways that, even now, strike us as being outside the normal "woman's role." I marveled at the freedom they found to follow the Lord's call on their lives. I found myself weeping with love for Jesus as I witnessed the respect with which he treated women. And through my study of spiritual gifts, *I began to discover that God gives gifts not based on gender but based on the work he has called us to do.*

What I was learning just didn't fit with the emphasis on the silence and subordination of women with which I had grown up. After I finished writing that Bible study,[3] I kept right on studying until I came to the point where I understood enough to be at peace with God, to be able to follow his call on my own life with courage, *and* to teach my daughters that they, too, could become anything that God called them to be. As women, we all need to know at least that much. It is one of the truths that will set us free.

Creation

I began my study with creation, for it is there that we get our first glimpses of what it means to be human beings created male and female. In Genesis 1 and 2 we see God's original and best plan for gender relations: a partnership model in which a man and a woman function together as a team of equals. In Genesis 1, we learn that God created humankind in two sexes—male and female—and that both were created equally in his image (verses 26-27). God blessed the man and the woman and gave them both the responsibility to be fruitful and multiply, to fill the earth, subdue it, and rule together over all living things (verses 28-29). When God surveyed all that he had made, including his newest addition of this "marriage team," for the first time in the entire creation story he commented that it was "very good" (verses 31).

Genesis 2 gives a more detailed account of the creation of man and woman. Verse 18 tells us God recognized that it was not good for man to be alone, and so he created woman—"a helper suitable for him" (NIV). While some theologians have interpreted this passage to mean that woman was somehow subordinate to man because she was created to be his helper (ezer), elsewhere in Scripture the same Hebrew word (ezer) is most often used in reference to God himself. For example, in Exodus 18:4, Jethro named his son Eliezer because "the God of my father was my help [ezer]." And in Psalm 40:17, as in many other places, the psalmist refers to God as "my help [ezer] and my deliverer." It is also important to note that the word ezer is translated in other places in Scripture as "succorer," "rescuer," "deliverer," "strength," and "power."[4]

As Ruth Tucker points out, in contemporary usage the word helper most often connotes strength. A parent helps a child with his homework.

A doctor is a helper to a patient. A rich nation is a helper to refugees. A person who is in distress psychologically or spiritually looks to a pastor or a counselor for help. "The one who helps is the one who has something to offer the one who is helpless or needs help. Adam needed help. He had no partner. God created a partner—a helper. There is no hint of either superiority or subordination."[5]

When God brought Eve to Adam, he was astounded and overjoyed to find someone who was like him: "This is now bone of my bones, and flesh of my flesh" (Genesis 2:23, NASB). But he also recognized and named the gender difference when he called her "Woman, because she was taken out of Man." For this reason [because of their fundamental unity] the man is instructed to leave his own family and cleave or cling to his wife (verse 24). Rather than pull a woman into the authority structure of the husband's family (the norm in the patriarchal system that developed later), Genesis teaches that the man is the one who should move away from his family toward his wife and cling to her in a new relationship that is characterized by interdependence. "Therefore a man leaves his father and his mother and clings to his wife, and they become one flesh" (2:24).

Paul expands on this interdependence in 1 Corinthians 11:11-12 when he points out that, "in the Lord, neither is woman independent of man, nor is man independent of woman. For as the woman originates from the man, so also the man has his birth through the woman" (NASB). This interdependence is pictured in the phrase "and they shall become one flesh." Nothing here suggests that one is "over" the other. In fact, any introduction of hierarchy seems completely contradictory to the oneness and interdependence pictured here.

The Fall

Eve's choice and Adam's choice to disobey God caused dire consequences for the human race. Among these was the introduction of sin and guilt, shame and blame into the male-female relationship. Although popular interpretations of this incident have taught that Eve was somehow "more guilty" than Adam because she ate the fruit first and then offered it to him, Genesis 3:6 reveals that Adam was with Eve during her temptation, apparently offering no help. Eve was left to hold her own in conversation with the serpent, and when she offered Adam the fruit, he took it without argument: "She also gave some to her husband, who was with her, and he ate."

When Paul observed that "it was not Adam who was deceived, but the woman being deceived, fell into transgression" (1 Timothy 2:14, NASB), the question comes to mind: Which is worse: to sin knowingly or to be deceived? If Paul is attributing "greater guilt" to Eve, how are we to interpret Romans 5:12-19 ("sin came into the world through one man") and other passages in which Paul ascribed primary guilt to Adam? This apparent contradiction can be resolved by recognizing that Adam and Eve were equally responsible for their personal choices in the Garden of Eden.

The consequences of the Fall outlined in Genesis 3:14-19 are *predictions* of how things would be in a sinful world rather than a prescription or a commandment for how God wanted things to be. In no way did this description of these natural consequences mean that women were prohibited from finding ways to avoid the pain of childbirth or free themselves from wrongful domination by their husbands. By the same token, God predicted that men would have to work very hard to get the ground to bear fruit, but he did not prohibit them from finding ways to make work easier—which they have. More significantly, within this sad scenario came another prediction—a promise even!—that one day Someone would come who would break the power of the Evil One (Genesis 3:15). That Someone has come and the church is still discovering how his life, death, and resurrection can redeem all areas of life—including relationships between the sexes.

The Life of Christ

In Old Testament days, the effects of sin in the lives of men and women were clearly seen. Women were viewed and treated as possessions—as "less than" men. Consequently, they were the victims of terrible abuse and violence (Genesis 16; Genesis 19:1-8; Judges 11:29-40; Judges 19). Even so, women like Miriam, Huldah, Abigail, Esther, and Deborah demonstrated that "you can't keep a good woman down." When a woman was the right person for the job, whether it was leading in worship, prophesying, exhorting, saving a nation from genocide, or leading soldiers into battle, God didn't hesitate to use her. And the results were impressive.

This reality was all but lost on Jewish men who, at the time of Christ, were still thanking God regularly "that I was not born a woman." They were forbidden to teach the words of the law to a woman publicly.

When Christ came, he broke man-made rules for gender relations and made new ones that reflected more accurately God's heart toward women. That is why we see him talking to an immoral woman about theology, worship, the state of her relationships, and the state of her soul (John 4). That is why we see him pointing out to the men that a woman caught in adultery was no more guilty than they were (John 8:1-11), and why we see him receiving Mary's act of worship as much more meaningful than anything that was going on in the synagogues (John 12:1-8). That is why some of his best friends were women—women were last at the cross and first at the tomb (Mark 15:40-47). And he appeared first to a woman and gave her the joyful responsibility of informing the disciples that he was alive! (Mark 16:1-8)

Christ, who was God come to earth in human form, was untainted by the sexism that characterized the society in which he lived. He raised a new standard for men and women to follow in their relationships. The impact of his life on gender relations can be summed up in Galatians 3:27-28: "For all of you who were baptized into Christ have clothed yourself with

Christ. There is neither Jew nor Greek, there is neither slave nor free man, there is neither male nor female; for you are all one in Christ Jesus" (NASB). These words are revolutionary from a cultural, political, and religious standpoint. The church is still in the process of applying these verses as we deal with the discrimination and partiality (all kinds) that exist in direct contradiction to the equality spoken of here.

The New Community

After Christ's death, the disciples returned to Jerusalem to await the Holy Spirit. Acts 1:14 says that they "all with one mind were continually devoting themselves to prayer, along with the women" (NASB). When the day of Pentecost came, they were all together in one place and tongues of fire rested on each one of them. All of them were filled with the Holy Spirit and were speaking in tongues (Acts 2:4). When Peter got up to preach, he explained these events to those who were watching. He said that this was a fulfillment of Joel's prophecy that when God poured forth his Spirit upon all humanity, sons and daughters, men and women would prophesy (that is, speak forth the mind of God) (Acts 2:16-18). And they did!

As the early church grew, women worked right alongside the men in spreading the gospel and planting churches. In many cases it was a woman (such as Lydia in Philippi) who was the prime mover in getting a church started and hosting it in her home. Other women taught theology (Priscilla), served as ministers or deacons (Phoebe), prophesied (Phillip's daughters), and simply worked very hard (see Romans 16:1-16).

First Corinthians 12 puts into words what was already in evidence in the early church: To each one is given the manifestation of the Spirit (spiritual gift) without regard to gender. It was entirely consistent with Peter's assertion that "God is not one to show partiality" (Acts 10:34, NASB) and that we are all members of the royal priesthood called out of darkness by God to proclaim his excellencies (1 Peter 2:9-10).

When Paul described the team concept in 1 Corinthians 12 and Ephesians 4 it was much more than just a theory—it was the way the men and women in the early church had worked together from the very beginning. Like the early church, we, too, can embrace a community that celebrates and utilizes the gifts of everyone. The reality that men and women can work together is one of the truths that can set us free. (For practical considerations of men and women working together, see appendix A.)

Redemption

At the heart of the gospel is a message of freedom for all who are oppressed (Galatians 5:1), and one doesn't need to look far to see that women have been greatly oppressed. Not only did Christ model a new kind of relationship between men and women, but through his death he redeemed us from the oppressive effects of the curse (Galatians 3:13). *When we require women to pay over and over again for Eve's transgression with their silence and submission, we negate the full redemptive power of the gospel.* Rather than becoming an example of relationships that have been redeemed, we model the reality of the curse. Rather than living out God's ideal (as seen in Genesis 1) so that our presence in society begins to transform it, we allow ourselves to be squeezed into the world's mold of sexism and discrimination.

Several biblical texts can be confusing to us as we seek to understand how men and women are to function together in marriage, ministry, and society. One of the most difficult to interpret is 1 Timothy 2:11-12, which seems to say that women are not allowed to teach or exercise authority over men. While the study of the particular passage and others is extremely important, basic principles of biblical interpretation teach us that we must always interpret difficult passages in light of broad theological themes such as the ones we have just observed—themes rooted in creation, the character of God (his justice and impartiality), the life and teachings of Christ, the leading of the Holy Spirit in the early church, and

general New Testament teaching regarding spiritual gifts and the priesthood of all believers.

A thematic approach to Scripture reveals that "more than a hundred
passages in the Bible affirm women in roles of leadership, and fewer than
half a dozen appear to be in opposition."[6] Yet as Christians, we have built
an elaborate system of belief and practice on only a few passages, such as
1 Timothy 2:11-12 and 1 Corinthians 11:2-16. These passages have loomed
so large that we have allowed them to color everything else we read. I am
not suggesting we merely dismiss these passages because we do not understand them. They are still part of the Scriptures, and we must continue to
wrestle with their true meaning. (For a fuller discussion of 1 Timothy
2:11-12, see appendix B.) But an even greater temptation that we must
resist is the temptation to lift these passages out of their own context, out
of the context of the broader themes of Scripture, or to elevate them to
the point that they become more important than the overall message of
the Scriptures.

Since we understand from other scriptures (such as 1 Corinthians
11:5) that women did pray and prophesy in church, Paul would have been
contradicting himself if he was saying that women could not teach or be in
positions of authority both now and forever. Additional information about
historical context, meanings of keywords, and grammatical structure (such
as what is included in appendix B) helps us understand that Paul was
addressing the *content* of their teaching since he was speaking to the issue
of heresy that was swirling around this fledgling church. He was also addressing the manner in which any new believers should learn—quietly and
in submission to the authority of Scripture.

This in itself was the start of something new. As we noted earlier, ordi-
narily Jewish women were not taught the Scriptures. But now Paul is saying that women who were new to the faith should be encouraged to learn
quietly[7] until they were ready to participate fully in the life of the church,

as mature women such as Phoebe (Romans 16:1-2) and Priscilla (Acts 18:24-26) were already participating.

Understanding the subjective elements of the translation process should, at the very least, make us cautious about developing an elaborate system of rules for gender relations based on words that have a range of possible meanings and passages that seem to be at odds with other scriptures. Indeed, it should lead to a desire to explore any new evidence—such as the continuing discoveries made by linguists and translators—and trusting the Holy Spirit to lead us into truth.

COMING OUT ON THE OTHER SIDE

It all sounds so simple now, so factual and convincing. But the process of searching for truth is never as linear as it sounds. My theological and intellectual journey had an emotional and spiritual side as well. Perhaps the fact that I was a preacher's kid and experienced my church almost as extended family made it more difficult for me than for some women to ask the questions I needed to ask, to claim my beliefs and then live them out. Even as things became clearer theologically, I was aware that I had a lot to lose.

I had to face the fact that I might lose the respect of those who would categorize me as "a liberal" or "a feminist"—whatever such ill-defined categories might mean. Opportunities for ministry might be fewer, at least in the short term, as people responded and reacted to the fact that I was "taking a position" on this controversial subject.

I knew that some of my significant relationships would be affected as well. It would require hard work to process the changes that were taking place in my life in response to the truth that I was trying to live into. I already knew that some might not have the flexibility to accommodate the freedom I was finding as I responded to God's call beyond what was traditionally viewed as acceptable for women. All of a sudden I began to understand more clearly what Jesus meant when he taught his disciples about the radical nature of following him—that sometimes it meant the willingness to "leave" those we love in order to follow God's risky invitations in our lives. I had always assumed that this teaching had to do with *physically* leaving to follow God's call to a foreign mission field or an opportunity for service across the country. But now I had to grapple with the fact that sometimes following God's risky invitations in our lives has to do with challenging ideology or theology that is too small to contain the reality of God, breaking with tradition that limits God's expression of the life he wants to live through us, or disappointing the expectations of those who thought they knew what God's will for us was.

The awareness of what I had to lose caused me to hesitate, and the place in which I hesitated was a very dark valley indeed. It was full of the anger and fragmentation that comes when we do not live out of our core beliefs. I couldn't pray. I couldn't worship. All I could do was shout my questions and wrestle with the Scriptures and God himself.

And there was grief. Grief over a world that should have been and could have been, but wasn't—a world where a young woman could pour out her love for God in service with no thought to gender. Grief over the time I had spent, in the psalmist's words, "as a beast before Thee" (73:22) stewing rather than serving. Grief over my own mistakes and the mistakes of others as I went through this process of growth. And most of all, grief over the fact that my understanding of God had, in some ways, been terribly distorted by the church's depiction of God's heart toward women.

Then one spring afternoon, several years after I had begun my search in earnest, the Holy Spirit communicated with me in the deep places of my soul, that place where God's Spirit witnesses with our spirit with sighs or utterances that are beyond words. It was a way of communicating that I had grown to recognize and trust throughout these years of quiet listening, an unmistakable impression upon my spirit: "I have spent years teaching you and leading you into truth. Now let that truth lead you out of this valley. It is time to stand for what you believe and never look back." If it had been any clearer, it would have been audible.

So I left the valley of darkness and unfreedom to stand on the truth that the Holy Spirit had spoken to my heart: the truth that *women and men are equally sinful and yet equally redeemed for full participation in every facet of life, love, and service.* As painful as the process had been, how glad I was that I had taken the time to wrestle with God over these issues. For like Jacob, who had wrestled with God's angel or God himself (Genesis 32:24), I walked away with the blessing of knowing where I stand in the presence of God and in the community of faith. Like Jacob, I have a painful place that is still sensitive, reminding me of the wrestling I have done. But I wouldn't trade this part of my journey for anything because understanding this truth has become a necessary part of growing in my love for God and in the freedom of serving him wholeheartedly. After all, it's hard to worship a God whom you do not feel free to serve.

A FOUNDATIONAL TRUTH

For women who want to know God more deeply, to grow in relationship with him, and to participate in shaping the next generation of women for Christ, there is nothing more important (aside from the issue of salvation) than knowing how God views us and whether we are free to serve him in the way that he calls us. The way we answer this question affects all areas of life: self-esteem, emotions, our relationships with husband, children, and parents, worship and service to God, and our view of ourselves at work and in society. It just doesn't get any more foundational than that!

But I also believe that the need to wrestle with this issue will pass over time. My parents once returned from a trip to Florida where they viewed pictures of ships on which slaves were brought to the United States from

Africa. They described how the slaves were transported with their arms and legs tied, forced to lie flat on the deck like cords of wood. Of course, to those of us living in the twenty-first century this is a horrifying image, and I was reminded of how far we have come. Even though we still have a long way to go in rooting out racism, it is hard to imagine a time when such open brutality was accepted.

Similarly, I believe that there will come a day when women will enjoy the full rights of God that "sons" know—those who receive the blessing of their family inheritance. And in that day, it will be hard to remember a time when anyone was barred from ministry or other life callings, simply because they were women. Jesus said, "You will know the truth, and the truth will set you free" (John 8:32, NIV). History shows us that freedom never comes without a fight. But it does come.

SPIRITUAL EXERCISES

Alone with God

Silence. As you come to the end of this chapter, take a few moments to sit with God in the silence of your own heart and reflect on one or more of these questions:

- What are some of your earliest memories of yourself as a little girl growing up, noticing and learning about what it meant to be a woman?
- Where did the strongest messages come from?
- What emotions do you feel as you scroll back through your childhood and notice these things?
- Who was God for you in the midst of these messages and experiences?
- Did you identify him with any aspect of these messages or did you find him to be different from what you were experiencing?

Prayer and journaling. Review this chapter, noticing the places of resonance and resistance that you highlighted. In your journal, tell God about the thoughts, feelings, desires, and questions that this chapter has raised for you. Notice the places where your experiences and questions were the same or different than the author's. Allow yourself to experience any emotions that come and to explore without judgment the source(s) of your emotions with words or by drawing pictures.

- What might your reaction indicate about what is going on in the deeper places of your soul?
- What is God inviting you to look at in yourself and in your experiences as a woman?

Invitations. *God, are you inviting me to hear or do anything in response to this chapter?*

With Your Spiritual Friend(s)

Begin your time together with a moment of silence and a simple prayer of invitation for God to join you.

Listening. Take turns giving each other your undivided attention. Share with each other a brief summary of what has happened between you and God this week in the context of your spiritual practices and your reading of this chapter.

- What did God say to you in your times of solitude and silence?
- What were your experiences of resonance and resistance as you read this chapter? How did you process those with God in your journal?
- What memories did this chapter trigger in you about yourself as a little girl learning what it meant to be a woman?
- What were the strongest messages you received?

- Which of these messages do you agree with or disagree with now that you are a grown woman looking to God for your truest identity?
- What questions do you still have?
- How does God seem to be inviting you to process those questions with him?

Prayer. Pray for one another.

THE FREEDOM TO LIVE IN TRUTH

In a restaurant let your mate or date do the ordering. You may know more about vintage wine than the wine steward, but if you are smart you'll let your man do the choosing and be ecstatic over his selection, even if it tastes like shampoo.

—ARLENE DAHL, *Always Ask a Man*

Do not lie to one another, seeing that you have stripped off the old self with its practices and have clothed yourselves with the new self, which is being renewed in knowledge according to the image of its creator.

—COLOSSIANS 3:9-10

One of my earliest moments of awareness that women have unique challenges relative to telling the truth came when I was in my late twenties. My husband and I had been identified as potential leaders in our fledgling church, so we were invited to take a class on leadership taught by the pastor. As a part of this class we were invited to take the PERFORMAX (DISC) personality test in order to understand our leadership styles better. We learned that according to this particular test, there are four personality types: D (dominant, Type-A personality), I (influencing), S (steady), and C (compliant). Each of us has one of these as our primary personality type and another that is secondary.

The results of my test were unmistakable: I definitely had the high D (dominant), Type-A personality. This wasn't exactly news to me; I was aware that my gifts and personality traits clustered around leadership. However, I had spent years trying to tone down that part of my personality. After all, what Christian woman wants to be called dominant when compliance and submissiveness are so much more highly valued in women? It took me a week to get over my embarrassment now that everyone knew my well-kept secret. My only comfort was the knowledge that most people in the class had guessed that I was an I personality (influencing, inspirational) which seemed to be a lot more acceptable in a woman. I congratulated myself on the fact that I had done a pretty good job of hiding myself.

This moment was startling in its clarity because I had to face the fact that I had an uneasy relationship with truth. In fact, I had to acknowledge that it was more natural for me to try to make reality more palatable to others based on their sensitivities than it was for me to live fully and freely in the truth—whatever it was in any given moment. As I began to pay attention to how I lived my own life in ways that were less than truthful, I noticed that I wasn't the only one.

Linda, a beautiful woman in her forties, shared similar tactics for trying to manage the truth of who she was in the context of her marriage. "My husband has always been a quiet man and I've always been outgoing and involved. I enjoy being in the center of things, but I've learned to be quiet so that he can be the leader and my children can see that he is the head of our home."

I could hear the wistfulness in her voice as she talked about her accomplishments involving leadership and communication during her high-school and young-adult years. She wanted me to understand that those strengths were just as much a part of her as was this newly chosen "quietness." Although she intended for her comments and behavior to be respectful of her husband, it really communicated the opposite. I couldn't help thinking, *You mean the only way your husband can be a leader is for you to withhold your strength?* It just didn't seem honest. Did her husband know of the self-confessed sadness that surfaced every now and then when she remembered lost opportunities for personal development? He was a loving husband; how would he feel if he ever realized that the price of his development was his wife's atrophy?

As distressing as Linda's comments were, I could relate to her need to minimize her own strengths. I became more and more curious about the dynamics that cause so many women—including myself—to hide the truth or at least soften it or minimize it. I was reminded of a Bible story that provides a window of insight into the dynamics and also the results of the struggle with truth-telling that women seem to share across the generations. You may be familiar with the story of Rebekah, who was married to Isaac. Together they had twin sons, Esau and Jacob. The problem was that they each had a favorite. Isaac preferred Esau because he was a hunter, and Rebekah favored Jacob, perhaps because he stayed closer to home. This favoritism brought out the worst in everyone—especially Rebekah. She was determined that her favorite, Jacob, would get the blessing that rightfully belonged to Esau.[1] God had already promised that Jacob would get the blessing (Genesis 25:23), but Rebekah, rather than trusting and waiting for God to fulfill his purposes, decided to help things along.

When Isaac was old, nearly blind, and ready to bestow his blessing on Esau, Rebekah sent Jacob to his father masquerading as Esau so that he would receive his brother's blessing. Jacob carried off the whole charade with precision. Shortly after Isaac had finished blessing Jacob, Esau returned from the fields ready to receive his blessing, and Isaac realized that there was something dreadfully wrong. He began to tremble violently as his mind pieced together what had happened and he realized that he had irreversibly blessed the wrong son (Genesis 27:33).

When Esau heard what had happened, "he cried out with an exceedingly great and bitter cry, and said to his father, 'Bless me, me also, father!' " (verse 34). But it was too late. Isaac had to give Esau the devastating news that his brother had come deceitfully and taken away his blessing. With gut-wrenching emotion Esau pleaded with his father to bless him with at least one blessing. Isaac did bless him, but it fell far short of the blessing Esau should have received (27:39-40) and it did nothing to heal the wounds that Rebekah's and Jacob's manipulation had inflicted. Esau was so full of rage against Jacob that he purposed to kill him after Isaac's death. In order to protect Jacob, Rebekah sent him away until Esau's fury died down.

In a time and culture where women had little power, Rebekah may have felt that this was the only way she could have influence; however, her manipulation cost her dearly. She lost her opportunity to trust God and see him come through with his best. She forfeited her own integrity. She failed to be an influence for good in the lives of those she loved. And she jeopardized every relationship that was important to her. As far as we know, when she sent Jacob away to escape Esau's murderous rage, it was the last time she saw her favored son.[2] And, in a turn of poetic justice, Jacob was deceived years later when his father-in-law-to-be gave him the wrong daughter as a bride (Genesis 29:15-30), which set off rivalry between sisters that embittered their home for decades.

GAMES WOMEN PLAY

Why is it that women often feel they have to resort to subtlety, indirectness, or even deceit to get what they want? One reason is that we receive strong messages from our culture encouraging us to pretend to be something we're not. As psychologist Harriet Goldhor Lerner describes it, there are certain aspects of a woman's socialization that quite naturally result in this kind of behavior.

> Pretending reflects deep prohibitions, real and imagined, against a more direct and forthright assertion of self. Pretending stems naturally from the false and constricted definitions of self that women often absorb without question. "Pretending" is so closely associated with "femininity" that it is, quite simply, what the culture teaches women to do.[3]

As another woman shares, our schooling in the fine art of manipulation and pretending often begins at home.

> In my family it was "unladylike" to say out loud what you wanted. I was admonished time and again that if someone wanted to give me something—candy, take me somewhere, read me a story, whatever—they would offer it of their own accord or just know that I wanted it. I got very good at hinting, pouting, and whining to get people to offer what I wanted without saying it straight out. Today as an adult, I've [been told] so many times, "Why can't you just say what you mean?"[4]

When you add these cultural messages to the ones that many of us received as a part of our religious upbringing, it's no wonder that we are a little hesitant about full disclosure!

GOD'S ALTERNATIVE TO PLAYING GAMES

Authentic relationships provide some of the greatest joys and deepest feelings of fulfillment that we can experience in this life. "We yearn for relationships where we can be completely honest, open and vulnerable. Where we can share failures as well as successes, shortcomings as well as strengths. Where we can reveal doubts and fears. Where we can find empathy and confidentiality."[5]

Sometimes, in our desire to cultivate such relationships, we opt for peace at any price because it seems less risky. Somehow it even seems more "Christian" to hide the truth about ourselves, to deny feelings, and to over-look offenses in an effort to avoid rocking the boat. However, when we skirt the truth and play games, the depth that we long for in our relation-ships will never develop.

From the Scriptures we learn that the key to deep and meaningful rela-tionships is truth-telling. It is only as we speak the truth in love that we grow up in relation to others, that we become knit together with them, and that we each can offer our unique strengths to the process of working together (Ephesians 4:15). But unfortunately, game playing comes more naturally to us as human beings than truth-telling. Why? Because telling the truth is scary, especially in relationships in which truth has not been the pattern. We might think:

- If I told my boss that I don't appreciate his suggestive comments, I could get passed over for a promotion.
- If I told my parents that it still bothers me that they were too busy for me, they would get mad and deny it.
- If I told my friend that some of her comments hurt me, she would just think I am overly sensitive.
- If I admitted to my small group that I was really struggling, they wouldn't think I was very spiritual.
- If I told my husband that I would like to pursue some of my own interests, he would panic.
- If I admitted how disturbed I am over the fact that we don't have any women elders at church, everyone would think I'm a feminist.

Yes, truth-telling can be frightening, but the alternative is much worse. When we cannot bring ourselves to tell the truth in our relationships, they will stay at a surface level at best; it is even more likely that they will deteriorate and die. Misunderstandings arise but are never resolved. Feelings beg to be shared but are left to fester inside. Offenses occur but nobody talks about them. Our true personalities are hidden and never invited to flourish in the warmth of acceptance. Avoidance patterns set in. Hurt and misunderstanding lead to detachment, distrust, and bitterness. And love begins to die.

A realistic look at the results of game playing motivates us to take courage in hand and cultivate greater levels of truth in our relationships.

TRUTH IN THE INWARD BEING

Truth-telling begins with telling *ourselves* the truth. Psalm 51:6 reminds us that God desires truth in the inward being—truth about our beliefs and doubts, truth about what is happening in our relationships, truth about how we feel, what bothers us, and how we need to change. It also includes telling God the truth, for as we are learning to speak truthfully with God, we begin being more honest with ourselves. The experience of talking to Someone who loves us unconditionally, coupled with the deep work of the Holy Spirit (his job, after all, is to lead us into truth) causes things to become clearer and leads us to greater honesty with ourselves.

It is fascinating to observe the healing powers of truth-telling in the life of David. In Psalm 73, for example, David is consumed by jealousy toward wicked people whose lives seem to be going so well while he, a man who is trying to live a godly life, seems to have one problem after another. He rages on and on for fourteen verses, laying it all out before God. Finally, in the quiet that usually follows a true catharsis, God showed him a bigger picture, a picture that included a long-range perspective ("Then I perceived their end...how they are destroyed in a moment," verses 17,19), self-knowledge ("I was like a brute beast toward you," verse 22), and heightened spiritual awareness ("There is nothing on earth that I desire other than you. My flesh and my heart may fail, but God is the strength of my heart," verses 25-26). No wonder David concluded that "for me it is good to be near God," (verse 28) for it was in his most honest moments that God was able to teach him wisdom "in my secret heart" (Psalm 51:6). And so it is with us.

TELLING OUR TRUE STORIES

Sometimes the hardest truth to tell ourselves and others is the truth about our experiences as women. So much of our literature, history, political context, and religious beliefs have been written and developed from a male perspective that we struggle to find a voice of our own—to talk about life the way we see it. Men have translated the Scriptures for us. Male pastors and teachers tell us how we should feel about being mothers. Male doctors evaluate our physical health and tell us how to be sexually fulfilled. Male psychologists tell us what it means to be psychologically well. We accept the roles assigned to us and believe it when we are told there must be something wrong with us if we're not satisfied with them. But every so often we wonder: *Why doesn't this fit for me? Why is mothering such a struggle for me? Why do I feel "less than" in my family, my church, or my work? Why am I uncomfortable going to a man for pastoral care? Why does fitting into the role carved out for me seem like shoving a square peg into a round hole? And why don't we hear the stories about all the brave, strong things women have done for God and humankind? Why are their struggles and triumphs saved for the women's coffee hour?*

When questions like these surface for ourselves or for others, it seems much safer to silence them with thoughts or words like, *Don't be ridiculous.*

This is what's best for us—everybody says so! But where is "truth in the inward being" (Psalm 51:6) if we don't give ourselves and others the freedom to ask our truest questions, to raise a hand (however timidly) and say, "Maybe that works for you, but my experience, my story, is very different"?

It is hard to tell the truth when all the voices around us seem to be saying something different. I know because I've tried it. As I have already described, one of the hardest truths I have ever struggled to tell myself, God, my husband, and others was how much it was hurting me to be a woman in the evangelical Christian subculture in which I had been raised. From my preteen years on I started noticing that there was something terribly wrong with the way women were treated in the church and it was tearing my soul apart. But the truth I was trying to tell about myself and the questions I was trying to ask were labeled "rebellion" almost as soon as I uttered them, so I quickly withdrew them and stuffed them down for a while longer.

It took me years to come right out and say that I just didn't believe all that I had been taught about "a woman's place" in marriage and in the church, that I saw something different when I read the Scriptures. But how does a woman go about exploring the reality of her experiences when everyone around her says she is wrong and "shouldn't feel that way"? Or when other women insist that their lives are completely fulfilling and the whole system is working for them?

At the time, I believed that other women were as satisfied as they said they were, but now I know that others also struggled. Some kept a stiff upper lip in public and cried their bitter tears alone. Some tried to tell their stories to "the powers that be" but found that they were never really heard. Others melted away quietly from Christian fellowships, not always sure of the forces at work against them but knowing they would die inside if they stayed. The few brave souls who refused to be silenced had been so completely excised that I was only aware of them to the extent that they had been labeled liberal and dangerous. Understandably, I felt very much alone in my turmoil—as though I was the strange one.

It wasn't until I was grown and well established in ministry that women began to tell me their true stories. A fiftyish woman who had taught with passion "wives submit to your husbands in all things" cried on my couch about a husband who made major life decisions without even consulting her. A single woman told me about having ministry opportunities withheld because she didn't have a man to team with. Several gifted women communicators told me about their rage and tears over being silenced in the church but asked me not to quote them because they feared the consequences of such honesty. A middle-aged woman admitted that her whole identity had been wrapped up in her children and now that they were gone, she was struggling desperately to keep depression at bay. As the director of women's ministry at one church where I served, I was cornered by a new Christian after a church service and was asked in hushed tones, "Could you tell me why we don't have any women pastors or elders? I mean, I love our pastors, but I could never go to one of them if I needed to talk about a problem." A young married woman told me her story of a husband who hit her when he got mad and the pastoral counselor who asked, "Well, what are you doing that causes him to do that?" And well into my married life, my own mother began to realize that wifely submission—as it had been taught in her generation—was an inadequate foundation for healthy relationships.

Why hadn't I heard these true stories when I needed them most? When I needed to know that my questions were legitimate and my unfolding story wasn't so unusual after all? Who was benefiting from this conspiracy of silence? And where is wholeness and integrity when we as women say we believe something and uphold it on an intellectual level but on an experiential level, we know it doesn't work?

It is very difficult to challenge what has already been accepted in society as the whole truth. Carol Gilligan, in her book *In a Different Voice,* demonstrates the impact of this problem in the field of psychology. She notes that psychological theory has been developed largely from the study of men so that women never seem to fit existing models of human growth. Rather than recognizing the imbalance in the studies, experts have assumed that the problem was with women's development.

Harriet Goldhor Lerner puts it this way, "Once something is defined as unfeminine or gender inappropriate, the old rules cannot easily be challenged. When women differ from the theories, the exceptions only prove rather than probe the rule, and it is the women—not the theories—who are brought into question. Women are still trying to fit into the predominant theories of the day rather than the other way around."[6] This at least partially explains why it can be frightening to present a different view than what is normally accepted; there is always the very distinct possibility that someone will say, "The problem is not with the way things are; the problem is you."

In addition, "females in our culture are reinforced in their avoidance of their own power. Not openly expressing dissent (or a different view of reality) is applauded as being cooperative, and not risking hurting others is seen as being self-sacrificial.... For men, being seen as outspoken is not felt as pejoratively as it is for women."[7]

There are very real reasons that we find it so hard to speak the truth about our experiences and questions. Yet truth, integrity, and wholeness call to us just like fresh air calls to us on a spring day. Integrity or wholeness is a strong theme in the Bible. Proverbs 20:7 states, "The righteous walk in integrity." William Backus points out that *integrity,* as it is used in such verses, means "manifesting in life and words the truth a person knows in [her] heart. When [she] knows the truth about what is in [her] heart and then allows that truth to surface, [she] has integrity." He continues:

The word *integrity* comes from the Latin *integer* meaning a whole number, not a fraction. The concept behind integrity is wholeness. When a person is the same without and within, when what others know about [her] is the same as what [she] knows about [herself], [she] has integrity. When someone knows the truth about [herself] and tries to hide it from others, [she] lacks integrity.[8]

When we lack a true understanding of ourselves and are afraid to show others who we really are, we end up "faking it" much of the time, which leads to the kinds of manipulation already discussed in this chapter.

When we do work up the courage to be honest with ourselves and with others, our honesty may lead to a "crisis of faith" or, as Bill Hybels calls it, "the tunnel of chaos" in our relationship with God, with others, and within ourselves. It certainly did for me. At times my own truth-telling took the form of angry shouting, lots of crying, unbelievable sadness, frenzied study- ing (because I just had to know), and admitting (much more than I wanted to) that I just *didn't* know. It tested my relationships to their limit. But God was deeper than the abyss I thought I was falling into, faith was stronger than my fears, and I did come out on the other side. When I first went into the tunnel of chaos ("where hurts are unburied, hostilities revealed, and tough questions asked"[9]), I wasn't sure there would be anything on the other side.

But I found that, even though it sometimes feels like I have more ques- tions than answers, the air is clearer on the other side of the tunnel (life is pretty hazy when we're not telling the truth), and the world is bigger, so big that at times I can't get my arms around it. (Truth is, after all, bigger than any of us). And I am more alive—spiritually, intellectually, emotionally, relationally—than I have ever been. That's what telling the truth does to you in the inward being.

TELLING EACH OTHER THE TRUTH

Telling ourselves and each other the truth—about who we are, how we feel, what we know, what we're questioning, what is working and what is tearing us apart in relationships and life—well, it takes raw courage at times. And it takes courage plus diligence and discipline to bring that kind of honesty into our everyday communications. Psychologist William Backus points out that

> our customs of speech frequently skirt the truth! We say, "I'd love to have you come," when we don't want the other person to come at all. We say, "Your wishes are all that matter to me," and then get angry when the other person tells us honestly what he wants. We hide what we really want and then act cross when others fail to discern our heart's desires. We fear honest refusals so we agree to do things we dislike. We explain to others why we simply must do something when the truth is we want to do it and there is no must to it. We manipulate others with expressions intended to arouse guilt before God, when our real motive is to control their behavior.
>
> Is it any wonder our relationships often hang by a thread? Or that our attempts at communication don't work? Is it any wonder nobody really knows us? Or that we can't be as close to other human beings as we can to our dogs and cats? The truth can set relationships free, as it can set the individual free,...not harsh truth, but truth spoken in love.[10]

A good place to begin the journey toward greater truth in our relationships is to police ourselves for accuracy in our everyday communications.

We can learn to let go of manipulative and less-than-honest communication patterns in favor of a more honest, straightforward approach. For instance:

- Instead of indirect communication such as dropping hints and "shoulding" ("You should stop watching so much television"), we can choose a more direct approach ("I am really concerned about how much time the television is on in our home. It seems to keep us from spending time talking, reading, or doing other things together. Would you be willing to discuss setting some limits on the television?").

- Instead of "guilting" ("After all I do for you, the least you could do is…"), we can be honest about our feelings of being unappreciated ("Sometimes I feel like I do so much for you, but then when I need help, you're too busy. You probably don't mean it that way, but that's the way I'm feeling right now").

- Instead of withholding ourselves by administering the silent treatment, pouting, or making ourselves sexually unavailable, we can talk about what is going on in the relationship ("I don't like it when you criticize me in public as you did today. It makes it very difficult for me to open up to you").

- Instead of intimidating, exaggerating, or issuing ultimatums ("If you do that again, I'm quitting!"), we can say something that is more honest and realistic ("I am not willing to be verbally abused just to keep my job. If you do not stop, I will need to speak to our supervisor").

- Instead of secretly enlisting the help of others in pushing our agenda ("I just can't get through to my husband on this. Do you think you could talk to him about…?"), we can talk directly to him ("Since we seem to be stuck on this issue, would you be willing for the two of us to get help from a counselor?").

- Instead of telling those little white lies ("Sure, it will be no problem to take care of your kids this afternoon," when you know it could just put you over the edge), we can tell the truth ("I wish I could help you out, but I don't think I'd better take that on this afternoon.").
- Instead of faking sexual enjoyment, we can be honest ("I'm really committed to having a great sex life with you, and that's why I need to tell you that this just isn't working for me. Could we try something else?").

At first these new communication patterns may feel as uncomfortable as a new pair of shoes, but the more we walk in them, the more comfortable they will become. Intimacy, trust, and kinship will grow because when we feel hurt, rather than withdrawing and losing closeness, we will talk about it, gain insight, and establish new patterns that protect love. When we say, "Yes, I would love to!" others won't have to ask "Are you sure?" because they will know they can trust what we say. And when, in the process of speaking truthfully, we get glimpses of the true selves that are often hiding behind facades, we will experience connection with fellow human beings that is unspeakably fulfilling.

WHEN THE TRUTH IS HARD TO HEAR

Of course, the other side of our being "direct and forthright" is that we welcome others to be just as honest with us. We need to demonstrate that authenticity and growth in our relationships are more important than the personal comfort that can only be maintained through denial and defensiveness. We need to accept honest refusals when they are given. And we need to listen and receive others in the manner in which we want to be listened to and received.

I learned this lesson the hard way one Sunday when I deeply offended some of the women in my church with comments I made during our weekend service. Speaking on the topic of "heroes," I made the point that heroes are often people we look up to because they have succeeded in areas in which we would like to succeed. To illustrate my point, I mentioned a Christian author whose teaching on womanhood and marriage I had respected until she had gotten a divorce. I mentioned that I no longer looked up to her in the way that I used to.

One woman who had gone through a divorce was so angry that she couldn't wait until the service was over to speak with me. She left her seat to request in whispered tones that we step into the hallway to talk. Then, her voice trembling with emotion, she said, "Do you have any idea what it was like to sit there with my children and listen to what you said today? I have worked so hard to regain my dignity after my divorce, to create a stable life for my children and to find my place here in this church. Then to have you get up there and say that you didn't think you had anything to learn from someone like me! I had hoped that you could respect me and maybe learn something from my mistakes. And those of us who have gone through a divorce—well, we would like to be married again someday, and we would like to be able to learn from those of you who are still married about how to make a marriage work."

There was more, but I think you get the idea. It was a painful experience, but—praise God!—the first thing that happened (after I told myself to calm down and just listen) was that I saw myself in this dear woman.

I saw that her pain (of being viewed as "less than" in the church) was very similar to the pain I had experienced in the church all these years. The fact that I had been honest about the pain in my life made me much more sensitive to hers. I, too, had been an outsider—a woman in a male-dominated system. Here she was, another outsider (a divorced woman in a system that valued women who had managed to stay married) trying to tell her story to one of those insiders (a married woman who happened to be in charge of the Women's Ministry). It was a story I needed to hear.

Of course I would have liked to defend myself, as anyone would, but there was no adequate defense. My comments had been thoughtless and insensitive; the fact that I hadn't meant them to be was completely beside the point. I needed to listen to her pain, to hear myself through her ears as she sat in the auditorium that day, and to tell her how sorry I was. I needed to tell her that, yes, there was a lot I could learn from her and the struggles she had been through. In fact, I was already learning.

I shed tears that day. Some were tears of disappointment in myself for making such a hurtful mistake, some were tears for the women who came to church that day hoping for a word that would minister grace to their souls but instead received a barb. But there were also tears of gratefulness that this friend (and friend she was) didn't let me walk out the door ignorant of the pain I had caused, doomed to inflict it again at some other time and place.

I was honored that, rather than letting our relationship go the way of churning anger that would eventually cool into a numb distance, she struggled with the truth of her experience and then offered it to me. In that moment, I knew that even though the externals of our lives were so different, we were sisters who had many similarities. I knew that here was a friendship full of integrity—that when the truth needed to be told, this relationship could handle it. And I knew that the experience of hearing and being heard—of having an effect and being affected—was very rich for both of us that day, richer than any word I could have spoken from any podium.

A RICHER LIFE EXPERIENCE

The struggle toward truth-telling is at the center of our deepest longing for intimacy with others. It is not that we have to tell everything, or tell it all at once, or even know beforehand all we need to tell. But an honorable relationship is one in which we are trying all the time to extend the possibilities of truth—and life—between us.[11] The point is not merely to get what we want (although that may very well happen). The goal of truth-telling is greater personal integrity and wholeness, life-giving intimacy with others, and the richness that comes when we accept the differences in experience that many people bring to our society, as well as to the body of Christ.

A power comes from saying what we believe and believing what we say. This is the strength we have to offer our world. When we give that up, we become fragmented at our very core. It is painful and exhausting for a woman to begin to uncover the truth of her own experiences in a culture that has assigned more importance to what men think, feel, and say. But the relationships, the Christian communities, and the social and political structures worth having require that we engage in this difficult yet rewarding process. As women of integrity, we cannot settle for anything less.

⌒ S P I R I T U A L   E X E R C I S E S ⌒

Alone with God

Silence. As you come to the end of this chapter, take a few moments to sit with God in the silence of your own heart.

- Is there an area in your life where you know a truth needs to be told—within yourself, in your relationship with God, in your relationship with others?
- Where do you play games with truth rather than walking freely in truth?

Do not feel like you have to do anything with the truth that you just identified. Don't jump to any conclusions about the implications of telling this truth. Just sit with the truth in God's presence and allow yourself all the thoughts and emotions that come. As you sit with this truth, do you have any glimpses of the kind of freedom that might be waiting on the other side of your willingness to walk in this truth?

Prayer and journaling. Review the chapter that you have just read, noticing the places of resonance and resistance that you have highlighted. In your journal, tell God about the thoughts, feelings, desires, and questions that this chapter has raised for you. Notice the places where your experiences and questions were the same as or different from the women described here. In your journal, express your feelings as well as your arguments and places of agreement or disagreement.

Invitations. *God, are there any areas of my life where you are inviting me to walk more freely in truth?* (As you ask God to invite you into truth, you might be thinking about the potential risks of truth-telling. You could express those concerns to God in prayer. You may also want to think about the potential rewards of truth-telling. Allow these to inspire you to do what you need to do.)

With Your Spiritual Friend(s)

Begin your time together with a moment of silence and a simple prayer of invitation for God to join you.

Listening. Take turns giving each other your undivided attention. Share with each other a brief summary of what has happened between you and God this week in the context of your spiritual practices and your reading of this chapter.

- What did God say to you in your times of solitude and silence?
- What were your experiences of resonance and resistance as you read this chapter? How did you process those with God in your journal?

- What is the area of your life where God is speaking to you about the need to walk in truth?
- What is it like for you to consider telling more truth or living into more truth in this area?
- What kind of support do you need?

Prayer. Pray for one another.

SIX

～

FREEDOM FROM THE TYRANNY OF THE "NEVER-ENOUGH" WORLD

The trouble with being in the rat race is that even if you win, you're still a rat.

—LILY TOMLIN

When my husband and I were first married and living in a small apartment, I thought that if we could just buy a house I would be satisfied. We had married right out of college and started our family shortly thereafter so the dream of owning a home seemed far off indeed. But miracles do still find their way into modern life: some acquaintances, who needed to quickly sell a home they owned, offered to help us with the down payment. Consequently, we became proud homeowners much sooner than we had expected. Even though it was a modest, three-bedroom ranch in need of decorating and repair, it felt so good to have space! To walk out our front door into a grassy yard rather than a dank hallway seemed like heaven on earth. For the privilege of owning a home I could live with peeling paint, yellow and green wallpaper, and an outdated kitchen.

Or could I?

It didn't take long for me to realize that I'm not that easily satisfied. I was fine as long as the first flush of purchasing excitement lasted. But pretty soon, desire began to overtake me again. If we could just replace the shag carpeting, get rid of those avocado-colored appliances, and remodel the kitchen, then I'd be satisfied.

Well, ten years later we had done all those things (and more!), and I had a startling realization: It doesn't matter how much we buy, there is always plenty more I want. The pull of things in my life is so deep and so strong that, at times, I have despaired of ever being free of it. I am very much a part of the "never-enough" world and chances are, so are you. Do you ever wonder why, even though you understand the dangers of debt, you spend money that you don't have? Or why, when you are lonely or depressed, it seems to help to go shopping? Why, before the paint is even dry on one remodeling project, you are plotting the next one? Why you feel so much more credible when you're wearing full makeup and a business suit than when you're wearing a jogging suit and the face God gave you? Or why your husband feels that he can never satisfy your material wants? Do you ever wish for the freedom that comes from being content with what you have? I wonder about myself sometimes, especially when my daughter once commented (with a perception beyond her years), "Daddy works so Mommy can buy the things she wants."

ALWAYS CONSUMING, NEVER SATISFIED

There are reasons why, with all that we have in life, it seems there are so many more things we just can't live without. In the never-enough world, the twin gospels of materialism and consumerism are preached nearly every time we open a magazine, turn on the television, or talk to a neighbor. Materialism[1] lulls us into believing that the physical, material world is the most "real," while consumerism, the dominant economic theory in North

America, entices us with the idea that the accumulation of more and better things is a worthy goal for our lives. Mix in a little bit of spiritual or psychological flavoring and you get the idea that material things provide the answers to life's basic questions:

- *What am I worth?* The most expensive hair color product.
- *What is success?* Being able to buy dinner for my husband with my own credit card.
- *How do I find peace of mind?* Buy more insurance.
- *How do I show someone how much I love them?* Send them "the very best" greeting card.
- *What do I do when the going gets tough?* Go shopping, of course.

Materialism and consumerism dovetail in their promises that if we can just achieve a higher income level, get our dream house, wear the right clothes, and enjoy the right kinds of leisure activities, we will be satisfied. But these two outlooks often produce families that are unable to get off the treadmill because they are deeply in debt…parents who have no time for each other or their children…families with nicer things than their parents had at that age but little time to enjoy them…men and women who know how to dress for success but are full of inner doubts and questions. Alongside our many acquisitions exists a profound sense of dissatisfaction that is never quelled for very long.

In *The Hidden Persuaders,* Vance Packard documents the way in which Americans are programmed to "consume, consume, consume, whether we need or even desire the products almost forced upon us."[2] He observes that after World War II American manufacturers were able to produce many more goods than people were consuming so they began exploring the question, "How can we stimulate the American people to buy more?"

They engaged sociologists and psychologists to teach them how to stimulate consumer buying by creating wants in people that they didn't realize existed. These trainers, who called themselves "motivation researchers," taught merchandisers to probe people's subsurface desires, needs, and drives in order to find their points of vulnerability. What the merchandisers identified were the very deepest human longings: our longings for love, our dreams of fitting in and "being somebody," our desire for power, and our need for emotional security. "Once these points of vulnerability were isolated, the psychological hooks were fashioned and baited and placed deep in the merchandising sea for unwary customers."[3]

The way they began to hook us was to offer considerably more than the actual item involved.

A car becomes more than just a car; it becomes an expression of your truest self. A particular hair coloring product becomes more than a beauty product; it tells me how much I'm worth. An exotic vacation becomes more than just some needed rest and relaxation; it becomes the panacea for all relational ills. A certain beverage becomes more than just a way to quench one's thirst; it promises adventure and maybe even some "community" in the midst of the adventure. Obviously, these manufacturers are trying to sell us much more than a car or a beauty product or a beverage; they are "selling to our hidden needs" quite unashamedly.

It is important for us to realize that a lack of contentment is now a part of our American cultural fabric. Manufacturers depend on the consumer (you and me) to be dissatisfied so that we will buy more and thus stimulate the economy. As one ad executive proclaims, "What makes this country great is the creation of wants and desires, the creation of dissatisfaction with the old and outmoded."[4] So, if you are dissatisfied, it is a sure sign that you were born in the U.S.A.!

GREAT EXPECTATIONS

Not only do hidden messages from our culture influence us, but our individual generation influences us as well. With the baby-boomer generation came a propensity toward an attitude of entitlement that has influenced us all. Researcher Landon Jones comments on this relatively new phenomenon: "For most of human history, people had thought that life was hard, brutal and tragic. The baby boom's early affluence [in the postwar years of the '50s and '60s] developed within it what some have called 'the psychology of entitlement.' What other generations had thought privileges, the baby boomers thought were rights."[5]

In the words of author Mike Bellah, we have created generations of overexpecters:

> We baby boomers were raised to believe we deserved a college education—for us and for our children—whether we could afford it or not. We deserved a secure retirement. We deserved the best medical care. We deserved a nice home in the suburbs. We deserved not just the pursuit of happiness; we deserved to be happy.[6]

I certainly see myself fitting into that description. I expected our "starter home" to be just that—a steppingstone along the way to something bigger. When we ended up living there much longer than I expected (fifteen years to be exact) I had to ask myself, "Who says?" People all over the world and right here in our own inner cities live with their extended families in small apartments. They never "expect" even to own a home, let alone the suburban type of home on which I and so many of my fellow baby boomers have our hearts set. Who says life owes that to me?

The generation younger than baby boomers, often called "Generation X," is now in its twenties and thirties. As this generation seeks business success and family stability, they, too, hunger for the money and possessions that my generation wanted. Although younger generations often emphasize values other than money, we all find ourselves greedy at times for what we think is rightfully ours.

The more we understand the messages of consumerism and materialism, the more we are able to spot their lies and free ourselves from their tyranny. Rather than being manipulated by these messages on a subconscious level, we will be able to "decode them by trying to cut through the layers of alibis, half-truth and image to get to the facts beneath."[7] It is only then that we are in a position to make real choices.

BEWARE OF DANGER

We also need to realize that remaining unaware of the undercurrent of materialism can be dangerous. The most obvious danger is that the undercurrent can pull us into its powerful undertow before we even know it. Consider the biblical story of Lot's wife, a woman who was so attached to her things that it spelled major disaster for her and her family. Although we don't know much about her spiritual sensitivities, we do know that Lot was a godly man whose soul eventually grew deeply disturbed by the filthy lives of the Sodomites. But he was a soul divided. Even though he was deeply disturbed by what was going on around him, "He liked the good life of Sodom's society. He preferred making money off its citizens to staying in the hills where there would be no filthy living but also no 'good life.'"[8] But he had a terrible price to pay for this indulgence. Rather than acting as an influence for good, Lot lost his own moral moorings, and God had to send two angels to forcibly lead Lot and his family out of Sodom before it was destroyed by the consuming fire of God. They literally grabbed Lot, his wife, and their two daughters by the hands and physically forced them to leave, warning them in no uncertain terms, "Flee for your life; do not look back or stop anywhere in the Plain; flee to the hills, or else you will be consumed" (Genesis 19:17).

As the family hurried to safety, Sodom and Gomorrah and the entire plain in which these cities were located were consumed by fire and sulfur.

But Lot's wife, trailing behind, looked back and was overtaken by sulfurous vapors. Encrusted with salt, she died there on the plain, captured in the pose that symbolized her attachment to the wealth, society, and sin that had been her whole life.

We are not left to wonder about what was in the heart of Lot's wife that day. Christ himself interprets this story for us. When teaching his disciples about the coming of the kingdom of God, he warns them about being so caught up in the material world that they are out of touch with spiritual realities. As an example, he mentions the people living in Lot's day, specifically Lot's wife:

> Just as it was in the days of Lot: they were eating and drinking, buying and selling, planting and building [in other words, completely caught up in the material world], but on the day that Lot left Sodom, it rained fire and sulfur from heaven and destroyed all of them—it will be like that on the day that the Son of Man is revealed. On that day, anyone on the housetop who has belongings in the house must not come down to take them away; and likewise anyone in the field must not turn back. Remember Lot's wife. (Luke 17:28-32)

Christ instructed the disciples to remember Lot's wife as an example of one whose attachment to material things had anesthetized her to spiritual realities. She had lived for physical realities for so long that she was unaware of the decay in her soul. Even when she came face to face with impending doom, she was unable to disentangle herself from the hold that the material world had on her heart. Her treasures were in Sodom and with them, her loyalty and affection. So she looked back, and it spelled her destruction.

It would be tempting to distance ourselves from this woman with protests like "I don't know her. I don't understand her. I would never…" But we *do* know her; she is our sister, and we share with her the same tendency to be deeply enamored with the things that we can see and physically know. Our doom may not be as sudden or dramatic as hers, but we are in just as much danger.

As one more contemporary woman shares, "Credit ruined my marriage, my self-image, and our family's future. It was a dreadful spiral that almost led to the loss of our home." She first applied for credit to pay off her overspending on Christmas presents. She was amazed at how easy it was to obtain credit and how accommodating the company was in hiding the loan from her husband:

> Not only did I get it (cash in hand the following day!) but they also agreed to use my office address rather than my home address, so the deception began. From time to time they offered me further funds, which I was too weak to refuse, and I had by that time also contracted with various stores for credit card debts as well. Soon it was completely out of control, and I had to borrow further just to meet monthly payments.[9]

The worse the problem became, the harder it was to tell her husband the truth; it was only when she was close to a mental breakdown that the truth came out. In her desperation, she turned to her church, where the pastor and treasurer took charge of the finances. Although they were able to negotiate a workable repayment schedule with her creditors, she still had at least ten years of repayment ahead of her. However, the worst part was the damage this situation caused to her relationship with her husband. In her own words, "The most awful thing to deal with is the lack of trust and forgiveness toward me by my husband, but who can blame him? Debt turned me from an honest trustworthy person into a deceitful liar.... Whatever I hear about people's shortcomings these days, my reaction is 'there but for the grace of God go I.' It's so easy to fall into the debt trap."[10]

This woman's story speaks to some of the most obvious pitfalls in a materialistic society: debt and the accompanying rat race, loss of integrity, and fractured relationships. Our human desire for more things and nicer things coupled with our existence in a society that encourages us to "buy now, pay later" is a highly combustible combination. There but for the grace of God go many of us, some of whom are already teetering right on the edge of financial disaster.

RECOGNIZING OUR EMPTINESS OF SOUL

But other dangers lurk beneath the shimmering surface of the material sea. They are harder to spot, to be sure, but they are no less real. What I've noticed about myself is that when I get too caught up in the constant noisiness of the activity and purchasing that is characteristic of modern culture, my soul becomes numb. The stillness in which the voice of God can be heard never comes. The truth that is born of quietness and expectant waiting is lost in the din of a frantic world. The opportunity to spend my life for a cause that is greater than myself is forfeited when I keep grabbing for those things that will give me instant but short-lived gratification. It's a vicious cycle: The more I give myself over to the material world, the emptier I feel inside. The emptier I feel, the more I am attracted to those things that will distract me from those feelings. The more distracted I am from the emptiness I'm feeling, the less opportunity there is to fill it with what is truly satisfying and I find myself caught in a vicious cycle. Even when I know that more commitments and more spending are not good for me, I'm not always able to say no.

While it has been sobering to face the fact that there are areas in my life that are out of control, this realization has become the motivation I have needed to quiet myself and ask the questions I have needed to ask. Oftentimes, the questions we are willing to ask ourselves are just as important as the answers we think we know. Questions such as:

- What do I expect out of life, and where do those expectations come from?
- What is success, and do I tend to measure it by outward trappings?
- How much of myself am I giving to my loved ones, and how much am I relying on expensive gifts to communicate love?
- What is happening inside me and in my relationships right before I go on an unnecessary shopping spree?
- What happens for me when I do let things get quiet? Is it peaceful, or is there unresolved pain that surfaces?
- What is the real source of emptiness or drivenness that I feel?

In the noisiness of our lives, it is hard to quiet ourselves and wait for the answers to questions as important as these. The truth that has come in my own quiet listening is this: As much as I am influenced by the tide of cultural messages, the source of my discontent goes far deeper than that. In the quietness I have found a woman who has allowed the affluence of her community to shape her expectations and feed her dissatisfaction. I have found a woman who can be unsure of her worth when she is not achieving. A Christian who knows how to do all the Christian "stuff," but has a lot to learn about being still and experiencing the presence of God as completely satisfying. A wife who finds it much easier to buy things for her husband than to offer unconditional love, acceptance, and physical affection. A mother who has let her children slip into the same frantic pace to which she was so prone, rather than building a life for them in which the material world is balanced with relationships, participation in the work of family life, and quiet time for reading, reflection, and cultivating spiritual awareness.

These are the places where I have needed to start stemming the tide of materialism in my own life. As I have learned to receive God's unconditional love for me and embrace the beauty of who I am as a created being uniquely called by God (which, by the way, has nothing to do with hair color), as I have experienced the soul satisfaction of giving more of myself to the people I love, as I have worked within the structure of our family life to include more of what matters most, as I have spent more time quietly in God's presence (not doing, just being)…the pull of the material world has begun to lessen.

REAL ANSWERS

In some ways, it would be easier if someone would just come along and tell us exactly how much is enough so that we could fall into line. But answers that fit into simple categories of right and wrong or 1-2-3 solutions are not real answers. Neither are answers that hold up someone else's lifestyle for us to copy. These rob us of the opportunity to stop our own material madness long enough to experience the empty places in our soul—the insecurity that is masked by all those "dress for success" clothes, the disappointment of an unfulfilling marriage that is numbed by constant activity, or the depression that is kept at bay by the "rush" we get when we go shopping. It is only when we have quieted ourselves long enough to listen to what is happening within us that real answers begin to emerge.

The truth is that we are created to be in relationship with God and others in ways that fill our souls. Just as our individual hereditary characteristics are embedded in our chromosomes, so our need and ability for relationship is embedded in the DNA of our souls. When sin, rebellion, or lack of attention causes rifts in our most important relationships, the emptiness of soul that results can be very painful. We may try to fill our emptiness by acquiring more things. But there will never be enough material things to satisfy the longings of the human soul. That is why Hebrews 13:5 draws such a strong connection between freedom from materialism and our relationship with God: "Keep your lives free from the love of money, and be content with what you have; for [or because] he has said, 'I will never leave you or forsake you.'"

The questions that materialism claims to answer are important questions indeed, but the answers can only be satisfied in a personal relationship with God that is growing deeper every day. *What am I worth?* I am worth so much that God sent his Son to experience the pain of sin and then take my penalty. *What is success?* Truly knowing God and accomplishing his purposes for my life. *How do I find peace of mind?* In knowing that God will never leave me. *How do I show someone I love them?* By giving myself sacrificially as Christ did. *And what do I do when the going gets tough?* I place my confidence in a loving God who has promised to help.

These real questions help us acknowledge the emptiness of soul that makes us so vulnerable to the hooks embedded in the messages of our culture. Real answers offer insights about ourselves, the material world, and the spiritual world that free us to choose a lifestyle consistent with our core values rather than cultural norms. Real answers help us keep our perspective in a world where desire is out of control. Real answers take us deeper into the relationships for which we were created. Real answers are found in becoming more consistent and intentional about pursuing the relationships for which we were created. Over time, almost imperceptibly at first, we become less obsessed with money and things and begin finding true satisfaction for the empty places of our souls.

KEEPING THINGS IN PERSPECTIVE

I would be unrealistic if I did not admit how much I enjoy the things money buys. Our home with its grassy lawn and good neighbors has been a wonderful place to raise our family and host our friends. The "sacred space" where I write and receive people in spiritual direction has become a true haven for myself and others to pray and listen for God's voice. Money spent on trips and vacations has been money invested in relationships, soul care, and appreciation of our created world. And life would certainly be more difficult without adequate, regular income. I enjoy these gifts without guilt because God "richly provides us with everything for our enjoyment" (1 Timothy 6:17).

But a balanced perspective reminds me that money does have its limitations. It can buy clothes but not confidence, cosmetics but not true beauty, an exotic vacation but not the ability to relax and sleep. Money provides alarm systems but not peace of mind, a shopping trip but not a friend to go with you, a *Better Homes and Gardens* house but not a mom who has time and energy left to play games or read stories. It buys expensive gifts but not love.

A balanced perspective also keeps me from being consumed by my materialistic desires and warns me about sacrificing what really matters in life for things that never quite satisfy. The material world offers a lot to women today—jobs, titles, sophisticated clothes, beautiful houses. It's tempting to try to grab for it all at once. But there is great potential for regret in this area, potential for getting to the end of our lives and realizing, "I put so much pressure on my husband (or myself) to make more money or go into more debt, that the rat race damaged our relationship." Or, "We got our dream house and car, but I had to go to work to pay for it all. I missed being home with my kids during the times they needed me most."

Contrary to the messages of materialism, it isn't the woman who dies with the most toys who wins. Freedom from the tyranny of the never-enough world comes in wanting only what you have rather than being driven to acquire everything you want. As we grow more contented with what God has given us, rather than straining for what he has not given, we are less vulnerable to the dangers of debt, the demands of a consumerist culture, and the emptiness of soul that keeps us striving for more.

As we learn to allow our relationship with God and with others to satisfy the emptiness of our souls, the hooks embedded within our materialistic culture can no longer find a place inside us to attach themselves to. And then we are free indeed!

⌒ SPIRITUAL EXERCISES ⌒

Alone with God

Silence. As you come to the end of this chapter, take a few moments to sit with God in the silence of your own heart and ask, *Which of the dangers associated with the material world am I most vulnerable to right now?* Without feeling like you have to do anything, allow yourself to notice the ways in which this vulnerability plays itself out in your life.

Prayer and journaling. Review the chapter that you have just read, noticing the places of resonance and resistance that you have highlighted.

- Where in your life right now do you get "hooked" by cultural messages?
- Are you able to recognize those times when you use material things to distract you from your emptiness of soul?
- Which of the bulleted questions listed on page 106 do you recognize as questions you ask yourself?

Allow yourself time to journal your response to these questions and to tell God what you are noticing about yourself as you think about relating to the material world. Identify what you need most from him these days and then express your need to him in prayer.

Invitations. *God, are you inviting me to do anything in response to what I have read today? How do you want me to respond to your invitation?*

With Your Spiritual Friend(s)

Begin your time together with a moment of silence and a simple prayer of invitation for God to join you.

Listening. Take turns giving each other your undivided attention. Share with each other a brief summary of what has happened between you and God this week in the context of your spiritual practices and your reading of this chapter.

- What did God say to you in your times of solitude and silence?
- What were your experiences of resonance and resistance as you read this chapter? How did you process those with God in your journal?
- To what dangers of the material world are you most vulnerable right now?
- What empty places in your soul do you try to fill with something from the material world?
- How is God inviting you to fill those empty places with something that is truly satisfying? (Try to be as concrete as possible.)

Prayer. Pray for one another.

SEVEN

THE FREEDOM OF UNITY
IN MARRIAGE

*When I look at it [my wedding dress], it hurts that all that care
is taken to preserve a dress when so little care was taken to preserve a family, but I guess it's easier to store a dress than to make
a marriage work.*

—PATTI ROBERTS

Marriage certainly does receive mixed reviews in contemporary culture. As
women, we run the gamut from pinning all of our hopes on marriage to
rejecting marriage as a trap that relegates us to limited roles and responsibilities. Bachelor and bachelorette parties traditionally given for grooms
and brides on the eve of their wedding seem to reflect this tension. In many
cases, the spouse-to-be commemorates a final night of "freedom" by watching raunchy movies and joking about the marriage trap, yet this is contradictory to the dreams many of us have about getting married.

Undoubtedly, many of society's images of married life—the nagging
wife who lives in curlers and a bathrobe, the couch-potato husband whose
most effective communication is yelling for his beer, unruly kids, bills that
never end, perfunctory sex—do perpetuate the idea that marriage is a trap.
But in actuality most of us get married because we have a great deal of hope

that our marriage will be one of the exceptions—one of the few that really work. Deep down, most of us do not believe that marriage is a trap; we believe the truth that marriage is given to be a source of great joy and fulfillment. Otherwise, we probably wouldn't even consider it!

Sometimes—when a marriage isn't working—it *is* experienced as a trap. This happens when conflicts are left unresolved, faulty communication patterns become entrenched, pain and hurt are stuffed down instead of dealt with, and fitting into traditional roles is more important than understanding individuals. When we feel trapped we have a tendency to feel desperate. And desperation can tempt us to ease the pain of a marriage that isn't working by getting involved with someone else, physically leaving the marriage, or shutting down emotionally. However, in a marriage that is working there is great freedom: to love and be loved, to allow ourselves to be transformed in the context of a committed relationship with another person, and to support each other in finding the truest expression of our most authentic selves.

So what does "a marriage that works" look like?

A MARRIAGE BIG ENOUGH FOR BOTH OF US

A marriage that works is one that frees both women and men to continue to discover who they are and to function as a team according to their gifts, personalities, and strengths. Preconceived notions about male-female roles in marriage have the potential to thwart this process of discovery and teambuilding, putting people in boxes so small that real people cannot fit into them!

Listen in on Diane's story of a marriage in which there is a lot of room for her husband and very little room for anyone else:

I became a submissive wife [as a means of] survival. It meant learning to live and survive in peace and getting as much my way as I

could, without causing a lot of commotion. I would have to calcu-
late: Clifford will only let me have my way on so many things
within the next week, so I'd better decide what those things are
going to be. I gave up some things for myself—personhood
things—so the girls could have more.... I had stamina enough to
fight for what the girls needed, but not enough left over to get what
I needed. It meant a lot of manipulation and very little confrontation.... I know it wasn't healthy for me. After several years of this I
began having all sorts of physical symptoms, and I think they're
related to the stress that this submission caused. But I don't see any
other way I could have done it. Clifford is just too strong of a person for me.[1]

Clearly Diane's marriage isn't working at some very deep levels, leaving
both her and her husband extremely vulnerable. Diane is vulnerable to
emotional and physical breakdown, to falling for the first man who comes
along and treats her kindly, to getting to the point someday where she says,
"I've had it up to here and I'm leaving!" Clifford is vulnerable to the bore-
dom that comes from living with a woman who has lost herself and her
vitality because she has given most of it away for so long.

James Olthuis describes the dangers inherent in this kind of one-way
marriage:

Although at times it may seem easier to let one partner take over, a
husband and wife can jeopardize their entire relationship by establishing a male-dominated marriage. When a woman virtually sur-
renders her personality to her husband, she has less to give to the
relationship as the years pass. Outwardly she may seem rather content, but inwardly she grows more and more dependent until she is
only an adjunct. Often powerful feelings of hostility well up inside

her, against herself for succumbing and against her husband (and God) for demanding such subservience. She feels her marriage is a "trap" with four walls and a husband as keeper.

The situation becomes more complicated when the husband continues to grow through outside contacts while the wife languishes at home. He may have begun to grow away from her when he promised to keep his office problems out of the home. Unfortunately, after years of living separate lives, he may begin to feel that his wife no longer has the understanding to be his confidante and equal. Despite her dutiful obedience and continual adoration, he begins to see her as an embarrassment. Sometimes, feeling guilty, he pampers her even more (just the wrong thing if he wants her to grow up); at other times he suddenly drops her for "no apparent reason," using her childish behavior (accentuated by his pampering) to justify an affair.[2]

Diane isn't doing herself, her husband, or her children any favors by maintaining the status quo of a marriage that isn't working. In fact, by working so hard to fit into a dysfunctional family system, she is actually helping to perpetuate it and pass it on to future generations. She needs to consider whether God is calling her to lead the way into "the tunnel of chaos" in order to move toward a marriage that is really working rather than one that just looks good from the outside.

We don't want to ignore the kind of dysfunction that goes the other way—wives who become dominant while husbands become more and more distant from their partners and their children. Most of us have known families in which the husband spends most of his time in the garage or basement puttering, or sitting at a bar with people who give him a sense of importance and belonging, or glued to the television in numbed silence. Meanwhile, the wife runs the household, brings up the children, decides the social agenda, and frequently verbalizes what she sees to be her husband's weaknesses. Men aren't the only ones with strong personalities that can crush the life out of their relationships when left unchecked. A male-dominated marriage may be more common, but imbalance in either direction is unhealthy and not the plan God ever had for marriage.

Nourished by Love

Scriptural instruction on marriage is grounded in the context of mutual submission among believers who are bearing with one another, forgiving each other, loving each other, telling each other the truth, and teaching and admonishing each other with thankful hearts in the name of Christ. This is a far cry from the "submission for the sake of survival" that has Diane tiptoeing around a man who does a lot of taking and very little giving.

The biblical concept of headship is modeled on the example of Christ's relationship with the church—not the hierarchy of corporate America with its presidents and vice presidents. According to Ephesians 5:22-33, Christ's role as "head" of the church involves being her Savior (giver of life), her lover (to the point of laying down his life), and her nurturer (caring for her as he would care for his body). Contrary to popular interpretations, headship has nothing to do with demanding obedience, being the one who makes final decisions, or being the one who pursues his calling while the wife tries desperately to be supportive and fit in. Rather, the word *head* is virtually synonymous with "beginning" or "origin."[3] In the context of Christ, the church, and marriage, headship has to do with being the one who initiates and leads the way in loving. The woman responds (as the church does) to this kind of love with a heartfelt desire to please her husband.

Dr. Gilbert Bilezikian states in his careful word study:

The concept of headship in the New Testament refers to the function of Christ as the fountainhead of life and growth and to His servant role of provider and sustainer.... Because Christ is the wellspring of the church's life and provides it with existence and sustenance, in return the church serves Him in loving dependency and in recognition of Him as the source of its life. Because man as the fountainhead of the woman's existence was originally used to supply her with her very life, and because he continues to love her sacrificially as his own body in marriage, in return a Christian wife binds herself to her husband in a similar relationship of servant submission that expresses their oneness. The imposition of authority structure upon this exquisite balance of reciprocity would paganize the marriage relationship and make the Christ/church paradigm irrelevant to it.[4]

Now that sounds like a marriage that works! Two individuals love and give to each other in such a way that both souls are nourished. A husband commits himself to love, nurture, and see that his wife has what she needs to be all that she is meant to be—to the point of laying down his own comfort, indeed his very life. The wife gives to her husband out of the fullness that comes from being truly loved and nurtured into full personhood. Their balance and unity speak volumes to a world burdened with trying to find love in relationships fraught with domination, manipulation, power struggles, and selfishness.

Exploring the Possibility of Unity

But what about those times when you and your husband just can't agree? Many couples have been taught that in such moments the husband should be the one to make the decision; nothing in Scripture supports this idea. Rather, the Scriptures speak of unity as the goal for relationships among Christians, married or otherwise: "Be of the same mind, having the same love, being in full accord and of one mind. Do nothing from selfish ambition or conceit, but in humility regard others as better than yourselves. Let each of you look not to your own interests, but to the interests of others" (Philippians 2:2-4). This is the norm for Christian marriage.

How many decisions come along in life that are truly worth sacrificing the powerful unity that we have discussed so briefly here? How many are so important that we cannot wait for each other and listen and work lovingly to achieve the one mind spoken of in Philippians 2:3-5? My husband and I haven't come up against a decision yet that was worth such a sacrifice.

The rush to designate the husband as the one who makes the final decisions is rooted in simple fear—fear that unity and consensus is not possible. Fear that if we don't give more power to one or the other, we'll never be able to make decisions. Fear that if you don't keep women in some sort of authority structure, they will lead their men and their families down the path to destruction. While some of these fears may be understandable, they are woefully inadequate as a foundation for marital relations. They totally discount the efficacy of the Holy Spirit's work in creating unity among us. They discount the power of Christlike love and mutual submission.

Faith, on the other hand, holds out for God's ideal of agreement and oneness before moving ahead. Faith says, "I believe that unity is God's will for us, and he can bring our hearts and minds together."

Certainly, there are times when one spouse may say to the other, "You know what? I think this decision affects you more than it does me, so let's go your way on this one." But that is a concession voluntarily given, not forced upon another on the basis of gender or anything else. There is a world of difference between a marriage in which deference is freely given and one in which it is understood that the husband always holds the trump card in the nitty-gritty of decision making. There is a great difference between a marriage where issues are worked out in a reasonable way and one in which the husband is outwardly "head of the house," while his wife pulls all the strings through deception and manipulation.

Stuart Briscoe, whose marriage has been working for many years, offers this bit of advice for couples who are feeling pulled in two different directions:

> Sometimes the reticence of one partner can be alleviated with better information. And sometimes the spouse who is charging ahead is neglecting to consider issues of real concern. Clearly they have got to talk about it. Assuming they've each got that willing spirit, these problems can be worked out. But one spouse should never push the other into something. They should go slowly, working together. They say the Atlantic convoys of World War II used to go at the speed of the slowest ship. That's the way to go.[5]

A MARRIAGE FLEXIBLE ENOUGH TO ACCOMMODATE CHANGE

When Chris married me, he thought he was getting a traditional girl whose main goals in life were to be a good wife and mother. He thought that because that's what I told him! At the time I was barely twenty-one years old, and I guess I did have those goals. Can you imagine his surprise (and mine, too) at finding out later that even though I treasured and valued my marriage and my children, I needed more in my life? I discovered a great deal of fulfillment in work that involved leading causes that I was passionate about and capturing truth through speaking and writing. In fact, my desire to be involved in ministry was clarified and intensified at the same time that God was giving us children; our relationship had to stretch in order to accommodate these changes.

Neither of us could ever have envisioned the various configurations that have characterized our family life through the years. We have struggled to accommodate the ages and stages of our children in combination with our own different callings to contribute to the world beyond our home. At times we have appeared to be fairly traditional—Dad works while Mom stays home and makes child rearing her primary responsibility. The freelance nature of my work along with Chris's willingness to flex his hours in order to cover the home front when needed made this possible for a number of years.

Most recently, we have been deeply engaged in a dual-career dance with both of us managing vocations to which we feel deeply called. Although our children are older now, we are still committed to being the primary influences in their lives and to having our home be a well-supervised and open environment for our children and their friends. Just as in the early years, our two-career home requires commitment to each other, to God's call on each of our lives, to creative and flexible thinking and problem solving, and a big dose of that indispensable "can do" attitude. Of course, now it does not just involve Chris and me, but all of us. We are learning what it means to be a family where each person's calling—Mom, Dad, and children—is valued and supported.

This flexible kind of family life is not something that gets figured out once and for all, and then everything runs smoothly ever after. Rather, we are very much "in process," working on things as we go, communicating honestly when things aren't right, brainstorming solutions, and making adjustments as things change. We are accepting the fact that we're not perfect, but that we love each other and want to celebrate what God is doing in and through each of our lives.

One creative solution that worked well for us was the time when we arranged for our sixteen-year-old daughter to cover the home front two days a week as part of her paid summer work. *She* suggested this as we brainstormed about how to handle the summer break with two parents needing to work outside the home at least part of the time. The variety of the tasks—cooking, cleaning, shopping, driving, and overseeing the activities of two younger sisters—appealed to Charity's capacity for leadership and organization (more so than other summer jobs she could have held) and gave her valuable experience that will benefit her over the long haul.

The result of this creative solution? We would come home on the nights Charity had been in charge to find the house clean, dinner ready, two younger daughters who have done their chores and played with their older sister, and a sixteen year old who was tired, but proud of her accomplishments. We were pleased at what God was doing in our family even though our lives seemed so complex and busy.

It is not always easy for families to stretch enough to accommodate a woman's calling to commitments beyond the home. It requires a significant amount of giving and taking on everyone's part. But as we continue to work toward an arrangement that fits who we are and who we are becoming, it is anything but stifling!

FACING PROBLEMS AND GETTING HELP

As a young woman preparing for marriage, I didn't realize that marriage would be hard and that it would take more than love and a commitment to Christ to make it work. Either no one was saying it, or I just wasn't listening—probably a combination of both.

Now I know that most married couples (the honest ones anyway!) will sometimes encounter real marital difficulties: anger so deep that it cannot be fully dealt with "before the sun goes down," depression that cannot be lifted by one more sermon or book on victorious Christian living, sexual difficulties that are not alleviated by simplistic teaching about sex as God's beautiful gift, or a crisis that threatens to overwhelm them. I know this because Chris and I have experienced these kinds of difficulties. They were difficulties that brought us to the point of saying, "Look, we have a problem. We have tried everything we know to try and it's just not working. We need help."

It's a little traumatic at first—a real blow to the pride—to admit that you need help and then to seek it actively. Then there is the challenge of finding someone who has the expertise, experience, and perhaps professional training to be of real help, and placing yourself in the position of being guided and helped. But the beauty of having a helper for times of stress in marriage is that the helper can become a kind of "safety net" as we move toward greater levels of intimacy in the relationship. Rather than being afraid of new awareness and new issues that need to be dealt with in the marriage ("If I told my husband that I really don't like sex, he would be devastated." "If I told my wife about my struggle with pornography, she would never forgive me." "My husband would be revolted if I told him about my eating disorder." "How can I tell my wife it really bothers me that she has let her appearance go?"), we can bring issues out into the open, knowing that there is someone to help if we get stuck or the problems become bigger than we know how to handle.

We all have unresolved issues that keep us from experiencing the fullness in life we have always envisioned for ourselves. Much of the work of maturing and healing the hurts of the past can only be done in meaningful connection with another person over time. Dysfunctional thinking patterns, poor communication skills, and character weaknesses don't change overnight or in isolation. The beauty of a marriage that works is that these areas are viewed matter-of-factly rather than as disasters that cannot be coped with. Marriage then becomes one of the contexts for God's transforming work in us.

Yes, pride does die hard. That's why some people wait until it hurts so badly they can't stand it or until some kind of crisis forces the issue. But in marriages that are working well, admitting problems honestly and getting help is seen as a strength and not a shortcoming. "Wisdom is with those who receive counsel" (Proverbs 13:10, NASB). The sooner the better.

LEARNING TO LET GOD BE OUR SOURCE

As a young wife I thought that somehow I could take away all of my husband's pain, that my answers would solve his problems, that I could fill up his empty places. And I expected that he would do the same for me. These expectations were draining because, in reality, only God can do those things.

In *Families Where Grace Is in Place,* psychologist Jeff Van Vonderen observes that much of the tiredness and "trapped-ness" that married people feel is a result of having the wrong job description. Many of us enter into marriage thinking that it is our job to meet each other's deepest needs. Inevitably, we both fail to live up to these expectations, and so we try to fix each other. The problem with fixing is that it just doesn't work, and pretty soon everyone ends up feeling like a failure—the "fix-ee" because he or she hasn't lived up to his or her spouse's expectation, and the "fixer" because he or she hasn't been able to effect change.

Eventually we must face the truth that no human being is capable of "filling up" another human being no matter how much fixing we do. And we can't really change anyone but ourselves. I realize now that my "job" as a married woman is to keep learning to let God meet my needs and change my destructive behaviors. As I mature in my ability to deal with anger, communicate truthfully with love and respect, break annoying habits, and conquer my own selfishness, I find that I have much more to offer Chris. As I see more clearly what I can't do for him (fixing and filling), I am freed to offer what I am best equipped to offer: my presence on the journey, a listening ear, any tools or insights I have gained along the way, and my support and participation in wrestling with life's great questions.

Does this mean that we are not concerned about each other's needs? In a marriage that works, both the husband's and the wife's needs are very important. However, even as we express our deep care for one another, we are realistic about what one human being can do for another. We can love each other wholeheartedly, *but that love cannot be expected to fully ease the pain of a mother or a father who could not love.* One human being can be a source of deep joy to another *but cannot singlehandedly stave off depression.* Being a husband or a wife can be a part of our identity for the time that God gives us to be together, *but it cannot give ultimate meaning to our lives.* We can cultivate our sexual relationship, *but we cannot accept responsibility for the other's choice to go outside the marriage for sexual fulfillment when the going gets tough.* We can ease each other's pain with our presence, *but we must each take responsibility for whatever work needs to be done in our own lives—be it forgiveness, righting past wrongs, grieving loss, or wrestling with God.* Parts of the journey we each must take alone, and God is the only one who can go with us.

For those of us who are used to fixing and controlling, the idea of letting go of those responsibilities can be frightening. We may fear that our spouse or our marriage will never change unless we're right in the middle of things pushing, manipulating, or giving advice! But faith can free us: faith in God's power to change people, faith in each other's capacity to change, and faith in the whole process of being changed by marriage.

FREEDOM WORTH FIGHTING FOR

It has been said that you have to choose your battles carefully. Some things are not worth doing battle over, but other situations call for all-out war. In a society that does little to promote faithful commitment to one spouse, the battle for our marriages is a battle worth fighting with every effective weapon we have.

A cover article in *Fortune* magazine titled "The CEO's Second Wife" confirms that though there used to be some pressure to stay married at least for the sake of appearances, today we are being pressured in the opposite direction. In this article Helen Singer Kaplan, second wife of the founder and chairman of Toys"R"Us, notes: "The change has been radical. There's no longer a prejudice against divorce and remarriage—almost the reverse. In some cases the man with the old, nice matronly wife is looked down on. He's seen as not keeping up appearances. Why can't he do better for himself?"[6]

George Barna, in his book *The Frog in the Kettle,* takes this trend a step further, predicting that in the new millennium,

> Americans will generally believe that a life spent with the same partner is both unusual and unnecessary.… People will begin to consciously acknowledge that they are likely to have several spouses over the course of their lifetime and will choose partners who will best satisfy their needs during the different periods of their lives.[7]

Those of us who are willing to fight for the freedoms that come in a healthy marriage will need to work at keeping our marriages fulfilling and fun. This means discovering the kinds of activities that we both find to be life-giving and that we can enjoy doing together and then making significant time, energy, and money available for them despite the challenges of living in such a fast-paced culture. We can also work at developing mutual interests so that the phenomenon of "creeping separateness"—the tendency to be so engrossed in our own activities and interests that we have less and less in common with our spouse—doesn't set in.

Stay Alert to Subtle Dangers

Staying informed of societal trends helps us to be aware of subtle dangers to our marriages. For instance, the *Fortune* magazine article mentioned in in the previous section alerts us to ways in which a woman leaves her marriage vulnerable to societal pressures and temptations. The men interviewed for this article indicated that while the first wife was "cold and unresponsive," the second wife was "supportive and sexy." The first wife was seen as unable to adjust to her husband's changing interests and unsupportive of the demands of his professional life, often becoming his self-appointed critic and conscience. In short, "she didn't keep up."[8] While these are not acceptable excuses for a man to leave "the wife of his youth" it does make us aware of the need to be attentive to the quality of our presence with our husbands and to the ways in which we can deepen the attraction to one another that drew us together in the first place.

Be Aware of Yourself

Many times we think that men are the only ones vulnerable to the temptation to betray the marriage relationship, but the truth is that women are vulnerable, too, in the midst of a changing society. As one woman observes:

> When you live life in a dog-tired, gotta-meet-everybody-else's-needs state, you lose a sense of who you are and what you're about in life. That makes you depressed and vulnerable to whoever comes along and tells you great things about yourself…. Women use affairs as an escape hatch…especially when a woman's life is stressful, trying to work, take care of the kids, be the good wife, whatever. They freak out and want no responsibility at all, which is what an affair is.[9]

Self-awareness is the key here. It may be that one of the most important things a woman can do for her marriage is to be assertive enough to say, "Hey, I'm running on empty too much of the time—we need to make some adjustments." When a couple is serious about protecting their marriage, they assimilate this information and brainstorm ways to prevent the tiredness and emptiness (in the individual and in the marriage) that may leave a woman open to making a choice that she will later regret.

Keep Talking

Even in good marriages, it is probable that a spouse will be attracted to someone else at some point. As difficult as it is to talk about this reality, these are the times when it is most important to keep talking—to keep telling the truth in love. Issues that we leave unacknowledged and unspoken have more power over us than those things we bring into the light.

A woman who faced the possibility of having an affair with a married Christian man reflects on her situation:

> Although many things were strong in my marriage, there was not a
> real cherishing of each other. After so many years of marriage and so
> many children, maybe we were taking each other for granted. And
> here comes someone who opens my doors, and treats me with
> respect, and understands a lot about me. I could have done two
> things: I could have kept my temptation secret or I could have
> shared the whole thing with Chuck. I chose to tell my husband.
> And things really changed for us. We started spending more time
> together, we spent hours in the bedroom talking.... We came out
> with an appreciation for our relationship we hadn't had before. We
> realized that to lose what we had would be totally devastating.[10]

Denying that we or our partner is vulnerable to outside attractions is just that—denial. While we may wish to spare each other from information that is painful, such secrecy actually weakens the marriage (because we are hiding something important about ourselves), reduces opportunity for accountability, and gives these attractions greater power over us.

Peggy Vaughn writes, "Only honesty can create the groundwork for monogamy. Attractions kept secret from a partner are far more likely to be acted upon."[11] But an honest look at sexuality requires courage and a common commitment to increasing intimacy. The one doing the telling must communicate that he or she is doing so out of a commitment to honesty and a desire to protect the marriage. The one listening must work hard to share his or her honest response without trying to punish, control, or withdraw. Both should have the freedom to ask each other about outside attractions and to remind each other that honesty, faithfulness, and true intimacy are among their highest shared values.

A BATTLE FOR THE BRAVE OF HEART

Sometimes when we experience the normal stresses and strains of becoming truly intimate with another person, we begin to believe that marriage *is* a trap. We begin to believe that if we could only get out of the marriage or try a new partner we would be free. The truth is that even if we did get out of the marriage, we would still have to live with ourselves and those things in ourselves that keep us from joy, intimacy, and effectiveness. In most cases true freedom is still to be found in a marriage where we continue to change and transform, even through difficulty.

Fighting for the kind of a marriage relationship described here is not for the faint of heart. It is for hearty souls with courage enough to explore new frontiers and conquer the enemies of intimacy. It is for those who know deep in their hearts that where there is no risk there is no reward. And it is for all of us who know what it is to push past our own limits of courage and strength because, over time, a marriage that works provides the context and also the catalyst for the transformation of growing souls.

⌒ S P I R I T U A L   E X E R C I S E S ⌒

Alone with God

Silence. As you come to the end of this chapter, take a few moments to sit with God in the silence of your own heart. If you are married, allow yourself to wonder, *Is my marriage a place of freedom these days? What's working in my marriage right now and what's not?* Without feeling like you have to do anything about it, notice your longings, your joys, your questions about your marriage these days. If you are unmarried, reflect on the thoughts, feelings, and questions you have about marriage. What can you do now to prepare yourself for a marriage that will be a place of freedom for you? What have you learned from married friends that will help you if and when you marry in the future? If you are single again due to divorce or the death of your spouse, reflect on your experience of marriage. Was it a place of freedom for you? What worked? What didn't? Are there any unresolved issues that remain?

Prayer and journaling. Review the chapter that you have just read, noticing the places of resonance and resistance that you have highlighted. Allow yourself time to journal your response to the following questions and to tell God what's true about you and your marriage right now. Express to him your deepest desires.

- Where were places where you felt affirmed in the rightness of something you were already doing or challenged to consider something new?
- Do any of the truths presented in this chapter enable you to move into a greater level of freedom than what you are experiencing now?
- Do you feel hopeful or hopeless or something in between?
- If you are single or single again, what do you want to say to God about your present circumstances?

Invitations. *God, are you inviting me to do anything in response to what I have read today? What is my response to you?*

With Your Spiritual Friend(s)

Begin your time together with a moment of silence and a simple prayer of invitation for God to join you.

Listening. Take turns giving each other your undivided attention. Share with each other a brief summary of what has happened between you and God this week in the context of your spiritual practices and your reading of this chapter.

- What did God say to you in your times of solitude and silence?
- As you read about fears, hopes, ideals, and ambivalence about marriage in this chapter, which emotions and concepts resonated with you? Which ones did you find yourself resisting?
- What questions do you want to bring to God about your thoughts and emotions toward marriage?
- If you are married, how do you work with the issues of headship and submission in your marriage?
- In what areas of your marriage do you feel freedom and joy?
- In what areas of your marriage do you feel sad or stuck?
- How is God meeting you in this midst of the joys and pain of living so intimately with another human being? What are his invitations to you?

Prayer. Pray for one another.

The Freedom to Embrace Our Sexuality

I praise you, for I am fearfully and wonderfully made. Wonderful are your works; that I know very well.

—PSALM 139:14

On the eve of my wedding, a friend shared with me a great truth of human sexuality. She said, "You know, Ruth, before marriage the temptation is to have sex. After marriage, the temptation is not to."

At the time, I scoffed at this little bit of marriage wisdom. Now I realize that it does capture the dilemma in which many women find themselves. If a woman is a Christian or has spent time in and around the Christian community, she has been taught that sex is "God's wonderful gift" to be shared only with her husband in the context of marriage. So she spends the first part of her life slightly uncomfortable with her sexuality, waiting for it to find its fullest expression in marriage. But then she gets married and finds, to her chagrin, that it does not always fulfill the expectation. What was meant to be a wonderful gift can begin to feel like a cruel hoax for single and married women alike. Single women may wonder why they are so sexually alive when they can't express their sexuality fully; married women over time may find their sex life to be disappointing or disillusioning.

A survey by popular columnist Ann Landers asked readers to respond to the question: "Has your sex life gone downhill after marriage? If so, why?" She obviously hit a raw nerve because she received an overwhelming 141,210 responses—52 percent from males and 48 from females—and the verdict was clear: 82 percent said that sex after marriage was less exciting, using adjectives such as boring, dull, monotonous, and routine.[1]

While Ann Landers's survey can hardly be considered "scientific" research, the results are telling and, I believe, representative of the reality in which many married people live. After some futile attempts to understand the forces at work, a woman may be tempted to dismiss the possibility of great sex as an unfortunate deception. But sex will not be dismissed that easily.

One can hardly pick up a book or magazine, watch television or a movie, go to the mall or to the beach without encountering something that is intended to arouse us sexually. And unless we are completely unaware of it, our sexuality continues to call to us with inexpressible longing for more meaningful expression, for deeper connection with another human being. Each of us, married and single, is created by God with a sexual dimension; we have the potential to unite—body and soul—with another human being. That is the way God made us. The question is, How can we embrace the gift of our sexuality in whatever season of life we are in?

BEGINNINGS

The sexual journey begins long before we think of ourselves as being sexually awakened. It begins with all the early verbal and nonverbal messages that we received about our physical bodies generally and our sexuality more specifically.

No one was born thinking sex is bad, or thinking sex is the greatest thing in the world either. Our attitudes toward sex, positive and negative alike, all were learned later from our culture…the earliest messages we got about sex, however, reached us when we were most impressionable, and they may stay with us well into adulthood—even when we wish they wouldn't. Unfortunately, those early messages were more likely than not negative ones.[2]

For many, feelings of shame, embarrassment, or confusion regarding their sexuality go way back to messages they received about sex from their family of origin, the church, society, early sexual experiences, and early experiences in marriage. For some, sex was a taboo subject that made everyone uncomfortable, leaving children feeling ashamed of their natural curiosity about their bodies and their discoveries about the sources of sexual pleasure. Others received verbal teaching that sex was good within marriage but received so many warnings about not falling into "sexual sin" that the whole thing seemed frightening and impossible to control. At the same time, they may have been observing a mother who pulled away from her husband whenever he tried to be physically affectionate or a father who grew distant from his daughters as they began to mature physically. Thus our *experiences* with sexual issues spoke louder than any verbal messages we were receiving.

Still others received overtly negative messages about sex being bad, sinful, suspect, or a duty to be endured. Many a woman shares Jody's experience of trying to disregard what her mother has told her her whole life: "My mother told me that sex is something we do to please our husbands and good women don't enjoy it. She never affirmed my sexuality, and my dad died when I was fifteen, so I grew up believing no man would find me attractive. It took a lot of years to unlearn what she taught me and find out sex could be joyful."[3]

In addition to the verbal and nonverbal messages we receive early on, certain kinds of experiences will shape us sexually as well. Early introduction into sexual activity by a family member, sexually arousing play with a member of the same sex, and sexual abuse are all experiences that influence who we become in terms of sexual knowledge and response.[4] Sexual abuse, in particular, is much more prevalent than most of us realize. Healing the pain of sexual abuse is a process that takes time, a willingness to tell the truth, and often expressions of anger and grief. For more insight into one woman's journey of healing from sexual abuse, see the endnote at the back of this book and pursue some of the other books listed in the resource guide.[5]

One important aspect of the sexual journey is to realize that each of us carries messages about sex from our early years as well as experiences that have shaped our attitudes about sex. Once we have taken an honest look at those early messages, we are able to decide, as adults, whether we agree with them. And once we have looked honestly at the experiences that have shaped us, they no longer have so much power over the way we think and act. This kind of search for the truth can give us insight into the ways that certain early experiences might be having debilitating effects on our present sexual functioning and our thoughts about our sexuality. *As we look at ourselves and our development honestly, we have the opportunity to embrace what is good and true, and move beyond what is no longer helpful.* We also have the opportunity to become more aware and purposeful about what we communicate to the next generation about their sexuality.

THE SEXUAL AND THE SPIRITUAL CONNECTION

For many of us who have grown up in and around the church, the relationship between sexuality and spirituality has been an uneasy one. Part of our religious heritage (at least for Protestant Christians and Catholics) has been "the sexless image of spirituality." In its most extreme form, true spirituality has been viewed as sexless, celibacy as the ultimate commitment to God, and bodily mortification and pain as conducive to spiritual purification. Women, the object of men's sexual yearnings, became particularly suspect in their sexuality. St. Thomas Aquinas stated, "God foresaw that woman would be an occasion of sin to man. Therefore he should not have made woman."[6]

Fortunately, the church has begun to offer some clearer thinking on sexuality, recognizing that it was created "good" and continues to be good. Particularly during the last couple of decades, we have witnessed a shift away from the overtly negative views that are driven by fear and thinly veiled disgust. Yet despite what (in many churches) amounts to a few statements about "God's wonderful gift of sex," discussion of topics related to sexuality are conspicuous in their absence. One notable exception is the annual "sex talk" for young people during which time a pastor or youth worker gives instruction about sexual abstinence. Although abstinence is an important subject, it fails to address many other facets of sexuality. Despite some progress in this area, many are still exceedingly uncomfortable with open discussion of sexual topics. A woman wrote to a Christian magazine with this comment: "I feel the topics covered in your [sexual issues] column have absolutely no place in a magazine for Christians. Questions about sexuality should be handled only in private conversation or counseling."[7]

This woman probably doesn't realize that her discomfort with matter-of-fact discussions of sexuality in a Christian magazine is due in part to a view that has remained strong in the church: the view that makes sharp distinctions between body and spirit and considers the spirit to be superior. This dualistic outlook causes us to avoid whole areas of life that are an important part of God's plan. As one writer states, "churches shy away from dealing vigorously with sexuality because it seems incidental or inappropriate to 'the life in the spirit.'"[8] And yet, it is obvious that we desperately need to "deal vigorously" with sexual issues within the context of the Christian community. The Christian church suffers just as much as the rest of society from problems related to sexuality—teenage pregnancy, sexual abuse, troubled marriages—and we need the Church to deal with sexuality openly, positively, and systematically, just as it would any other part of the Christian experience. Only by doing this can we learn to integrate the sexual and spiritual parts of our lives into the healthy combination God intended.

The Need to Think Spiritually About Sex

We've all heard the saying that the biggest sex organ is the brain. It's true! What we think and feel about sex probably has a greater effect on our sexual functioning than anything else. The problem is that many women *think* on an intellectual, rational level that sex is good, but they still *feel* uncomfortable with it. Exposing some of the early, faulty messages we received about sex will help with these uncomfortable feelings. It is also crucial that, as Christians, we gain a more accurate understanding of what God thinks about sex.

The foundation for embracing our sexuality more wholeheartedly can be found in the creation story where we are told that "the man and his wife were both naked, and they felt no shame." (Genesis 2:25, NIV) The fact that their sexual parts were exposed was as comfortable for them as the fact that they had bare feet! They knew none of the shame and discomfort that is so prevalent today. For Adam and Eve in their sinless state, sexuality was a wonderful reflection of God's image, as were other aspects of their created being. *Any discomfort they would later develop with their bodies and with their sexuality was a direct result of their sin and the subsequent shame it introduced* ("I was afraid because I was naked; so I hid" Genesis 3:10, NIV).

Somehow many of us have developed the idea that it is more spiritual to minimize our bodies and sexuality. But in fact, it is clear from this record of the earliest days of human existence that the opposite is true: the sexual side of ourselves cannot be separated from the spiritual—together they make up who we are. To try to divide ourselves leads to confusion, rather than spiritual health. From the creation story we understand that male-ness and female-ness and the dynamics between the two are a work of God that he pronounced very good. The very existence of the woman's clitoris is evidence that sex was given to us for our enjoyment. Unlike any other body part, the sole purpose of the clitoris is sexual pleasure.

Adam and Eve's comfort level with their nakedness is a beautiful picture for us of the openness and intimacy that is possible in marriage. The powerful experience of uniting one's body with another's is the physical manifestation of the "one-fleshness" that God intended for the man and woman who come together in mutuality and commitment. *God* is the one who connects these sexual, relational, and spiritual realities. Once we understand that sex is one of the best ideas God came up with, we need not feel embarrassed about getting all the information we can about this wonderful aspect of life. There is so much we need to know.

The Need for Reliable Information

"I was very naive sexually when I got married," says Nicolette.

> I wanted sex to be something wonderful, and it turned out to be a crock. It didn't stop hurting until after our first child was born. It sure wasn't fulfilling. I was on the pill.... I had no knowledge that being on the pill is like being semi-pregnant, in terms of hormones, and that being pregnant often brings a decrease in sexual interest. Nobody told me. I thought it was all me. I thought something was wrong with me. I was a pretty reserved person.... I *was* orgasmic once I got to the proper stage, but I was never aroused before the encounter, and that seemed like it would be so much fun! My hope was that I would be as interested in sex as Dave was, that our appetites would be the same.... All the time, I'd be thinking I've got to get better, I've got to get better. But there was no better to get; I was really stuck.[9]

Nicolette's comments reflect a lack of information, which is a predictable result of our discomfort with speaking plainly about sexual matters. Somehow moral people have developed an assumption that if we do what is right and save ourselves for marriage, then everything will just fall into place when the time comes. While this may be true for some, most women benefit from having as much information as is available.

There is all kinds of information that would have been helpful to Nicolette and her husband as they prepared for marriage and as they adjusted to each other sexually after marriage—information about the mechanics of sex, the effects of birth control on sexual functioning, a more accurate understanding of female orgasmic response, help with communicating about sex, and much more. Unfortunately, Nicolette had absorbed faulty information that had shaped her unrealistic expectations.

Ann, a vivacious and energetic woman in her thirties, describes the problems misinformation caused in her sex life:

> My husband and I were both virgins when we got married. We were
> very excited about our newfound sexual freedom and enjoyed our
> physical relationship immensely. I did not experience orgasm right
> away but the closeness that we shared was so meaningful that I was
> not at all concerned. However, we were reading one of the few
> Christian sex books available at the time which stated that simulta-
> neous orgasm through intercourse was our "right" and we should
> pursue it. It also made a big distinction between "vaginal" orgasms
> and "clitoral" orgasms—vaginal orgasm (through intercourse alone)
> being the kind that mature women experienced. Well, we bought
> into this idea hook, line, and sinker until it began to rob us of the
> joy and uninhibitedness we had experienced early in our marriage.
> John started feeling pressured to produce such an orgasm and I
> started feeling pressured to have one. The orgasms I was having

regularly [through direct stimulation] suddenly seemed "less than." I felt like I wasn't a "real woman" yet.[10]

Misinformation about female orgasmic response has been prevalent in our culture and has caused some couples to be overly focused on the woman achieving the "right" kind of orgasm—one experienced simultaneously with her husband during intercourse. As one woman said, "I finally had an orgasm, but my doctor told me it was the wrong kind."

Freud in particular did a lot to propagate the "myth of the mutual orgasm."[11] However, in their research Masters and Johnson found that all orgasms women experience involve the same physical components, from muscular contraction to a rise in heart rate and blood pressure. A woman's physiological response is the same regardless of what brings her to climax. This is not to say that there isn't any difference on an emotional level. Many women find that they enjoy different ways of experiencing orgasm at different times; it is purely a matter of personal preference, rather than a "right" and "wrong" way of doing things.

For Ann, this understanding was very freeing. She admits that, "Sex became one big stress point until we got more accurate information about the fact that most women need direct clitoral stimulation.... We read authors who encouraged us to relax and enjoy all the ways that we receive pleasure from being together. We're having a great time now that we're not so goal-oriented."

MEN WANT IT; WOMEN DON'T (AND OTHER SEXUAL STEREOTYPES)

A stereotype is a conventional, formulaic, and usually oversimplified conception of a person based on his or her sex, race, religion, ethnic background, or other factors. Stereotyping on the basis of sex is so prevalent in our society that it is the relational air we breathe. Much of what we would like to call gender roles are no more than stereotypes, behaviors that we as a society have dubbed "normal" and "appropriate" over the years so that they have become widely accepted as the norm for human functioning. Some of the prevailing notions about men maintain that they are aggressive (or at least assertive), logical, unemotional, independent, dominant, competitive, objective, athletic, active, and above all, competent. Conversely, women are frequently viewed as passive, nonassertive, illogical, emotional, dependent, subordinate, warm, and nurturing.

What is so striking about the above lists is that we all know so many women and men who just do not fit them. That is the problem with stereotypes: They are simplistic and they fail to take individuality into account, making life more difficult than it needs to be for the person who does not fit the stereotypes. Furthermore, acceptance of such narrow gender-role expectations can have a profoundly negative effect on our sexual functioning.

"Women are less interested in sex than men are." One long-standing, slow-to-die assumption in many societies

> is the mistaken idea that women are inherently less sexually inclined
> than men. A related gender assumption is that "normal women" do
> not enjoy sex as much as men do. Such gender stereotypes may result
> in women being subjected to years of negative socialization during
> which they are taught to suppress or deny their sexual feelings.[12]

This was the case with Jody, the woman we heard from at the beginning of this chapter. She had learned from her mother that sex was for men, not women, to enjoy. This made it very hard for her to express interest in sex or actively seek her own pleasure, even after marriage. It made it hard for her to admit that she had any sexual needs or desires at all.

For the woman who is interested in sex and easily aroused, this stereotype can cause emotional ambivalence about her sexuality. She may have a hard time accepting her responsiveness as part of herself and is then prevented from relaxing and enjoying sex as it is meant to be enjoyed. She may even begin to use her energies to block or hide her normal response rather than risk feeling like she is more interested or responsive than a "virtuous" Christian woman ought to be.

The Penners, respected Christian authors in this area, describe the problem very well:

> The natural noises and behaviors typical of the sexual response cause in some women an inhibiting embarrassment that must be corrected.... As we—men and women—get aroused, we respond. Our heartbeat increases, we breathe faster and louder, we may experience muscular contractions, our bodies may feel like moving in thrusting or pushing motions, and we may have the urge to make gasping noises. Women who have difficulty allowing themselves to experience arousal or release are often unable to let themselves exhibit any or all of these behaviors. They are embarrassed and uncomfortable, and as with any other discomfort, they tend to avoid that which causes these negative feelings. Thus they will hold back their natural sexual responses.[13]

If a woman continues to cut herself off from her sexual feelings in this way it will become a vicious cycle; as she distances herself from her sexual feelings, she will experience less pleasure, and when she experiences less pleasure, she will lose interest. Buying into the "men want it, women don't" stereotype (consciously or unconsciously) can inhibit a woman from fully experiencing the sexual nature God has given her.

"Men are the initiators and women are the responders." Unfortunately, this stereotype encourages women to be passive and allow themselves to be "acted upon" rather than actively seeking pleasure during lovemaking. The

problem with accepting this stereotype is that being active and initiating at least some of the time is a key to enjoying the sexual experience fully. Indeed, Scripture makes it very clear that sexual pleasure and release is a need for women as well as men and is equally important for both. "The husband should give to his wife her conjugal rights, and likewise the wife to her husband. For the wife does not have authority over her own body, but the husband does; likewise the husband does not have authority over his own body, but the wife does. Do not deprive one another except perhaps by agreement" (1 Corinthians 7:3-5).

Again, the Penners' comments highlight the importance of rejecting stereotypes that cast men as aggressors and women as passive receivers:

> [You] who experience little arousal or are still preorgasmic…must take
> responsibility for and control of what you need. Your partner cannot
> give you arousal or release. He can participate in your having it, but
> only you can allow it to happen as you free yourself to experience it.
> This may seem obvious, and yet it is one of the most difficult mental
> shifts to make, because for so long the subtle teaching has been that it
> is the man's responsibility to bring the woman sexual pleasure.[14]

Another natural result of our belief that men are to be competent leaders and women are to be not-so-competent followers is that men are then expected to be "sexperts," which places an unnecessary burden upon them. Rejecting this stereotype is helpful for men because sometimes they tire of being so responsible for the success of the sexual relationship. As one man says,

> Sometimes sex is more like work than fun. I have to make all the
> decisions—when and where we are going to have sex and what we
> are going to do together. It's my responsibility to make sure it works

out good for both of us. This can put a lot of pressure on me and it gets real tiring always having to run the show. It would be nice to have someone else call the shots for a change.[15]

Indeed! When two adults are involved in a sexual relationship it is much more healthy and fulfilling if the responsibility for acquiring information and planning the fun is shared by both the woman and the man.

"Men cannot control themselves, so it is up to women to control them." This idea is particularly damaging to women. One of the strong messages many young girls receive as they grow up is that men are out of control when it comes to sex, and that it is their responsibility as young ladies to conduct themselves in such a way that doesn't cause men to lust or to exceed the limits that the girl sets. Men, they are told, will "take as much as they can get," and so the woman must make sure that she is not coerced into unacceptable activities. Consequently, for many young women this comes to mean that if a man does show signs of interest or (gasp!) lust, or begins behaving inappropriately, it is somehow the girl's responsibility and the girl's fault: She must not have been sitting properly, wasn't dressed discreetly enough, shouldn't have been so friendly, or *something*.

The natural result of this stereotypical view is that rather than feeling comfortable with their sexuality and viewing it as a dynamic that is a natural part of life, many women experience an uncomfortable mixture of shame and pleasure as their sexuality begins to awaken. Because of this ambivalence, they may increasingly distance themselves from their sexual feelings and minimize any sexual feelings that others might have toward them.

This concern with control is not uncommon for adolescent girls during their dating years, and it can be effective in helping them not to compromise. The problem is that, while there are some helpful elements to this stereotype (that's why stereotypes are so easy to fall into), sexuality is not a light switch that we can turn on and off at will. Therefore, it is not surprising that a woman who spends a great deal of time and energy reg-ulating sexual intimacy to preserve her "honor" may have difficulty expe-riencing sexual feelings when it becomes appropriate for her to let go of those controlling behaviors in marriage.

We need to reject the idea that men cannot control their urges and therefore women are responsible for them. On the contrary, men are just as capable of and responsible for controlling their own sexual urges as they are responsible for controlling any other area of their lives, such as the urge to spend too much money, to overeat, or to indulge in angry tirades. Yes, they have strong sexual desires and are stimulated by what they see perhaps more than women are. Women do well to be sensitive to this. But we must not confuse sensitivity with responsibility.

Young girls need to be encouraged to embrace their developing sexual interest and sensations as a part of becoming all that God created them to be, as cause for the celebration of growth and life that it is. When a young man experiences sexual desire for her, she will then perceive it as evidence that everything is functioning as God intended, *not that she has done some-thing wrong.* In the context of how exciting and right it all is, we have the perfect opportunity to discuss the benefits of saving the fullest expression of our sexuality for the commitment and intimacy of marriage. Then when the time comes, the sexual switch need not be turned on from having been completely off. Rather, the part of our sexual journey that includes mar-riage will be more like turning a dimmer switch from low to medium to high—a much more gentle transition.

WHAT SOME WOMEN HAVE LEARNED ABOUT SEXUAL SATISFACTION

Although lack of sexual fulfillment in marriage is very widespread (82 per-cent of couples in Ann Landers's column indicated problems; 50 percent in a more scientific study conducted by Masters and Johnson), there is a significant percentage of married couples who are having good sex. One woman from Dickinson, North Dakota, responded to Ann Landers this way: "Our sex life gets better all the time. Why? Because it is an honest expression of a love based on respect, courtesy, honesty, admiration, and mutual trust." Many single women as well, whether they have never married or are single again due to divorce or the death of a spouse, are able to embrace their sexuality even though they may or may not have a partner. What might we learn from them?

Women who are enjoying their sex life know that great sex develops in a loving, committed relationship. Even though Chris and I have been married for many years, we still find new levels of intimacy to share. It would be very disturbing if, after a time of connecting deeply on an emotional and physical level, there was a possibility that he would walk away with a vague promise of "I'll call you sometime." For women in particular, love and sexual intimacy cannot grow in a garden of uncertainty.

The reality is that plenty of women are trying it the other way. Many single women are struggling to reconcile the reality of their sexual desires with the circumstances of their singleness in a society that throws sex in their face at every turn. Periods of singleness—which will come to all of us at one time or another—are enormously difficult in this regard. But if the sexual revolution taught us anything, it taught us that there are very good reasons for God's ideal of saving sexual intimacy for those who commit themselves to each other in marriage.

The words of this woman who tried it both ways are haunting in their description of our very real need for connection and of the disillusionment that comes from trying to meet it in the wrong way:

Sexuality mimics love. It compels tenderness and embraces, it forces the lovers to hug one another, to allay one another's pain through the revelations of sexuality, as when true love is exchanged. What follows such experiences? Disappointments, a bitter aftertaste, mutual accusations of bleak loneliness, feelings of exploitation and defilement. Neither of the two gave true love but only expected to receive it, therefore, neither received it.[16]

On the other hand, sex therapist Dr. David Schnarch proclaims, "The greatest sexual ecstasy comes not with a *Cosmo* cover girl, but with your spouse." He describes the electrifying sexual connection that can be reached by two people in a close, intimate relationship. However, he goes on to say that the reason many married couples don't achieve it is "because they are scared to reach their sexual potential within the overwhelming intimacy of marriage." Intensely intimate marital sex is more threatening than people realize, and it only takes place as couples "work past their fears and the discomfort that comes from breaking barriers of intimacy together."[17] In other words, good marital sex only happens as we become "increasingly naked" in the presence of the other person and are not ashamed.

Women who are finding sexual fulfillment understand that the growth of a sexual relationship is not about technique but about two people learning how to be loving and intimate. They know it is a process complete with stops and starts, days when it seems like a lot is happening, and days when it seems like nothing is happening. They accept the fact that there are obstacles to overcome, heights of ecstasy to be scaled, and dry spells to wait through patiently. They understand that sexual freedom is not the freedom to have sex with anyone they want; it is the freedom to stay in the process of achieving true intimacy with another human being.

In addition, women who are experiencing sexual satisfaction do not worry about "how things ought to be." They are not agitating themselves with thoughts like: *We should make love more often. I should be experiencing multiple orgasms. We should be trying this new position or that new toy.* Even though they seek help when they need it, they enjoy their sex life as uniquely their own and not to be compared with national averages or the latest magazine article. They accept the changes that different seasons and circumstances bring—pregnancy and childbirth, infertility, stress, work that requires travel for either partner, differing sexual appetites at different times, menopause, midlife crisis, and aging. They do not view these as problems so much as opportunities to adjust, accept, or search for new ways of loving.

A woman who is enjoying herself sexually is also becoming increasingly at home in her body. We live in a culture in which it is extremely difficult for a woman to feel good about her body. Anorexic actresses and models parade before us on television and in magazines while busty *Playboy* bunnies scream at us, THIS IS WHAT A SEXUAL WOMAN LOOKS LIKE!

All of us, when we compare ourselves to these images, feel inadequate in some way. Many of us bring negative feelings and images with us from growing-up years when sexual organs and functions (such as menstruation) were considered dirty. It doesn't help that so much of the street talk and profanity we hear chooses sexuality as its main subject. And yet these bodies are our vehicle for enjoying sex, and they are part of the gift that we give when we make love. But how can we give ourselves over to the sexual experience when we feel that our bodies are ugly, inadequate, or the reason men can't control their thoughts and behaviors?

In many different ways, a woman can move toward accepting and enjoying the body God has given her. We can get to know our bodies, take stock and discover what we think is beautiful, and accept those things that aren't quite what we want them to be. We can learn a simple appreciation of our bodies in the many ways they function: "I really enjoy the things I can do in my body. I enjoy letting go and experiencing orgasm. I love a good game of softball or volleyball. I'm amazed that my body has given birth and nursed children. I'm so glad that I can comfort someone with a hug. Thank you, God, for this wonderful gift."

In addition, being physically fit or at least physically active is a wonderful way of experiencing ourselves as physical bodies. Walking, biking, and participating in sports can heighten our feelings of gratitude for the gift of life in our bodies and keep us more in touch with our physical, sexual selves. All of us—married or single—can embrace the "sexy" or sensual side of ourselves quite apart from the presence of a man in our lives. One woman notices, "Swimming in warm water, dressing in silks, exercising until I feel 'high'—all of those things are sexual feelings to me. Even if I'm not involved with someone else, I can still feel sexually alive."[18] Others are aware of their sexuality as an *energy*, and rather than being uncomfortable or ashamed of it, they channel it toward caring for those around them and making a difference in this world. We have many ways of learning to be at home in our bodies, and as we do so, we bring pleasure to the heart of God by enjoying the gift he has given.

Some women find that masturbation is another way of growing more comfortable with their bodies as well as managing their sexual energies when sexual expression with another person is not available or appropriate. Research indicates that although anywhere from 60 to 80 percent of women masturbate to orgasm, many women have strongly negative feelings about masturbation.[19] It's hard to know where all these negative feelings come from but it's almost certain that some of our shame or fear about touching ourselves may be formed very early in our development.

The Scriptures say nothing about this subject, and medically speaking we now know that there are no harmful physical or medical effects from masturbating. Actually, there is ample evidence that the practice can be beneficial—especially for women. One study found that married women who masturbate have greater marital and sexual satisfaction than women who do not. One of the reasons for this is that women can learn a lot about their own sexual responses—which kinds of touch feel good and which are irritating, which body movements and positions enhance sexual response—from self-pleasuring.[20] Too often women leave knowledge about their sexual anatomy to their husbands or doctors because of their phobias about touching themselves, and they miss out on knowledge that would be helpful to their marital relationship.

Self-stimulation can also be very helpful for the married woman who has not yet learned to experience orgasm.[21] For the woman who is uncomfortable with her body or with her body's sexual response, the freedom to explore in privacy may make it easier for her to share this knowledge with her husband and be responsive to him.

Unmarried adults often suffer in silence as it relates to this issue because there are two distinct schools of thought on singleness and masturbation. One belief is that the single person must be celibate in every sense of the word, avoiding sexual stimulation or experience of any kind. The other view sees sexuality as too much a part of the whole person to be completely repressed and ignored.

Christian writers and counselors fall into both camps. Some view the physical release of sexual tension as a gift from God for women who are single, helping them to embrace their sexuality. Masturbation is seen in some ways as a deterrent to sexual sin; some women have found that when they are feeling comfortable with and in control of their own sexuality, they are less likely to act inappropriately in their male-female friendships or to fall into sexual relationships out of desperation or the mere pressure of unmet sexual urges. At the same time, those who view masturbation as off-limits maintain that there are nonsexual ways of channeling the sex drive, such as physical exercise, expression of creative gifts, and service to others.[22]

Whichever view you take, if you are single it is most important that you think through the reasons for your decision to allow yourself this practice or prohibit it. We are in the most danger of being negatively influenced by our sexuality when we neglect to take an honest, well-reasoned look at it. This area, certainly as much as any other, should be explored in the context of prayer. God, who created us as sexual beings, will not turn away in embarrassment when we ask him for help and wisdom!

Women who are experiencing sexual fulfillment in their lives know not to use sex as a weapon. Because of the way relationships between men and women have traditionally been structured (the man being dominant and the woman being his supporter), it can be quite natural for a woman to see sex as her only weapon in a situation where she feels she has very little power.

In the workplace, a woman may be sorely tempted to flirt with the boss just a little, feeling that this is the only way for her to get into his good graces. In marriage it doesn't take long for a wife to figure out that withholding what her husband wants most puts her in a powerful position; she may begin to see this as her only way of registering a complaint or displeasure. These tactics often get results, making it easy to fall into a pattern of using sex or withholding it—without even being aware of what we are doing. The resulting sexual difficulties then are not really about sex but are indicators of other problems in the relationship, such as an imbalance of power or the inability to resolve conflict.

Ann Birk, director of a sex therapy program in Boston, says that the major predictor of sexual dysfunction in women is chronic and under-expressed anger. When a woman is angry with her husband or boyfriend and that anger cannot vent itself, it can have a direct and crippling effect on sexuality. Repressed anger and loving abandon just aren't able to exist side by side in most cases. Birk recalls the case of one young woman who was very angry with her husband because he was rarely home. "She could not bring herself to confront him with her anger and developed a vaginal condition that prevented her from having intercourse. As soon as she was able to confront him, to say, 'I need you home more,' the condition vanished almost immediately and she was able to function sexually."[23]

I do not want to make this process seem simpler than it is. It takes hard work to resolve these kinds of issues to the satisfaction of both parties in a relationship. However, many women have found that when they learn to deal more directly and effectively with anger and other relationship issues, they begin to flourish sexually.

Women who are experiencing sexual satisfaction know they have to conserve time and energy for it. A newspaper article titled "No Sex, Please, We're Tired Americans" highlights the fact that one of the biggest reasons married couples do not have sex is their pace of life. After the job, children, school functions, meals, and care of the home, couples end up in bed very tired. And when you're not getting enough sleep in life, it's easy to let sex go by the wayside or to have it but not put too much into it.

It's simple: Good sex takes energy. The sexually vital woman knows this and makes a conscious effort not to use up her last bit of energy at night washing the floor, putting last-minute touches on a presentation, or talking on the phone to a friend. There certainly are "crunch times" when it is inevitable that we fall into bed exhausted or don't even make it to bed at the same time. But the woman who is enjoying a fulfilling sex life does not allow this to become a pattern. She lets the floor go, gets up a little earlier in the morning, and gracefully excuses herself from the lengthy phone conversation. She doesn't just see sex as being for her husband; she understands that she needs it too. The warmth of being close, the release of tension, the reawakening of loving feelings that get lost in the rush of everyday tasks and schedules are elements of life that she cannot afford to lose touch with. And so, with at least some regularity, she saves part of herself for it.

THE JOY OF SEX

Psychiatrist M. Scott Peck tells the story of working for many months with a "rigid, frigid woman in her mid-thirties" who underwent a sudden and profound Christian conversion, and within three weeks of her conversion became orgasmic for the first time in her life. Peck observed that the timing was not accidental and concluded that when this woman became able to give herself wholeheartedly to God, in very short order she became able to give herself wholeheartedly to a human partner. He quotes these words of a friend: "The sexual and spiritual parts of ourselves lie so close together that it is hardly possible to arouse one without the other."[24]

The Bible tells us that our bodies are the "temple of the Holy Spirit" (1 Corinthians 6:19, NIV). In some unexplainable way, God's Spirit indwells us, making our bodies a place where we can meet and know him. Since sexuality is such an important aspect of our bodily selves, it, too, can become an area of our lives whereby we meet and know God in unique ways. All parts of the human experience are somehow connected. Thus all aspects of our humanity, including our sexuality, are spiritual and hold the possibility for abundant living, for the experience of grace, and for the imprint of the Divine. Reverend Alice Peterson, pastor and spiritual director, states,

> Many think that sexuality will go away or at least become quiescent as we grow spiritually. On the contrary! As we abide more closely to the God who is the source of all creative energy, the God of the Incarnation, we begin to experience sexual energy in a new way, as a holy, inalienable, generative force.[25]

As women, our delight in living in our bodies, our joy in physical expressions of love that are appropriate to the relationships that God has given us, the capacity for communion that keeps us seeking appropriate connection with others—all of these are ways of bringing glory to the Giver of the gift of our sexuality. They are a powerful testimony to the fullness that comes when we live our lives in harmony with him.

⌒ SPIRITUAL EXERCISES ⌒

Alone with God

Silence. As you come to the end of this chapter, take a few moments to sit with God in the silence of your own heart. You might want to reflect on one or more of these questions:

- How do you feel about the sexual, womanly part of yourself?
- Does it feel like a gift or a burden, a place of gladness or place of shame?
- What are the experiences in your life that seem to shape your perspective?

Prayer and journaling. Review what you have just read noticing the places of resonance and resistance that you have highlighted. Few of us have had the opportunity to reflect on our sexuality as a part of God's call to spiritual transformation.

- Where in this chapter did you identify (or not) with other women's experiences?
- What was your response to the idea that the sexual part of ourselves and the spiritual part of ourselves are connected?
- What difference would it make in the way you expressed yourself sexually if you really knew that to be true?
- Which of the stereotypes do you need to let go of in order to experience your sexuality more freely as a gift from God?
- Do you sense God calling you to a deeper place of healing for any early sexual influences that may have been imposed on you?

Allow yourself time to journal about your questions and desires in this area. Tell God what's true about you right now and what you long for. Then listen for his response.

Invitations. *God, are you inviting me to respond to what I have read today? In what way?*

With Your Spiritual Friend(s)

Begin your time together with a moment of silence and a simple prayer of invitation for God to join you.

Listening. Take turns giving each other your undivided attention. As appropriate, give each other a brief summary of what has happened between you and God this week in the context of your spiritual practices and your reading of this chapter.

- What did God say to you in your times of solitude and silence?
- What were your experiences of resonance and resistance as you read this chapter? How did you process those with God in your journal? In this area in particular, share only what you feel comfortable sharing.
- If you feel comfortable doing so, talk about one or more of the following questions:
  1. How are you experiencing your sexuality these days—as a gift, as a burden, as a complication?
  2. Do you experience your sexuality as being at all connected with your spirituality?
  3. Is there any piece of information or perspective offered in this chapter that you think will help you experience a greater level of freedom in living your life in God as a sexual being?

Prayer. Pray for one another.

NINE

FREEDOM FROM THE ROLE OF SUPERMOM

Of course a mother gives up a lot for her child: blood, sleep, tears, not to mention time, money, and peace of mind. But a mother must not feel obliged to give up herself. Not unless she wants to raise a motherless child.

—LISA CRONIN WOHL

It is difficult to admit how hard mothering has been for me. It's not the mechanics of it—the pregnancy, the birthing, knowing what to feed when, figuring out what to do when they're sick. No, what I've struggled with most is the relentlessness of the demands, the never-ending nature of the needs to which I must attend, the interruptions, the constant delayed gratification of my own desires, the uncertainty about how my children will turn out after all the parental words of wisdom have been said and all the hard work has been done.

I know I am not alone in my ambivalence. As one friend shared, "I think a lot of women struggle with their role as mother. For me, mothering is nothing like I thought it would be.... I always pictured myself spending hours reading to my daughter, but I don't. She wants me to get down on the floor and play with her, but I've discovered that I just don't like to play.... My self-concept has really suffered because I haven't lost the weight I put on during pregnancy. I hardly ever have reason to get dressed up, and nobody listens to me as though I have anything intelligent to say like they did when I was working."

A STRUGGLE WITHIN A STRUGGLE

The fact that many women find mothering to be more difficult than they had imagined is a truth of the female experience that can be hard to talk about. Society's expectations of us and our own expectations of ourselves are so different from our actual experience of things; media and child-care experts present images of motherhood that can be hard to live up to:

> A good mother is supposed to be totally devoted to her children; she is not allowed to get tired or bored by childcare and housework. Nor is she supposed to feel anything but love for her children. A woman who feels—as most mothers do—moments of boredom, anger, frustration, resentment, and other "negative" emotions toward her children is taught not that she is a normal mother, but that she is a bad mother.[1]

From both cultural and religious points of view, motherhood has been emphasized as a woman's highest calling in a more all-consuming way than fatherhood has been for men. We hear the biblical message that children are a gift from God but when our experience doesn't match our belief system, we're not quite sure what to do with ourselves. How-to books and magazine articles written by earth-mother types who have an unlimited supply of ideas for planning day-trips, craft projects, holiday traditions, and morning devotionals rarely encourage us. They just further overwhelm us with an unattainable ideal.

The struggle that women experience on an individual level also takes place within a culture that is grappling with the issue of "what to do with the children." A quick glance at magazine and newspaper headlines over the last decade reveals a powerful picture that requires little commentary: "Are We Forgetting the Kids?" "After School Orphans," "Who's Minding America's Children?" and "Forever Theirs: The Dark Side of the Job from Which You Cannot Resign." (This one was accompanied by a large drawing of a mother gagged and bound to a chair, held captive by a child with a gun!)

As women we have been told that we can have it all—a good marriage, children, a successful career, material possessions, and other personal achievements—and that children don't have to interfere with any of these pursuits. At best, children are often viewed as an option that we can fit in at our convenience or decide against altogether; at worst, they are seen as a nuisance or an interruption.

In an article in *Time* magazine titled "Shameful Bequests to the Next Generation," the author describes our legacy to the young: bad schools, poor health care, deadly addictions, crushing debts—and utter indifference. The author goes on to note:

> Mothers and fathers worry about the toxic residue left from too much television, too many ghastly movies, too many violent videos, too little discipline. They wonder how to raise children who are strong and imaginative and loving. They worry about the possibility that their children will grow wild and distant and angry. Perhaps they fear most that they will get the children they deserve. "Children who go unheeded," warns Harvard psychiatrist Robert Coles, "are children who are going to turn on the world that has neglected them." And that anger will come when today's children are old enough to realize how relentlessly their needs have been ignored.[2]

Is it any wonder, then, that "guilt and uncertainty make child rearing the number one topic of conversation among young mothers today? Today's parents are raising children in ways that little resemble their own youth. The question that haunts them: Will the kids be all right?"[3]

If we are at all aware, we understand that the chances of "the kids being all right" are slimmer than they have ever been. James Dobson notes, "It has become a daunting task to shield the younger generation from 'safe-sex' instruction in school, from profane and sacreligious language in the neighborhood, from immorality and violence on television, from homosexual and lesbian propaganda, and from wickedness and evil of every stripe."[4]

After reading the litany of threats facing our children today—drive-by shootings, illegal drugs, sexual molesters and kidnappers, murderers and rapists taking children from their own bedrooms, degrading television programming, and commercials featuring dancing condoms—it is easy to feel overwhelmed by the responsibilities of parenting, the majority of which still fall to women in our society. The fact that our culture no longer supports morality and religious truth as it has in the past just adds to the gravity of the situation. As Christians we labor under the weighty realization that, to a certain extent, the future of our children depends on our ability to counter the culture in which they live and breathe. How do we experience truth and freedom in the midst of such pressure?

THE PARADOX OF MOTHERHOOD

I have struggled, questioned, argued, and cried during my years of parenting. Yet it is in the midst of God's call to mothering that I am being transformed—invited to a place of greater freedom—as I trust in God's sovereignty and receive the blessings he bestows through my children.

In the early years of parenting, a kind of awe develops as we realize that *this* child—*our* child—is given to us and to this world for a purpose that

God himself knows and intends to make known in his time. It's not only that children in general are a blessing but that the specific children God sends to us are given as his blessing for our lives. Some of these blessings are fleeting in nature—the pleasure of soft baby cheeks perfect for nuzzling and pug noses perfect for kissing, the pride that fills our hearts as we watch a child—our child—run with strength and grace down a soccer field, the fullness that we feel as we don pajamas and cuddle under blankets to watch a movie together on a snowy night, the amazement of seeing strengths surface in our child that are so different from our own.

Moments of blessedness come when we are least expecting them. They are the moments of joy that give us perspective when the stress and tedium of child rearing threaten to overwhelm us. Sometimes these moments are gone as quickly as they come, but we can hold them in our hearts as evidence that God sent these children to bless us in ways we couldn't imagine until we experienced them.

Other blessings are of the long-lasting sort, blessings we carry with us into eternity. The greatest of these is the blessedness of knowing that we have influenced another soul to embrace Christ as Savior; this is the one treasure that you *can* "take with you." At the time of this writing, Chris and I have just sent our oldest daughter, Charity, off to college. It is hard for me to express the gratitude and awe, the deep love and satisfaction that I feel about sending this daughter into the world—one who is strong and beautiful and clear about who she is in God, willing and ready to do her part in turning her world upside down for Christ. As I expressed to her in a letter written on her eighteenth birthday, "You are becoming yourself in ways that some women take all their lives to achieve. (Some never do!) I truly cannot figure out where you came from! I see glimpses of myself in you, but you are also much *more* than what I am and I am reminded that you came from God."

So, it is quite a paradox to find that an area where I have struggled so deeply has become one of my deepest sources of joy and pride. Even as I am aware of the deep levels of satisfaction I have as my daughters emerge into such true expressions of the persons God created them to be, I am also aware that mothering has provided yet another context for my own transformation. It has required me to confront levels of selfishness and pride that might have been left unchallenged were it not for the unique opportunities that mothering presents. The experience of being a mother has called me to new levels of faith and perseverance that might have otherwise gone unexplored. Working on my character deficiencies as they surface as I relate to my children and listening to my daughters' unedited evaluation of my Christianity as it is lived out before them has provided me with wonderful growth—when I have been able to remain open!

These are the blessings God intends for us when he gives us the gift of children. And in a culture like ours where it seems that children are "God's least-wanted blessing," it is the eye of faith that knows how to see them and the believing heart that knows how to receive them.

God's Invitation to Love Children

The story of Hannah is a true parenting success story. Perhaps you remember the story of this woman who struggled with infertility and promised God that if he gave her a son she would then dedicate him to the Lord's service (see 1 Samuel 1 and 2). The Lord answered her prayer and gave her a son whom she named Samuel. When Samuel was weaned, Hannah kept her promise and took Samuel to the temple in Shiloh to serve God with the priest Eli. Hannah's early training stood Samuel in good stead and, despite Eli's spiritual deadness and some poor influences (Eli's unruly sons), he went on to become one of the greatest prophets, priests, and judges Israel ever knew.

Although the details of Samuel's upbringing are a bit unusual, the story of Hannah and her son reminds us that God can work in a variety of situations to produce children who will serve him faithfully throughout their lives. This is of particular comfort to single parents who labor under the added pressure of trying to fill the roles of mother and father while at the same time trying to generate all or most of the family income. When a situation seems impossible, Hannah's story reminds us that God can be trusted to bring our children through whatever the disadvantages of our situation happen to be. Hannah's story also underscores some basic elements of effective parenting and leads us to ask ourselves if we are willing to love our children in some very practical ways.

Love Them Enough to Welcome Them

Sometimes in the throes of mothering we forget that children are human beings created and known by God. Hannah knew even before her child was born that God was involved in the life that formed in her. Psalm 139 indicates that God knows and forms each child in the womb. Before they are born, God already has a plan for them. As he pointed out to Jeremiah: "Before I formed you in the womb I knew you, and before you were born I consecrated you; I appointed you a prophet to the nations" (1:5). Men and women of the Bible were highly aware of the fact that life does not begin merely because of human action—God is always involved in conception and birth. Eve said, "I have gotten a manchild with the help of the Lord" (Genesis 4:1, NASB), the Lord was the one who opened Leah's womb (Genesis 29:31), and Ruth 4:13 says "the LORD enabled her [Ruth] to conceive, and she gave birth to a son" (NASB). Recognizing that God is the source of our children's lives is foundational to understanding the magnitude and the privilege of the call to parent.

Believing that children are a blessing, Hannah prayed that God would give her this gift and welcomed her son when he was born. Her response mirrored Christ's welcoming attitude toward children in Matthew 19.

Even though the disciples were anxious to shoo them away, Christ used them as an example of faith and said that when we welcome children, we welcome him.

As women we have a unique opportunity to welcome the little ones by bearing them in our bodies. This is the first sacrifice we make, and it *is* a sacrifice! In a body-worshipping culture such as ours, it is no small thing to realize that your breasts and belly may never be the same! But that is only the beginning. In her book *Sacred Dwelling: A Spirituality of Family Life,* Wendy Wright speaks about what this welcoming really means:

> To welcome a child is to accept responsibility for another person twenty-four hours a day, seven days a week, for a good many years. Ultimately, it is to welcome the unfolding mystery of an entire lifetime's joys and pains as your own. To welcome a child is to give priority to the unpredictability of another life, to tend to it in sickness, no matter what you had otherwise planned, to allow your plans and dreams to be altered, even set aside, because of another's need. To welcome a child is to learn to think and speak in response to a different and constantly changing worldview, to be outside of your own frame of reference. You learn patience and judgment and are confronted with your own very real and heretofore untested limitations. To welcome a child is to recognize the surprising expansiveness of your own capacity to love and to confront the shattering truth of your own violence and self-centeredness. To welcome a child is to have your heart stretched, made capable of loving in a new and unrepeatable way.[5]

God calls fathers and mothers to welcome children into their lives, making a place where their emotional, spiritual, and physical needs are met.

Love Them Enough to Make Them a Priority

Hannah was forced by her unusual circumstances to see her time with Samuel as a window of opportunity for training and loving that was very short-lived, and she took full advantage of it. In Jewish culture, weaning (which literally means "dealt fully with") was accomplished when the child was around three years old. Until Hannah felt that she had dealt fully with her son, she didn't even take the annual trip to Shiloh to worship at the temple. She knew that the time would come when it would be right for her to go and fulfill her promise. But until the Lord freed her to do that, she made Samuel her priority.

Although our window of opportunity may not be as small as it was for Hannah and Samuel, it is relatively short in the whole scheme of things. In the early years especially, most children want to be with their parents more than anyone else and are wide open to our influence. What a privilege this is! It's not long before children enter into the developmental stage in which they are embarrassed to be seen with parents and want to hang out with their friends rather than their family. What could possibly be worth giving up being with my children when they want to be with me more than anyone else in the world?

Love Them Enough to Discipline Them

The story of Samuel (1 Samuel 1–4) offers a poignant study in contrast. While Samuel ministered to the Lord and experienced his presence, Eli's sons grew up to be scoundrels. The Bible says that they had no regard for the Lord or for the duties of a priest to the people. They stole from the offerings people brought and seduced the women who served at the place of worship. Eli knew about his sons' sinful behavior but only offered a weak reprimand. Finally God intervened and said to Eli, "I chose your family out of all the families in Israel to perform the sacred duties of priests. I revealed myself in a special way to your ancestors. Why then have you honored your sons more than me by fattening yourselves on the choicest parts of every offering of my people Israel?" (1 Samuel 2:27-29, author's paraphrase).

To Samuel, God communicated this message, "I am about to punish his [Eli's] house forever, for the iniquity that he knew, because his sons were blaspheming God, and he did not restrain them" (3:13, author's paraphrase). And that is exactly what happened. It wasn't long before Hophni and Phineas were killed in battle. When Eli heard the news he fell from his seat, broke his neck and died. A tragic ending to tragic lives.

The point is that we don't do anyone any favors by refusing to discipline our children. In fact, we do our children, ourselves, and our society a great disservice when we allow them to be disrespectful, immoral, and undisciplined. We have the same problem today that Eli had, although perhaps for our own set of reasons. Leading pediatricians T. Berry Brazelton and Benjamin Spock worry about the disappearance of discipline, particularly when both parents work. "Parents don't want to spend the little time they have with their children reprimanding them," says Spock. "This encourages children to push limits and test parental authority."[6]

Children have an uncanny ability to play on the guilt feelings to which today's parents are so susceptible. I've noticed that when I am stressed out because I have taken on too much in life and I am not sure if the kids are getting what they need, it is very easy to give in when they accuse us of being unfair in requiring them to pull their weight around the house, behave respectfully, or live without something they want. Then, in an effort to assuage my own guilt, I tend to spend the time when I am available overcompensating. However, when I am more consistently available for my children's legitimate needs, I am much more confident about insisting that they do the dishes, accept the fact that they cannot have another sleepover, or respond respectfully to the limits we have set in our home. When I know they are getting what they really need from us—time, attention, limits, physical needs (not necessarily wants) met—then I am a lot less likely to give in to doubt when it comes time for strong discipline or saying no.

Limits set by loving parents are good for children because young people who do not know how to work, how to respect authority, and how to control themselves will not get very far in life. In fact, these qualities are becoming so rare that just by cultivating them, our children will distinguish themselves and be well on their way to success in work, marriage, family life, and spiritual service. We cannot expect them to have this long-range perspective while they are young; that's why we must keep it for them until they are old enough to realize how important it is.

Love Them Enough to Share Our Spiritual Journey

We do not know how many years Hannah was able to spend with Samuel before she took him to the temple. However, we do know that in whatever time she had, she trained him effectively and cultivated his spiritual life. Even though he was surrounded by poor influences at the temple, Samuel continued to serve the Lord faithfully. And even though Eli was ineffective as a father and as a spiritual leader ("the word of the Lord was rare in those days; visions were not widespread," 1 Samuel 3:1), it was Samuel who began to hear and respond to God's voice. In fact, "as Samuel grew up, the LORD was with him and let none of his words fall to the ground. And all Israel…knew that Samuel was a trustworthy prophet of the LORD…. For the LORD revealed himself to Samuel at Shiloh…and the word of Samuel came to all Israel" (1 Samuel 3:19–4:1).

The amazing truth here is that God had given up trying to communicate with the elderly priest Eli, and so he chose to communicate with this young boy who had a heart that was sensitized to the voice of God. It was through this mere child that the horror of spiritual drought in the land of Israel was relieved. Where do you think Samuel's strong character and spiritual receptivity came from? My guess is that it was a combination of the heart God gave him and the training he received in his home.

Just think! Our children also have the potential to be those through whom God speaks and from whom a river of life can flow to those who thirst for a taste of God's presence. But raising up the kind of children who will know God and bless others doesn't happen by accident. It happens in homes where children are important, where limits are set, and where spiritual awareness is cultivated.

Another observation comes from Deuteronomy 6:6-9: Effective child training is a mixture of structured and spontaneous instruction. This verse presupposes that both parents are with their children enough to be able to teach them throughout the day as they walk together, talk together, and as they drop off to sleep and wake in the morning. These informal times of training and instilling values are just as important as more structured family prayers and Bible reading.

As children grow older it can also be appropriate to share those places where we are still in process—wrestling with our own unanswered questions and the unfinished places in our own souls. During the time when I was questioning my long-held beliefs about God's view of women, I did not know where the questions would take me spiritually or how they would affect my relationships. As my struggle deepened, it became impossible to hide my emerging emotions from those closest to me—including my three daughters. As much as I might have wished that I could travel this part of my journey in seclusion, that was not my situation. I had three little girls watching their mother fight for her spiritual life.

At one point in particular, when I needed to drop out of church for a while in order to let old wounds heal, I remember crying out to God with questions about how this would impact my girls' spiritual development. How would they possibly understand the fact that their dad took them to church while their mom stayed home? What meanings would they place on this later on?

At that point, I knew I needed to take what seemed like a huge step of faith as a mother. I had to believe and trust that if I stayed faithful to the way in which God was calling me to go deeper with him, healing the pains of the past and forming something new for the future, then something good would be in that for my daughters. Perhaps letting them in on my own struggle would give them more freedom to wrestle with God if and when they needed to, and ultimately find that "one cannot go far before falling into [God's] arms."[7] Thus, in age-appropriate ways, I began to be more intentional about sharing this portion of my faith journey with our daughters, letting them see my struggle and hear my questions. I began trusting in God's care for them, trusting that they could benefit from knowing the truth of my experience and its impact on our family. And I have no regrets.

Today, as I witness their emerging strength and clarity about who they are as young women, I know these things have something to do with parts of my journey they have witnessed. I am convinced that the best thing we as mothers have to give our children is our own transforming selves. Whatever we leave unresolved within ourselves—due to fear or laziness or lack of initiative—will be passed on to them as unresolved issues. On the other hand, opening up to God's transforming work in our lives can become one of the greatest treasures we could ever offer.

Love Them Enough to Let Them Go

As we dropped Charity off at college this fall, I couldn't help but remember her first day of kindergarten. I had walked to pick her up and as we walked home, she insisted on walking a couple blocks ahead. I called her back and tried to convince her to walk and talk with me, but she said, "Can we do that when we get home? I want to be a big girl." There was no malice. No impertinence. Just the honest expression of a little girl trying to grow up.

So we walked that way and I had the pleasure of watching her walk ahead of me—ponytail bobbing, backpack carried proudly. Every block or so she would turn around and wave—just making sure I was there. And I would wave back, trying to communicate with every wave that I loved her and was proud of her and that it was okay that she wanted to walk alone. It was a picture of the process parents and children begin at birth: the process of letting go, of allowing our children to gain their independence little by little. It is, after all, what we raise them for, and we must never forget it.

For Hannah, the moment of letting go all the way came much sooner than it does for most of us. After weaning Samuel she took him back to the temple to dedicate him to the Lord's work just as she had promised. It is hard to imagine that she was unaware of Eli's lack of spiritual effectiveness or Hophni and Phineas's sinful behavior. Yet the time had come for her to trust that the training she had done and Samuel's own personal relationship with God would give him the moorings he needed. Certainly that is what we must trust when we face those moments of saying good-bye.

Fortunately, letting go comes gradually for most of us, one good-bye preparing us for the next. The first time we leave our baby with Grandma prepares us for the church nursery. The first day of school prepares us for that first overnight. Dropping them off at the big junior high or high school prepares us for the day we drop them off at college. Teaching them to choose their dates wisely and then letting them go prepares us to let them go with the one they choose to marry. Dedicating our children to the Lord at birth, as Hannah did, helps prepare us for the day when he calls them into service that may take them far from us.

We seek to achieve a balance between letting our children go in age-appropriate ways and providing the undergirding for their explorations.

We must not hold them too tightly, yet always be there in the background, waving at them with support and love, ready to come to their aid when they need us, protecting them from dangers they are not quite ready to handle. And somewhere along the way, as we negotiate their transition into adulthood, we become more than parents and children. We become friends.

GIVING TO OUR CHILDREN WITHOUT LOSING OURSELVES

As you can see, I have experienced a wide range of thoughts and feelings about my role as mother. I have spent time thinking that the grass looks greener on the side of the fence where women carry briefcases and dress in something besides jeans. In fact, I have been back and forth over the fence several times. I have also taken a long hard look at the inequities women have experienced as a result of having so much of the responsibility for home-making and parenting placed on them. I have had days when anger and frustration have threatened to overwhelm me. And in the midst of all that I have come to realize that there is no other area in my life in which the ramifications of my choices are so far-reaching and the potential for regret so great.

While motherhood is a privilege that offers great joys and great challenges, it is important for us to remain clear about the fact that motherhood is one part of a whole life lived for kingdom purposes. Just as it is a grave mistake to invest our relationships with men with the weight of our need for self-esteem, identity, and purpose, it is also a mistake to invest our mothering with all of our hopes and dreams for meaning in this life. While motherhood is a deeply rewarding experience to which God calls most women, motherhood is only half a life's work.

One author notes that thirty-five is the age at which most women send their last child off to school, leaving many years for them to make other meaningful contributions to the kingdom of God here on earth. Many who have not kept their mothering in perspective with the greater call of God on their lives find themselves feeling useless after their children leave the nest and have very little sense of what they should do next. Many end up biding time in dead-end jobs that do not capitalize on their giftedness or do not give them a sense that they are contributing to a cause that really matters. The sense of how much of themselves they "gave up" to be a mother can be overwhelming when they begin to realize it.

Sometimes it seems like all these issues together do nothing more than create a Catch-22 situation that is impossible to find our way out of. We feel anything but free. We fear that the truths we want to embrace will conflict with the realities of daily life. All I can do in such times is carry it all into God's presence over and over again. I do this because I trust him. I do this because I know that he cares equally about me and about my children; he alone can give me perspective and help me put my life and the lives of my children together in a way that is best for all of us in the long run. I need his help to find the middle road that women must walk, a road that runs between two harmful extremes—neglecting our children or neglecting ourselves.

The only way to find the middle road and stay on it is to keep looking to God for guidance as each choice presents itself. I cling to his promise in Psalm 32: "I will instruct you…in the way which you should go; I will counsel you with my Eye upon you" (verse 8, NASB). With his loving eyes upon me and my eyes on him I have gotten better at knowing, "Yes, this ministry will fit right now… No, this class would take too much of my energy… Two evenings out this week, not three… No committee work now but maybe after this project is finished… Time to put my own reading away and read to the children… The kids have gotten what they need from me today, now I can give some time to other work… Oops, I overdid it today, I'll do some adjusting tomorrow." God continues to lead me into new ways of balancing and embracing the unique dimensions of my gifts and family callings.

As I have continued to bring my wrestlings to God and open my heart to what he wants to teach me about being a mother, I've noticed that some concerns pale into insignificance while other concerns give birth to certainty. One truth I have become more certain of is that *children in our culture are in danger.* And that danger is not just "out there" in the big, bad world. Our children are also in danger because as a generation they have suffered our neglect, our indifference, and our inability to do what it takes to keep our families together.

Recent studies show that during unsupervised hours, latchkey children of all social and economic groups are twice as likely to abuse drugs, engage in sexual intercourse (one psychologist mentions that usually a girl has her first sexual experience in her or her boyfriend's empty house), join gangs, or contribute to the astonishing increase in the juvenile violent crime arrest rate in the last several years. In addition, these children may be extraordinarily isolated and lose out on valuable life-shaping experiences with friends and role models during the critical period of adolescent development.

The message of these facts is simple: Our children need us! I consider myself to be a liberated woman. But there is no way I can, nor would I want to, "liberate" myself from the fact that I have children and they need me.

The answer to the question of what to do with children is not for women to pull out and renege on our God-given responsibility. The answer is for men and women together to fall on our faces before God and confess selfishness and upside-down values where they exist. To believe the truth that children are a blessing and to translate that belief into the obedience of making them a priority in our lives. To slow down our frantic rush for success, money, and power so that we can adequately supervise our children all the way through their teenage years. To share parenting responsibilities so that women and men alike can nurture other parts of themselves even as they nurture children. To cast ourselves upon God for wisdom and strength. To daily inquire of God, "What will it require of me to nurture the emotional, physical, and spiritual well-being of my children? How do you want to transform me in the process?"

ACCEPTING THE RESPONSIBILITY

The call on our lives as mothers invites us to rest in the sovereignty of God in giving us children but also to accept the responsibility to make informed choices. Bill Hybels wisely encourages newly married couples not to make the choice to have children unadvisedly. He mentions several important considerations that should inform such a decision. "First," he says, "newly married couples should devote themselves to solidifying their marriage before they even consider having children. Raising a healthy, well-adjusted, Christ-honoring child in today's world almost demands a strong marriage and family unit." He also recommends that couples consider whether either of them carries "the deep trauma of a painful or tragic past" that they have not yet worked through fully.[8] They need to consider the implications of passing on their debilitations to another generation and make the investment in dealing with unresolved issues before bringing a child into such a complicated scene. (These issues might be substance abuse, sexual abuse, domestic violence, parents who were unable to give love, or other similar struggles and traumas.)

The fact of the matter is that "it takes time and energy to raise children. Young couples hoping to find a system of child rearing that doesn't inconvenience them or overload their already full schedules should rethink their decision. It may be they're missing the whole point of having children."[9]

A couple may also decide, after listening to God and paying careful attention to what he is doing in their lives, to make "the legitimate choice" not to have children in order to participate in building Christ's kingdom by pursuing full-time careers in ministry or in the marketplace. It is unfortunate that, in some Christian circles, couples who choose not to have children are considered incomplete, selfish, or unfaithful to the whole idea of marriage. Yet, we can't ignore the "normal" families that have turned out to be quite unhealthy because someone didn't count the cost—either to the children or the parents—of adding family members to a life already consumed in ministry and career.

IS THIS A JOB FOR SUPERMOM?

I am convinced that one of the reasons we as women today struggle so greatly with our role as mothers is because the weight of responsibility of nurturing and rearing children tends to fall primarily on us. God's instruction for us to attend to our children is huge and multifaceted, but when men and women are committed to it together, it is much less overwhelming.

I do not need another book on how to be a better mother. I do not need a support group. What I have needed is my husband, the father of these children, to participate more fully with me in this great call of God upon our lives. I have needed to hear him say with words and with action, "You are not alone. These children are just as much my responsibility as they are yours. Together we have received the high call of parenting."

Just as the men and women of Israel together received such detailed instruction for caring for children (Deuteronomy 6:6-9),[10] so I have needed to know and experience in relationship with Chris that raising children is not "women's work" but kingdom work that is worthy of the very best we both have to offer. And it has been in working together—rather than in listening to one more sermon or reading one more book—that my feelings of being overwhelmed and isolated and inadequate have begun to subside.[11]

Nurturing children, generating income, and following God's call to minister to a lost world can be blended into a rich family life in a multitude of ways. It should not necessarily be assumed that the wife's ministry or career is the one that must come to a grinding halt. In some cases it is feasible for the husband, the wife, or both, to slow down, adjust, and find ways to give and take in order to accommodate the arrival of children.

One couple I know (both pastors now) has made a variety of arrangements throughout the life of their family. Steve finished his graduate work B.C. (before children), but Jamie had not finished hers when they had their first child. During the early months of his son's life, Steve worked part-time and helped out with child care while Jamie finished her degree. Then for four years, Steve worked in his career of choice while Jamie stayed home with child number one and added another. At a previously arranged time they switched and Steve stayed at home for three years while Jamie got her career off the ground.

Today the children are well on their way to adulthood, and both Jamie and Steve are settled into their respective pastorates. Steve looks back on the years he stayed home with his children as "the best years of my life" and says, "I know that I did something that was right for my children, my wife, and even me." He concludes,

> More and more fathers are investing themselves in parenting
> because they realize there is joy and satisfaction there that can be
> found nowhere else. And they realize that their children need them
> in ways that are important and unique…. Who better than a father
> to mold healthy self-image through play and everyday activities like
> these (playing horsey on the living room floor)? Who better than a
> father to teach his children that they are important and worthwhile
> by investing his time and energy into them?… Fathers who stay at
> home with their children have the same goal as everyone else—to
> bring up happy, well-adjusted children. When parenting is shared,
> [this] objective may be more easily attained.[12]

Mary Stewart Van Leeuwen offers this challenging perspective for families today:

> The root issue is not primarily…some historically fixed way of
> structuring family economic, domestic, and childrearing tasks. The
> root question is one of priorities. How can a given Christian family,
> with its particular constellation of talents, limitations, and needs, so
> structure itself that it contributes to the advancement of God's king-
> dom on earth? Perhaps the best environment for children is not one
> in which the mother stays home, but one in which the whole
> family, as part of the larger family of God, reaches out to meet the
> needs of others. Just how an individual family accomplishes this at
> various stages of family life is a matter of responsible Christian free-
> dom. There is no one, "best" answer that fits every case.[13]

The privilege of parenting with another person is a God-given gift. When women and men share the responsibility of providing for the physical, spiritual, and emotional well-being of their children, neither has to be weighted down with burdens heavier than God intended for them to bear alone. Together we can open ourselves to the transformation God invites us to through the blessings and the wonders of our children.

SPIRITUAL EXERCISES

Alone with God

Silence. As you come to the end of this chapter, take a few moments to sit with God in the silence of your own heart and allow yourself to experience the full range of your feelings and thoughts about being a mother at this particular stage of your mothering experience. Don't judge yourself at all. Let yourself feel the joy and privilege, the frustration and pain, the longing and the satisfaction, the things that you're sure of and the things you're questioning.

Prayer and journaling. Review what you have just read, noticing the places of resonance and resistance that you have highlighted. Allow yourself the time to reflect on and journal about your experiences and longings as a woman who is also a mother. Tell God what's true about you right now and what you long for. Then listen for his response.

- Where were places in the reading that touched places of deep concern in you?
- What places sparked joy?
- What was your heart's response to some of the research that was presented along with the biblical truth?
- Where did God seem to be touching a place of desire and commitment in you?
- What opportunities for transformation are being given to you now in the midst of your mothering?

Invitations. *God, how are you inviting me to respond to what I've read today?*

With Your Spiritual Friend(s)

Begin your time together with a moment of silence and a simple prayer of invitation for God to join you.

Listening. Take turns giving each other your undivided attention. As appropriate, tell each other some of what has happened between you and God this week in the context of your spiritual practices and your reading of this chapter.

- What did God say to you in your times of solitude and silence?

- What were your experiences of resonance and resistance as you read this chapter? How did you process those with God in your journal?
- How is God transforming you in the midst of your mothering?
- What is the area of your deepest joy as a mother these days?
- What is your deepest question or concern?
- When you ask God, "What will it require of me to nurture the emotional, physical, and spiritual well-being of my children?" what do you hear?

Prayer. Pray for one another.

Freedom in the Midst of Difficulty

Be patient towards all that is unsolved in your heart and try to love the questions themselves...do not now seek the answers, which cannot be given you because you would not be able to live them. Live the questions now. Perhaps you will then gradually, without noticing it, live along some distant day into the answer.

—Ranier Maria Rilke, *Letters to a Young Poet*

Every now and then I enjoy window shopping in jewelry stores. I am always amazed at how the cut stones, especially the diamonds, shine so brilliantly. Even the cheapest, most ordinary diamonds look beautiful under the bright lights when displayed against a background of black velvet.

It can be that way with people, too. Sometimes, against the backdrop of pain, tragedy, or difficulty, a beauty shines forth that is accentuated by the darkness of the surrounding circumstances. Abigail was such a woman—a diamond whose beauty and worth shone against the backdrop of a difficult, heartbreaking marriage. Abigail was everything I would like to be—godly, intelligent, and beautiful. However, the most striking thing about her is that she managed to live a godly life in what, to me, would have been an intolerable situation. How did she do it?

STRONG UNDER PRESSURE

Abigail's story is found in 1 Samuel 25. The writer describes her as "intelligent and beautiful in appearance," while her husband, Nabal, was "harsh and evil in his dealings" (25:3, NASB). As the story unfolds we see more evidence that Nabal was no knight in shining armor: He was impossible to reason with, he was selfish and rude, and he was an alcoholic who became abusive when he was drunk.

It is not hard to imagine the disappointment and loneliness Abigail lived with on a daily basis. Certainly she had the same hopes that we all do for tenderness, intimacy, companionship, and spiritual oneness in marriage. How she must have wished that her life were different and perhaps, at times, she cried out to God to deliver her from the pain of such a hurtful, unhealthy relationship.

One day, the normal stress of living with a difficult man escalated into a true crisis. David, who was running from a jealous King Saul, happened to be hiding out in the desert of Paran, which bordered Nabal's property. During that time, David and the six hundred men who were with him provided protection for Nabal's shepherds while they were in the fields. At one point David politely requested payment for services rendered and Nabal responded with rudeness and ungratefulness, denying any knowledge at all of David or the protection his men had provided. This sent David into a murderous rage and he quickly organized four hundred of his men to kill all the males in Nabal's household (verses 13,21-22).

One of Nabal's servants understood the gravity of the situation but also understood that Nabal was "such a worthless man that no one can speak to him" (verse 17, NASB). So he went straight to Abigail and explained the situation. She obviously had the complete confidence of her household staff, and with good reason. She immediately swung into action, initiating a plan that was characterized by insight, godly wisdom, courage, and diplomacy. Her direct and insightful intervention with David (verses 18,25-38) quickly diffused this volatile situation.

David, this great man of God, was impressed by Abigail's discernment, and he listened and responded to the wisdom of her words. He realized that what she was saying was true. If he did act out of uncontrolled anger as he had planned, he would shed innocent blood rather than leaving vengeance up to God. At best, this would place a permanent blot on his character; at worst, it could disqualify him as a leader for the people of Israel. So he blessed her and received the provisions she had brought, turning away from his murderous intent.

Abigail must have been very relieved at the outcome of her peacekeeping mission, but when she got home, she faced another problem. Nabal had been partying and he was drunk; it was not a good time to tell him about the disaster they had so narrowly escaped (verse 36). She wisely waited until the next morning to fill Nabal in, and when he heard it, "his heart died within him so that he became as a stone" (verse 37, NASB). Apparently he was paralyzed by a stroke and then died ten days later. When David heard about what had become of Nabal, he was thankful that he had waited and allowed God to avenge his cause. He also sent a proposal of marriage to Abigail, and she accepted in what appears to have been a very happy ending.

From Difficulties to Diamonds

Despite the fact that Abigail's marriage was probably arranged, as was the custom of the day, her situation is all too contemporary. Even women who have had the opportunity to choose their marriage partner end up with unexpected difficulties. One author describes Abigail as the perfect candidate for an Al-Anon recovery group or a support group for "women who love too much," citing Abigail's rush from an abusive marriage into a polygamous one as a foolish choice.[1]

But there was more to Abigail than that. She was not living in denial, and she didn't shy away from a realistic assessment of her situation: "Please do not let my lord pay attention to this worthless man, Nabal, for as his name is, so is he. Nabal is his name and folly is with him" (verse 25, NASB). She was a woman with excellent management and interpersonal skills, as evidenced by the way she handled conflict and related with the household staff. She worked effectively for peace by clarifying the issues in a nonthreatening way and showed tremendous spiritual discernment regarding God's plans for David. But she also knew that he was on the verge of making a critical error in judgment by taking his own revenge rather than leaving it up to God. Abigail, a master of tact and timing, chose carefully how she would broach sensitive subjects and when she should act on her own initiative. And she chose to stay committed to Nabal rather than run from her problems.

Rather than seeing a woman who loves too much, I see a woman with limited options who exercised the few she had quite effectively. In those days, a woman without a husband had no options. She couldn't obtain a restraining order, find a shelter for battered women, get a job, and start a new life. Back then, a wife belonged to her husband in the same way that he "owned" his slaves and his cattle, and he was free to do with her as he wished. Had Abigail left Nabal, she would have been totally without support and protection, and Nabal could have killed or severely punished her if he caught up with her. The option of leaving was not available to her.

However, Abigail still had the option of choosing how she would respond to her circumstances. She never used her husband's boorish behavior as an excuse to act the same way. Rather, she kept growing in a positive direction so that when the moment of crisis came, she was ready with the skills and spiritual maturity to handle it. Because she had been exercising her inner options, the moment of crisis also became a moment of opportunity—an opportunity to save her family and to be an influence for good in the life of a great man of God.

Obviously, it's not only difficult marriages that cause the backdrop of some people's lives to be so black. For others it is chronic pain, depression, or a physical disability. For some it's a painful childhood memory or a past mistake. It could be a child, a spouse, or an in-law who is a constant source of emotional pain. Maybe there is something in their lives that hurts so badly they've begged the Lord to take it away, but it's still there.

At some point all of us face difficulties that cause deep pain and seem unfixable. Sometimes we wonder if we're going to make it through or if we're going to fly to pieces. In the midst of the unfixables of life we ask, "How can I be with God in the midst of this? How can I allow the beauty of the Christ-life to emerge against the backdrop of this difficulty—rather than allowing it to become a black hole that just sucks me into the darkness? How can I experience the freedom Christ offers me when I feel so overwhelmed and trapped in my pain?"

We may not have answers to every dark situation we're in, but we can find ways to open ourselves to the reality of God's activity in the midst of our struggle.

Allow Yourself to Be Honest with God

One thing is true: God has the power to change our circumstances. The story of Abigail tells us that. And it is perfectly acceptable for us to ask him to do just that. Paul asked the Lord three times to take away his "thorn in the flesh" (2 Corinthians 12:7, NASB). Christ prayed the night before he was crucified, "My Father, if it is possible, let this cup pass from me; yet not what I want but what you want" (Matthew 26:39). Even in their willingness to do God's will, they expressed their desire for God to take the hard thing away. This kind of desire is not condemned or forbidden by God.

In the case of both Paul and Christ, God chose not to grant their request. But that did not lessen the importance of expressing it to him. They still needed to be in communication, to open up their truest questions, and to experience God's presence with them in the midst of their pain and grief and frustration. To understand the importance of this dynamic in our relationship with God, we might think of our relationship with our children. Even when we have to say no to a request, we're not upset that they asked. We still want to talk and to tell them that we care and that they are not alone. Sometimes we are able to offer another perspective or a ray of hope— and sometimes we aren't. But knowing that we're in it together becomes a comfort and a bond. So it is with God. We talk to him first of all because he is our most intimate friend and we want to share all things with him. And that is how relationships develop.

We also talk to him because he has the power to take our pain away; we express our faith and trust in his goodness when we make our requests known to him. Be even when he doesn't respond exactly as we would like, we might find that turning to God in the midst of difficulty has a way of kick-starting our relationship with him into a new gear. Remembering the worst storms of her difficult marriage, one woman recalls, "I had a choice between talking to myself or talking to God, so I chose to talk to God. He became like my husband in a way, and as I look back on those times, my relationship with God seemed so much closer than it does now that I'm through the storm."

A difficult marriage or any other kind of hardship gives us the opportunity to learn to trust God and love him despite the circumstances of life. In so doing, we move beyond the honeymoon stage of our faith ("I'll follow God as long as things are going well") to a more mature relationship that transcends hardship and is able to trust even through dark times.

Allow Difficulties to Produce Character

It would be easy for us to let the fact that God delivered Abigail from her difficult marriage take our focus off other important facets of this story. For me, the main point is not that she was delivered but that she did not allow the circumstances of her life to determine what she would become. Rather than becoming hard, bitter, cynical, or stagnant, she allowed God to chisel away at her character, making her brilliantly beautiful against the dark background of a difficult life.

Interestingly enough, the character qualities that circumstances produced in Abigail's life were precisely the ones she needed in order to deal with her crisis situation. These qualities were so much a part of who she was that she didn't even need to stop and think. Undoubtedly, years of living with a difficult man had given her plenty of opportunity to develop the wisdom, tact, and courage it took to approach David effectively. And years of talking with God kept her so in tune with what he was doing in her world that she could offer a spiritual perspective when it was needed. She had not allowed the negative forces in her life to shape her but rather she allowed them to produce godly character.

Just as physical muscles are developed in the hard work of pulling or pushing against weight or gravity, so our spiritual muscles are developed in the hard work of living in less-than-perfect circumstances. Some character traits can be developed no other way. Romans 5:3-4 says: "We also exult in our tribulations, knowing that tribulation brings about perseverance; and perseverance, proven character; and proven character, hope" (NASB).

Allow Difficulties to Bond You with Others

One of the most profound experiences of my life was the opportunity to accompany a friend into the delivery room where she gave birth to a baby girl who was too young to survive outside the womb. It was an intense human drama: What is usually a life-giving process produced death. For a few suspended moments we gazed unabashedly into each other's souls, bound together by vulnerability and shared pain. Life and death were there, so closely intertwined. And the tears were there as together we grieved the loss of this baby who was already greatly loved. But there was also trust and hope in the Lord that was deeper than words. And, even in her pain, I saw beauty and strength in my friend that was different from any physical attribute I had ever seen. Her choice to allow me to be with her in that moment was one of the most valuable gifts I have ever been given.

Everyone has pain and difficulty in life, but usually we try to keep it hidden for as long as possible. What a loss that is to all of us because opening up our pain to others can level the ground between us as human beings and allow us to see each other more clearly. Tim Hansel discovered this through the ongoing physical pain he experiences as the result of a climbing accident:

> Pain, if allowed, produces an identification with the sufferings of others, and even the sufferings of Christ, that we could not experience any other way. One is allowed to see dignity in the midst of human struggle and see beyond the false barriers that are oftentimes imposed between human beings.[2]

When we experience pain in our lives—whether it is the pain of a difficult marriage or any number of other hardships—we have a choice about whether to experience it in isolation or to open it up and find the bond it can create with others. If we are struggling in some area of our lives, we can be sure that others are as well. Although often our first response is to offer advice, we should keep in mind that advice isn't always the best form of support; usually what we need most is the strength and courage that comes from knowing we're not alone and that others are also struggling to hang in there. When we make the choice to share our pain, the beauty and strength we see in each other is nothing less than inspiring!

Allow God to Be Strong Through Your Weakness

One thing I learned along the way in my life as a writer and spiritual companion is that people don't really want to hear about all the things I've got nailed down and no longer struggle with in life. A life that looks like it's all put together may be motivating to some, but to normal folks, it just seems overwhelming and unattainable. As a wise leader wrote, "It's easier to take up a cause led by a fellow human being than to follow someone who covers all signs of weakness."[3] It's not easy to let others see our difficulties and the areas where we are not strong. It seems more natural to hide those things rather than risk misunderstanding, embarrassment, or disrespect from those who don't know how to respond to the reality of human limitations—theirs and ours!

I've come to accept and expect that God will often use areas of weakness and vulnerability in my life—even the areas I'm ashamed of!—for his purposes. Of course I would like to put only my strengths out there for everyone to see. Wouldn't we all? But God has a different plan. Again we can learn from the apostle Paul and his own thorn in the flesh. He says that God wants us to boast about our weaknesses, in other words, put them right out there in plain view so that God's power can come shining through.

Even when God does say, "No, I'm not going to take the pain away for reasons that only I know right now," as we talk with him about it, he gives us the opportunity to take a step back and look at the larger picture. Sometimes he even allows us to understand his reasons. Although we can never completely understand the mind of God on these matters, we do know some things.

First of all, we know that pain and weakness keep us in touch with our vulnerability and in touch with our need for God and others. As Paul learned through his thorn in the flesh, pride lurks in dark corners of our hearts. Often the greater the work that God is doing in and through our lives, the more susceptible to pride we are. Paul realized this: "To keep me from exalting myself, there was given me a thorn in the flesh, a messenger of Satan to torment me—to keep me from exalting myself" (2 Corinthians 12:7, NASB). Another truth Paul realized was that his thorn in the flesh would keep him available as a means by which God could show his power. One pastor put it this way, "When we are truly in touch with our ordinariness, we become vulnerable, and [this very weakness] becomes a black velvet background against which the stunning diamond of the power of God is seen pouring through our lives."[4]

When the Going Gets *Too* Tough

As inspiring as Abigail's story is, it is important for us to realize that there is a difference between "good hard" and "destructive hard."[5] God calls us to remain in the midst of some difficulties—difficulties that over time transform us in ways that are beyond imagining. One friend, who lost her eighteen-year-old daughter in a car accident, held me in a tight hug several weeks after her loss and whispered in my ear, "I am not the same!" Her voice had a sense of awe and gratitude, a "given-overness" to God that indicated to me that rather than going the way of soul-numbing bitterness, she was allowing God to do his transforming work in her through this terribly hard thing that was bringing about a deep good in her life.

Another kind of "hard" needs to be acknowledged here, the kind of difficulty that is dark and evil and begins to tear at the very fabric of our souls. Violence and abuse of any kind—particularly domestic violence—is the kind of "destructive hard" that we have the right to war against and flee from for our own good and for the good of those around us.

Domestic violence is the greatest single cause of injury to American women—greater than auto accidents, rape, and mugging combined. These facts have led some to conclude that home is the most dangerous place a woman can be.[6] With this in mind, I want to clarify that *in no way do I wish my comments in this chapter to be construed as encouragement for any woman to stay in an abusive relationship.* Battering is a sin before God and a crime punishable by law. It is, without exception, intolerable. No woman should be encouraged to think that domestic violence is normal or what she deserves. The idea that if a woman would behave differently she could placate the violent man in her life is a trap. In actuality,

> violence is not legislated by the wife's action; it is a specific choice made by the abusive husband. If frustrating situations offered only one option, abusers would be equally violent on the job, driving in traffic or interacting with friends; but it is simply not true. The majority of abusers direct their violence specifically and purposefully toward their wives.[7]

In many cases, the more compliant and submissive a woman becomes, the more violent her husband gets. And once a pattern of violence has been established, it will continue until there is some sort of crisis (such as the wife leaving, an intervention, or an arrest).

It would be comforting to think that in Christian marriages these problems do not exist, but this simply is not the case. In 1981, Phyllis Alsdurf prepared an article for *Family Life Today* on wife abuse in Christian homes and was stunned at the magnitude of the problem.

> Wives told of being struck in the face, kicked, bruised, dragged across the floor by their hair, and even bitten. And by whom? Ordained ministers, Christian businessmen, some well-known evangelical leaders—all men who lived a lie and perpetuated abuse that was an abomination to God.[8]

The response to Phyllis's article on wife abuse convinced Phyllis and her husband, James (a clinical and forensic psychologist), that this problem existed in greater proportion among Christians than they had ever realized. It prompted them to spend eight years researching and writing the book

Battered into Submission, in which they document the problem of wife abuse among Christians and trace some of its major roots to faulty theology taught in many fundamentalist homes and churches. They observe that "the distribution of power can be badly skewed in the Christian home. Fortified by preaching that accepts all sort of cultural assumptions about what 'headship' means, abusers often use Scripture as ammunition for their misuse of power."[9]

One battered wife shared how her husband's (and her own!) theology contributed to the abuse she suffered:

After marriage, my husband treated me as a nonperson with no value other than through him. He cited Scripture passages in support of his treatment of me. Any time I objected to his behavior or to his decisions, he told me that I was to submit to him just as totally as if he were Jesus Christ. He firmly believed that if I were obedient and submissive, God himself would take care of me. Therefore he was free to behave as irresponsibly as he liked without fear of hurting me or our child. He felt God wouldn't allow us to be hurt unless it was God's will.

My husband took no responsibility for his actions at all. I spent many hours in prayer and fasting, seeking to drive out every vestige of sin from my life. I believed that when I finally learned what God was trying to teach me, my husband would respond with love. But the more I submitted to him, the more arrogantly he displayed his flagrant abusive behavior. I sought counsel from pastors and friends. Many didn't believe me. It's not hard to understand why. How could such an upstanding member of the church and community be capable of such a miscarriage of God's justice?... Those who did believe me offered no solace; only sympathy and empty platitudes. They affirmed my submissive reaction to my husband's abusive tyranny. No one at any time went to talk to my husband about his behavior in loving correction. I was always left empty-handed to return to my own personal hell.[10]

It is easy to see how the sin of wife abuse can go unchecked in circles where wives are taught to submit blindly to husbands, where divorce is preached against without any consideration given to circumstances, and where dominance by the husband is seen as his divine right and responsibility. In fact, such teachings provide good covering for abuse under the guise of bringing one's wife "into subjection." Thus the batterer does not consider his actions abusive; he is simply fulfilling his God-given responsibilities.[11]

Wife abuse is a symptom of deeper problems in the marriage—low self-esteem, poor problem-solving and conflict resolution skills, not knowing how to cope with intense emotion, patterns of violence learned in childhood, and so on. However, "it is too dangerous to discuss the problems of marriage until everyone is safe. Any problems with conflict resolution or communication cannot be realistically discussed while the husband is blatantly abusing power. Trust and confidence cannot be developed unless safety is achieved first."[12]

A battered woman's first step, then, is to gain safety for herself and for her children. She can do this through calling local domestic violence hotlines or women's shelters. If a hotline does not exist, calling 911 and asking for the number of a local domestic violence agency can also be effective. A woman must believe that she and her children are worth a better life (which is no small feat for a woman whose husband has been demeaning her for years) and be willing to do any or all of the following to get it: call the police, press assault charges, leave and refuse to consider returning until the abuser has completed a counseling program for offenders, or "go public" with the abuse to employers, relatives, and church community. This is the means by which "a woman offers her husband yet another opportunity to acknowledge the illegality and immorality of what he has done. These are acts of both self-preservation and love for her husband. Since he is participating in evil, forcing him to deal with it and not submitting to it is an act of love."[13]

The Alsdurfs are quick to point out, however, that once a victim has taken the first step, she holds virtually no power over whether the batterer will choose the path of true reconciliation. While expressing confidence in the power of God's love to redeem relationships characterized by abuse, they also acknowledge that most often reconciliation does not occur. When it does, it is not an event but a painful and slow process that involves more than willpower. For the abuser, it involves facing the horror of his sin, confessing it (both privately and publicly), expressing his intent to change, and committing himself to the process of learning new patterns for loving and relating to his family. This is accomplished through professional therapy, support groups, and strong accountability within a community of Christians. For the abused, it involves forgiving, not primarily for his sake but for her own. There is no easy way back, but there is a way. But it will never happen unless someone has the courage to say, "Enough."

A FORK IN THE ROAD

"Life is difficult," says M. Scott Peck in the opening line of *The Road Less Traveled.* He goes on to say that this is a great truth because "once we accept this truth, we transcend it.... Because once it is accepted, the fact that life is difficult no longer matters."[14] What does matter is what we do with it.

The difficulties and pains of our lives bring us to a fork in the road, a place where we must choose. And it's impossible to stay neutral. To allow our pain and difficulty to corrode our spirit, to make us hard and bitter, is to have chosen. To keep living for some future escape is to refuse the present. To allow God to transform us in the situation as we are honest with him, as we invite his perspective, as we deal forthrightly with our difficulties, and as we open our lives to others in strength and vulnerability—this is the road less traveled. And choosing that road will make all the difference.

SPIRITUAL EXERCISES

Alone with God

Silence. As you come to the end of this chapter, take a few moments to sit with God in the silence of your own heart and allow yourself to become aware of the area in your life that seems like it is unfixable. Allow the full gravity of your situation and all the emotions that you feel to come to the surface of your heart and mind. Don't try to fix anything or figure anything out. Just be with God right where you are; rest in him and allow him to comfort you as a parent would comfort a child.

Prayer and journaling. Review what you have just read in this chapter, noticing the places of resonance and resistance that you have highlighted. Allow yourself the time to reflect on and journal about your experiences and longings. Tell God what's true about you right now and what you long for. Then listen for his response.

- How did you feel as you read about Abigail?
- How is your situation the same or different?
- Who is God for you in the midst of this difficulty?
- What questions would you like to ask him?
- How is God using your difficulty to shape you and bless others?
- How do you feel when you think about putting your areas of weakness "out front" for others to see?
- Is your difficulty in the "good hard" category or is it in the "destructive hard" category?

Invitations. *God, are you inviting me to do anything in response to this chapter? How are you calling me to respond?*

With Your Spiritual Friend(s)

Begin your time together with a moment of silence and a simple prayer of invitation for God to join you.

Listening. Take turns giving each other your undivided attention. In this area in particular, share only that which you feel comfortable sharing. As appropriate, share the area of your life that this chapter seems to speak to. Give each other a brief summary of what has happened between you and God this week in the context of your spiritual practices and your reading of this chapter.

- What did God say to you in your times of solitude and silence?
- What were your experiences of resonance and resistance as you read this chapter? How did you process those with God in your journal?
- How is God meeting you in the midst of your difficulty?
- This chapter mentions several ways in which we can allow the beauty of Christ to emerge in us—being honest with God, letting difficulties produce character, allowing difficulties to bond us with others, allowing God to use our weaknesses. Which of these invitations to spiritual transformation seem to be God's invitation to you at this time?

Prayer. Pray for one another.

THE FREEDOM TO REACH ACROSS GENERATIONS

If the truth be told, we today are who we are—if we are anybody—
because some woman, somewhere, stooped down long enough that
we might climb on her back and ride piggyback into the future.

—RENITA WEEMS, *Just a Sister Away*

Perhaps you are familiar with the term *doublespeak*. Doublespeak is the practice of obscuring the unpleasantness of a subject by couching it in euphemistic terms. My personal favorite is the travel newsletter that refers to the over-sixty crowd not as senior citizens but as the "chronologically gifted." The reason I like this one is that, rather than obscuring the truth, this phrase actually clarifies a truth that would otherwise be lost: Older people *are* "chronologically gifted" with wisdom they have gained from weathering the seasons of life.

I have had the privilege of being in several life-changing relationships with women who are "chronologically gifted." In fact, as I look back over my spiritual development and try to pinpoint the factors that have influenced me the most, I seldom think of a particular Bible study or sermon. Instead it is older women who spent time sharing their lives with me that have had the most significant role in my spiritual transformation.

Ruth Anne was a woman who had been a close friend of our family for years. Realizing that even the best training at home needs to be supplemented by the input of other gifted Christians, my parents arranged for me to spend one of my college summers with Ruth Anne and her husband. Though I spent most of that summer working in a fast-food restaurant, it was one of the richest times of my life spiritually. Ruth Anne memorized Scripture a book at a time, so I memorized too. She gave me a copy of A. W. Tozer's *Knowledge of the Holy,* which helped deepen my relationship with God. Every evening we went for a three-mile walk in the Virginia hills surrounding their home and talked about everything from boyfriends to church government to the problem passages in Hebrews. She allowed me just to live and learn with her, and that summer was life changing. Later, I returned to her home for a week-long visit with my husband and three children. During that visit much of our conversation revolved around child rearing. I shared some of my fears and uncertainty; she made some observations and offered me encouragement, instruction, and resources. It was just the kind of challenge I needed!

Darlene shared her life with me in a different way. While I was in college, far from my own family, she took an interest in me and invited me to her home quite often. Our relationship was characterized by commitment, open sharing, and prayer. I saved all of my deep and not-so-deep questions for our get-togethers. Her perspective was a treasured source of help and encouragement. As an older woman she was able to teach me so much through the friendship she allowed to develop between us.

SHARING TRUTH TOGETHER

Of course, the idea of older women helping younger women is not a new one. It is a biblical principle that often gets lost in the shuffle from this meeting to that Bible study. Titus 2:3-5 instructs older women to be reverent in their behavior "that they may encourage the young women to love their husbands, to love their children, to be sensible, pure, workers at home, kind, being subject to their own husbands, so that the word of God will not be dishonored" (NASB). A few key observations stand out to me in this passage.

Life Experience Rather than Age

Paul does not define the age groups to which he is referring when he uses the words "older" and "younger." He doesn't say "Older women are those who have reached some magical age when they are suddenly deemed mature." This lack of definition indicates that all of us can be teaching and learning from each other back and forth on a continuum rather than seeing ourselves in rigid age categories. What qualifies us to teach others is maturity and life experience rather than chronological age.

Showing First Rather than Telling

The apostle is speaking here of a type of ministry in which you show it with your life before you tell it with your mouth. Paul's usage of the word *encourage,* which can be translated "teach what is good," indicates teaching by example as well as verbal instruction.[1] Paul's own life and writings illustrate how he helped younger Christians to maturity through relationships that were characterized by affection, tender care, and fatherly encouragement (1 Thessalonians 2:7-11). He opened up his very life so that others could learn from his example. And when it was necessary, he expressed his love through confrontation with tears (2 Corinthians 2:4). He knew that we do not necessarily need more Bible studies or preaching services; we need relationships that provide examples to follow.

Encouragement Rather than Mothering

Most young women do not need another mother, they just need an older friend. Win Couchman gives an effective image of the role of the older woman by telling the story of her drive home one Christmas Eve.

A deep San Francisco–style fog kept our car crawling blindly along the road. Suddenly another car pulled onto the road right ahead of us. Because we were now following a set of beautiful twin taillights, we could safely increase our speed from 15 to 25 miles an hour. A mentor is someone further on down the road from you who is going where you want to go and who is willing to give you some light to help you get there.[2]

The two cars had no official relationship—the passengers didn't ask to get in the other car or be hooked up by a tow rope. They were just following along behind someone who was a little farther along and who could light the way. In fact, the car in front probably didn't even realize anyone was following! But unknowingly, they were providing just the amount of light that was needed.

BUT CAN IT WORK TODAY?

This whole idea sounds so logical, so right, so comfortable. It conjures up images of a world where women share their experiences as they sit quilting or baking bread together—a world that, for most of us, is long gone.

Our world, by contrast, is transient, fast-paced, and filled with new challenges for women. Young women today tend to move across country instead of across town and find themselves cut off from their mothers and other women whom they have known and learned from all their lives. And the older women find themselves with very empty nests indeed. In addition, the number of working women has increased so dramatically that there is no longer the networking that used to occur so naturally. The woman who chooses to stay at home full time may find herself the only one home in her neighborhood during the day. In the meantime, working women find that they are barely holding themselves and their families together, without much energy and time for mutually beneficial relationships. Ironically, these very differences cause us to need helping relationships now more than ever.

Incorporating this timeless principle of intergenerational friendships into contemporary life is possible if we are willing to *be flexible and customize*. There is no precise formula for helping relationships grow because friendships are as diverse as personalities themselves. Some women get together to study the Bible and pray while others meet more spontaneously as situations arise. Sometimes a young woman may ask an older woman to share an area of expertise: some aspect of child rearing, entertaining, interior decorating, or professional advice. When a young woman is struggling with something specific, such as job stress, communication in marriage, sexual purity, materialism, or jealousy, she might approach an older woman to help her in that area. Some women begin with a time limit in mind; others continue indefinitely with periods of varying intensity. No matter what your stage in life, these relationships can be customized to meet the needs and lifestyles of those involved.

SETTING THE TONE FOR CROSS-GENERATIONAL RELATIONSHIPS

One of the most important things we can do to facilitate cross-generational relationships is to give some attention to our mind-set. Certain attitudes pervade our society that make it very difficult for women to encourage and learn from each other. Sometimes these attitudes exist and are conveyed to others unbeknownst to us, but their presence can greatly hinder mutually beneficial relationships.

One of the biggest barriers to relationships between women today is an attitude of self-sufficiency on the part of younger women. While it is good for women to have a sense of their own personal accountability before God so as not to be overly swayed by the opinions of others, there is a kind of independence that can be counterproductive. It is an independence rooted in pride, and it results in a disregard for the counsel of others who are older and/or wiser.

It isn't always easy for today's younger woman to learn from someone else—we're a pretty independent group! Never before have women been able to enjoy such success in careers and other personal achievements, and it is exhilarating. But it is easy to see how a growing self-confidence could translate into a false sense of control over one's life in which there is no need for anyone's help. We have allowed images of the professional woman who is out there "putting her best foot forward" to become our model for success.

For the Christian woman, these attitudes can carry over into our spiritual lives, and we can find ourselves maintaining the impression that we are attractive, poised, gifted, and spiritually mature. We maintain this image even during times of great difficulty so that it becomes almost impossible for us to accept help, encouragement, or training from older women. Of course, the older women sense these attitudes and feel that we do not want or need their help. Then when times of need do cause us to be more open, the older women are nowhere to be found.

I was at such a juncture after the birth of my second child. My husband and I had withdrawn from a lot of our activities because of increased family responsibilities. I was not recovering very quickly and was feeling lonely and overwhelmed; my self-sufficiency gave way to frightening feelings of isolation. I was desperate for friendship, encouragement, and practical help from older women, but none was forthcoming. At first I was angry. I assumed that these women were neglecting their responsibilities. But as I began to probe for reasons, I was told that people thought I had it all together and didn't need their help. Ironically enough, this is what I had wanted them to think. But now my carefully attended image of a confident, poised, self-sufficient young woman had backfired! It had made me unapproachable and beyond the reach of those who would have liked to offer encouragement.

It was through this experience that I discovered a dichotomy within myself. A part of me recognized my need for support and encouragement, but another part of me wanted to continue appearing totally competent and self-assured. I believe other young women experience the same inner struggle, and it is important for us to deal with the pride that can become a barrier between us and the older women whose encouragement we need.

We must guard against being wise in our own eyes (Proverbs 3:7)—so wise that we disregard the wisdom of others. We need to communicate to more mature women that they have a lot to offer and that we would greatly benefit from time spent with them. We must learn to listen and be open to what they are saying even when it hurts—when our first reaction is to get defensive and clam up. Developing a teachable attitude and accepting older women as role models may require a change for some of us. However, women who are humble and teachable are the ones who are growing and learning.

Older women can also be responsible for attitudes that are hidden enemies of fruitful relationships. When they allow themselves to pass judgment on younger women—even if that judgment is unspoken—the perceptive woman will sense this and not risk opening up. Marsha has a genuine love and concern for younger women, demonstrated by her willingness to invest time and energy into relationships with them. However, she has a low tolerance for new ideas and has difficulty understanding women whose struggles are different from her own. Consequently, when she reaches a point of disagreement with a younger woman, she withdraws her friendship and moves on to someone else who sees things more her way. She has had a string of friendships that follow this pattern, and several women have been deeply hurt. The following guidelines can help avoid this unhealthy kind of relationship.

Keep the goal in relationships clearly in mind. Those of us who are considered to be more experienced are responsible to encourage others by our example and verbal instruction. We are not to make others into carbon copies of ourselves or force them to make the same choices we have made in order to win our approval. It is good to remember that they are not accountable to us but to God. As Romans 14:4 says, "Who are you to judge the servant of another? To her own master she stands or falls; and she will stand, for the Lord is able to make her stand" (NASB, feminine pronouns mine). It is our responsibility to offer ourselves in relationships; it is God's responsibility to bring about growth and change.

Don't give too much advice too soon. Too often we offer advice before giving younger women the chance to express themselves fully. This is unfortunate because the very process of expressing feelings and talking through one's problems can be therapeutic. Learning to ask thoughtful questions will take us a long way in understanding what the other person is experiencing: "How does that make you feel? What is it that you really want? How do you think that decision will affect those closest to you? Has God brought any scriptures to mind regarding this decision?" Many times a woman can find her own answers if she is given time to verbalize her concerns and brainstorm a little. Also, if we do not take the time to listen first, we run the risk of giving answers that are simplistic or irrelevant. It is no wonder the Bible says, "He who gives an answer before he hears, it is folly and shame to him" (Proverbs 18:13, NASB).

MUTUAL TRANSFORMATION

In my experience, the best cross-generational relationships are those in which both the younger woman and the older woman are contributing to each other. No relationship is as healthy as it could be if it remains all taking and no giving indefinitely. Relationships characterized by an awareness that each has something to give and something to gain are invigorating rather than draining. They tend to last long after any formal arrangements for the relationship have fallen away. The age difference is not disregarded or forgotten, but both women come to understand that chronological age does not define what we have to offer one another.

My friendship with another Ruth has been marked by this kind of mutuality. Our relationship began somewhat typically—she was an elder's wife at the church we attended. Many young women were drawn to her because of her honesty, compassion, and obvious spiritual depth. When I accepted the responsibility of directing the Women's Ministry, I asked Ruth if she would be willing to be a part of this team because I knew her teaching and pastoral gifts would be a real asset. I asked her if she would meet with me regularly to pray, to offer her input and perspective, and to be supportive on a very personal level. I was delighted when she agreed, and thus began a friendship that has endured through challenges that neither one of us could have imagined at the outset.

Some of those challenges were related to the fact that she was an elder's wife in the church where I became a staff member. When staff and elders came down on different sides of an issue, it was awkward and stressful. Other challenges had to do with personality and generational differences. I was very direct in my communication and ready to plow ahead on issues that she needed to take more slowly. We both suffered because of gender inequities in the church, but she expressed her suffering through tears and sadness (which is generally more acceptable for women), and I expressed mine through anger, which was hard for her to deal with at times. We were at different stages in our lives, so she could not take some of the risks I was free to take. This was disappointing, but we loved and respected each other enough to accept that God was leading us down our individual paths.

It took us a while to learn that we were different—but one was not better than the other. We went through some painful transitions in our life together at church—disagreeing vehemently at times—but we learned to negotiate these rough spots with honesty, mutual respect, commitment to the relationship that transcended issues, and giving each other space when we needed it. What began as a younger woman looking to an older woman for encouragement grew into a relationship that was so valuable to both of us that we were determined not to let anything destroy it. Now that Ruth has moved away and some of the outside pressures on our relationship have been removed, I marvel at what we made it through.

What did we offer one another that was so valuable it was worth such a significant investment of time and emotional energy? For me, this relationship was honest on deeper levels than any relationship I had ever had with an older woman (other than my own mother). Ruth went through some very deep waters during the time we were meeting on a regular basis, and she was remarkably vulnerable in opening them up for me. She made no attempt to conceal her struggles or make them seem easier than they were. She had no simplistic solutions. The lessons I learned from seeing the unvarnished version of her experiences, from weeping with her and praying for her, are lessons that will be with me for the rest of my life. She led by her example, freeing me to share some of my most personal struggles as well. This vulnerability—which manifested itself in her friendships, her leadership style, and her teaching—had a significant impact on my own friendships and ministry style.

In addition, her graciousness in accepting and following the leadership of this young whippersnapper (which is what I was) gave me tremendous confidence. Knowing that she believed in me helped me believe in myself. I was amazed at her willingness to learn from me even though I was her junior by about fifteen years. We shared information, and both of us were open to being stretched by the new ideas and ways of looking at the world that we were picking up in our studies and other relationships. We were also able to be open about what was going on in the relationship: feelings of competitiveness, disappointment, anger, intimidation, being misunderstood. Our honesty was painful at times, but because our love and commitment was never in question, we were able to use these experiences to gain a deeper understanding of ourselves as well as each other.

It has always been obvious what I, the younger woman, gained in this friendship. But Ruth shared in a letter some things I had given her as well:

A cross-generational relationship, which I so much need to understand myself, my daughters, the world, God.

A desire for honest assessment of life and its foundational principles.

An open delving into a very difficult area of life…revealing your hurts, listening to and absorbing mine.

Opposite perspective or a "different" (not wrong) way of viewing a predicament.

Patience in accepting me and trying to understand my limits of conscience and actions due to prior commitments.

Vulnerability and truth-telling.

Steadfastness to continue the relationship when we hit hard and tall barriers in the church setting and, at times, found ourselves almost on opposite sides, staring through at each other.

The largeness of spirit to admit defeat and at other times to say, "I'm sorry. Forgive me."

The example of preparing clearly (to take a stand) and then opening your mouth to verbalize it. This has given me more courage.

The joy of having another woman beside me committed to the Scriptures.

Much hope that honest relationships can be built as you have not let me go, nor have I let you go…because we have weathered each other's "hard" counsel at times, asked forgiveness, explained ourselves, tried to understand each other, recognized that we are different but are both needed in the kingdom, and that we need each other.

You can probably tell that this was not a perfect relationship. It didn't happen at the perfect time, the perfect place, in the perfect way, or with two perfect people. It was not without its mistakes. But it happened with commitment, honesty, and mutuality—some of the best stuff we as women have to give each other. Together we learned that "women are in this thing together. And when we share information, when we console each other, encourage each other, talk to each other, we get stronger. We get powerful. Women are sisters to one another."[3]

GETTING STARTED

All of us have opportunities to know someone younger than ourselves who could benefit from time spent with us and someone older than ourselves from whom we could learn. As we begin to realize our responsibility to those younger than ourselves, we can ask God to show us someone in whom we can invest our time. A relatively young woman can keep her eyes open for a high-school or college girl who seems open to her input. Meet somewhere for a Coke. Or, if your schedule is crowded, invite her to go along with you while you shop or take your kids to the park. All of us can be sensitive to "divine appointments" and use situations in which we are thrown together with a younger woman (such as nursery duty, committee work, or traveling to a conference or retreat) as opportunities to take a special interest in them.

As younger women, we can take the initiative to identify a woman we respect and actively pursue a friendship with her. We can let the relationship unfold naturally or ask her to consider meeting with us on a regular basis. Our taking the attitude of a learner will make it easier for that older woman to share her life with us. Realizing that we each have something to offer in relationships, regardless of our age and stage, will encourage us to search out and cultivate friendships that are mutually fulfilling.

I've heard it said, "If you can't be a good example, then you'll just have to be a terrible warning." That's a frightening prospect! God's idea is for older women to be a good example of how he transforms everyday life— how he helps us build up our families by loving our husbands and children properly, how he helps us develop strong character, make right personal choices, and avoid the pitfalls that are so abundant these days. It's the real stuff of life that can't be learned in a classroom but is best learned by watching someone else. Even in our transient, fast-paced society, he wants us to be always reaching ahead to learn from those who are farther along in their journey and reaching back to those who are coming along behind. With God's help we can become the kind of encouraging, nonjudgmental, teachable women who can make it happen.

SPIRITUAL EXERCISES

Alone with God
Silence. As you come to the end of this chapter, take a few moments to sit with God in the silence of your own heart. Who is it that has reached across

the generations to provide guidance for your journey into spiritual transformation? Allow yourself to experience gratitude for the gift that this woman has been to you.

Prayer and journaling. Review what you have just read in this chapter, noticing the places of resonance and resistance that you have highlighted. Tell God what's true about you right now and what you long for. Then listen for his response.

- What are your hopes, dreams, longings for the kind of relationship described in this chapter?
- Do you have any previous experiences that cause you to doubt the possibilities?
- Is there any attitude that God is speaking to you about that might need to shift in order for you to engage in this kind of relationship?

Invitations. *God, are you inviting me to respond in some way to what I have read today?*

With Your Spiritual Friend(s)

Begin your time together with a moment of silence and a simple prayer of invitation for God to join you.

Listening. Take turns giving each other your undivided attention. Give each other a brief summary of what has happened between you and God this week in the context of your spiritual practices and your reading of this chapter.

- What did God say to you in your times of solitude and silence?
- What were your experiences of resonance and resistance as you read this chapter? How did you process those with God in your journal?
- Who are the older women who God seems to be using in your life to provide some light for your journey into spiritual transformation?

- Who are the younger women who seem to be looking to you for light?
- Are there any next steps that God is inviting you to take in any of these relationships?

Prayer. Pray for one another.

TWELVE

FREE TO BE CHRIST
IN THE WORLD

Sooner or later, if we follow Christ we have to risk everything in order to gain everything. We have to gamble on the invisible and risk all that we see and taste and feel. But we know the risk is worth it, because there is nothing more insecure than this transient world.

—THOMAS MERTON, *Thoughts in Solitude*

These are exciting and challenging days for women, days full of choice and opportunity. The controversies continue over the roles of women and men in marriage, ministry, and the marketplace, and the issues that have been raised will not go away. Their complexity demands that we continue in the spiritual practices and relationships that open us to true wisdom and discernment. The disciplines of solitude and silence, Scripture reflection, prayer, and spiritual friendship will help us hear and respond to the One True Voice in the midst of conflicting voices and expectations. Even as we move beyond the limits that others impose on us and seek to nurture a world in which the strengths of women can fully emerge, that Voice reminds us that our deepest calling is to allow the transformations of the Christ-life to unfold uniquely in our lives.

It is here that we part company with the feminist for whom the fight for fairness and equality has become an end in itself. It is here that our lives might become an uncomfortable challenge to women for whom personal comfort, "keeping the peace," or maintaining the status quo have become the highest value. Here, we choose not to look to the lives of others as a blueprint for our own, but dare to say yes to the risky invitations of God. As Jesus told the apostle Peter when Peter compared himself and his calling to that of the apostle John, "If it is my will that he [John] remain until I come, what is that to you? Follow me!" (John 21:22).

As we respond to Christ's invitation to follow him, we learn from his example, letting ourselves be transformed by the truth and the freedom he lived.

CHRIST GAVE HIMSELF FREELY TO THE WILL OF GOD

It is interesting to note that Christ was in a situation similar to that which women often face: For the most part, he was not recognized for who he was or what he had to offer. Yet the main purpose of his life was not to prove who he was or to glorify himself. He knew who he was in relation to God and humankind. This is an important first step for us to realize as we seek to be Christ-followers. He knew that he was here to do God's will in God's timing and that at the proper time his full identity and purpose would be revealed. In the meantime, he moved through life with single-mindedness unaffected by the opinion or persuasion of others.

Early in his ministry when Satan, the disciples, and even his family members tried to convince him to reveal his identity and set up his kingdom, Christ refused to be pushed. His answer was always some variation on the statement he made to his brothers when they encouraged him to show himself to the world at one of the Jewish festivals, "Go to the festival yourselves. I am not going to this festival, for my time has not yet fully come" (John 7:8).

When Peter first heard about Christ's impending death and protested the necessity of it—"God forbid it, Lord! This must never happen to you!" (Matthew 16:22)—Jesus refused to be sidetracked from the main purpose for which he had come. "Get behind me, Satan! You are a stumbling block to me; for you are setting your mind not on divine things but on human things" (verse 23).

When the Pharisees and religious leaders began to persecute him and try to arrest him, he was undeterred because he knew that, ultimately, God's will would be accomplished through him, regardless of human interference. Sometimes he withdrew for a while but never for very long. He always came back, faithfully ministering, healing, and speaking the message that people needed to hear.

I am tremendously comforted as well as challenged by this image of an unflappable Christ walking this earth with an unwavering commitment "to do the will of him who sent me" (John 4:34). He expected that those who didn't understand what he was trying to do would attempt to stop him— some out of ignorance and some out of malice. But because he was in such close communion with the Father and knew he was in the center of his will, a peace emanated from him.

As we observe this in Christ's life, we, too, can rest in the fact that people—even those who try to limit the ways in which women serve God—cannot ultimately prevent God from accomplishing his will in and through our lives. If he has given me spiritual gifts to use in service to others, he will give me opportunities to use them. Too often we look to people to recognize our gifts and give us the opportunity to use them, as if they had ultimate control. But God does not waste his gifts or his calling. As we engage in the process of spiritual transformation, he will place us where we can be of greatest use to him.

I am reminded of Joseph, whom God caused to find favor in the eyes of key people so that his purposes could be accomplished—despite jealous brothers who sold him to strangers, false accusations by an immoral woman, and a forgetful cupbearer. The vision God gave Joseph while he was still a young boy, the lessons he learned while he was second-in-command at Potiphar's house, the breaking he experienced during time spent in jail, and his meteoric rise to the top of Egyptian government were all part of God's plan for him that could not be thwarted. Later in his life he was able to say, without bitterness, to his brothers who had been so cruel, "You meant evil against me, but God meant it for good in order to bring about this present result" (Genesis 50:20, NASB). Like Joseph, I, too, can look past people and situations that seem limiting and see an all-powerful God.

CHRIST LEARNED OBEDIENCE THROUGH THE THINGS THAT HE SUFFERED

Scripture makes the surprising statement in Hebrews 5:8-9 that Christ "learned obedience through what he suffered; and having been made perfect, he became the source of eternal salvation for all who obey him." I find this statement about the reality and the purpose of Christ's suffering to be one of the most amazing and freeing truths about him found in Scripture. It is amazing because it is hard to comprehend why Jesus needed to learn if he was already perfect. At the same time, this statement is very freeing because it helps me realize that to learn or to have need of learning is nothing to be ashamed of.

This insight into Christ's life became a particular comfort and instruction to me some years ago. I wanted badly to serve on a committee that I cared very much about, and I felt I had the qualifications to make a positive contribution. I expressed this desire to the chairman of the committee but was never invited. I was sure this was because I was a woman and that it was yet another instance where "women had to do twice as well as men to be thought half as good." That may have been partially true, but that wasn't all.

When I got up the nerve to ask the chairman about it, he described weaknesses in my character that he felt would render me ineffective on that committee. These were hard words to hear. But as much as I wanted to run away from his words and categorically deny them, I needed to consider the truth in what he was saying and learn from his feedback. I knew that God wanted me to look past the people in the situation and see him disciplining and training me. The discipline was painful, not pleasant (as it says in Hebrews 12:11), but I needed it.

Our suffering cannot be compared with Christ's because of the intensity of Christ's suffering and the fact that our suffering is often connected with our own character weaknesses—yet it is encouraging to know that we are in very good company as we try to remain open to learning. Hebrews makes it clear that the things Christ learned through his suffering prepared him to be our perfect Savior—one who could understand what it means to suffer in obedience to God. Even though he was fully divine, there were some things he needed to learn through experience.[1] How much more true this will be for us!

If we want to be the kind of women who follow God courageously and live lives that are consistent with the way he has gifted and called us, there will always be this kind of learning to be done. We will seldom get it right the first time, and sometimes there may be consequences to suffer for our mistakes. At other times we will be called upon to suffer for doing what is right (as Christ did) and will have the opportunity to identify with Christ in new ways and grow in fellowship with him (Philippians 3:10). We can be encouraged by Christ's example not to become hardened and immovable in our approach to life but rather to relax into the process of growing and learning.

CHRIST WAS FULL OF GRACE AND TRUTH

Nothing got Christ into hot water more regularly than his consistency in speaking the truth. It was usually after some particularly honest moment—such as the times he revealed that he was God in the flesh or exposed the hypocrisy of the Pharisees—that crowds got violent, picked up stones to stone him, or tried to arrest him. For those whose hearts were open, however, his penetrating insight was one of the things that convinced them of his authenticity as the Son of God.

Although Christ was consistent in telling the truth, he told it in a variety of ways. He chose a communication style that was appropriate for each situation. With the Samaritan woman, Christ was very gentle and at times subtle in helping her understand the truth about who he was, who she was, and what she needed. With people like Nicodemus (the Pharisee who came to see Jesus by night in John 3) and the rich young ruler (Mark 10:17), he was polite but cut right to the heart of the matter. In response to Nicodemus's lack of understanding of the fundamentals of the gospel, he said, "You're a respected teacher of Israel and you don't know these basics? Listen carefully. I'm speaking sober truth to you. I speak only of what I know by experience; I give witness only to what I have seen with my own eyes.... Yet instead of facing the evidence and accepting it, you procrastinate with questions. If I tell you things that are plain as the hand before your face and you don't believe me, what use is there in telling you of things you can't see, the things of God?" (John 3:10-12, MSG).

To the rich young ruler, who wanted to know what he had to do to inherit eternal life, Christ had this to say: "You lack one thing; go, sell what you own, and give the money to the poor, and you will have treasure in heaven; then come, follow me" (Mark 10:21). Honest. Take it or leave it. (This guy left it.)

And then there were the religious leaders for whom Christ reserved his strongest brand of truth-telling. It seems that politeness and subtlety would not be effective with ones who were so hardheaded:

Woe to you Pharisees! For you tithe mint and rue and herbs of all kinds [they were legalistic to the point of tithing on every last spice], and neglect justice and the love of God; it is these you ought to have practiced, without neglecting the others. Woe to you Pharisees! For you love to have the seat of honor in the synagogues and to be greeted with respect in the marketplaces. Woe to you! For you are like unmarked graves, and people walk over them without realizing it. (Luke 11:42-44)

No wonder the Pharisees and Scribes began to be very hostile toward him.

At times speaking the truth was not enough; action was needed. For instance, when opportunists used the spiritual yearnings of poor people as an occasion to make money in the temple courts, Christ became so indignant and impassioned for justice that he strode through the temple court overturning their tables and chasing them out (Matthew 21:12). At that point the blind and the lame practically came out of the woodwork as though they had been waiting for someone who had pure motives to come and care for them. And Christ healed them. But where were the spiritual leaders with wisdom and courage enough to stand for what was right?

In an earlier chapter, we discussed the particular struggle that women in our culture have with telling the truth or taking a stand. In light of Christ's example, it would seem hard for us to justify cowering in a corner, cringing from telling the truth when there is hypocrisy or injustice to be exposed. For those of us who are asking, "What would Jesus do?" part of the answer is

"He would tell the truth." He would have several different styles from which to choose, and he would pick the one best suited to the situation. But he would do it. And so will we if we are following in his steps.

CHRIST ALLOWED HIMSELF TO BE MOVED WITH COMPASSION

The English language doesn't have a single word to describe the phenomenon of compassion in the life of Christ as he experienced being human. In fact, in its biblical usage as it relates to Christ's experience, *compassion* is a verb that means "to be moved as to one's inwards, to yearn with compassion, to suffer with another, to be affected similarly."[2]

Compassion was not something Christ *had;* it was a moving *within.* It caused him to weep, to reach out and touch, to heal, to raise from the dead, to cast out demons, to speak the truth that would set the multitudes and the individual free.

When he saw that the crowds were hungry, he was moved with compassion to mobilize his disciples to feed them (Matthew 15:32). When he saw with spiritual eyes the crowds of people who were like sheep lost without a shepherd, he spoke from a heart filled with compassion and began to teach them many things. He then called his disciples so they too could share in this vision, giving them power, authority, and a plan so they, too, could meet needs (Matthew 9:35–10:42). When the rich young ruler came for instruction on how to receive eternal life, Jesus looked at him, loved him, *and then* told him the hard truth (Mark 10:21). When he saw a widow on the way to bury her only son and envisioned what her life would be without him, he was moved with compassion to raise him from the dead (Luke 7:12-15).

One of the most wrenching descriptions of Christ's compassion came during his triumphal entry into Jerusalem. Finally, people were getting the idea that he was the Messiah, and they began waving palm branches and shouting "Hosanna!" or, "Save us, we pray!" But as Jesus approached that beloved city, in his omniscience he saw the tragedy that was in its future. Rather than being caught up in this moment of popularity and praise, he wept with compassion for what he saw, wishing with his whole heart that they could be spared:

> If you, even you, had only recognized on this day the things that make
> for peace! But now they are hidden from your eyes. Indeed, the days
> will come upon you, when your enemies will set up ramparts around
> you and surround you, and hem you in on every side. They will crush
> you to the ground, you and your children within you, and they will
> not leave within you one stone upon another; because you did not rec-
> ognize the time of your visitation from God. (Luke 19:42-44)

Christ never lost sight of the value of people and his compassion for them—not even on the cross. Certainly it was compassion that moved him to ask God to forgive the soldiers who nailed him to the cross "for they do not know what they are doing" (Luke 23:34, NIV). It was out of compassion that he promised paradise—as only he could—to a man who was dying the same death as he.

And so I am compelled to ask, How often is my teaching motivated by true compassion? When have I been perceptive enough to look past someone's material wealth and see their loneliness or their need for meaning in life? Do I look at people (my husband, children, parents, fellow Christians, difficult neighbors) and really love them before I speak truth that is hard to hear? Am I willing to take a good hard look at the person (made in the image of God) who is wasting away with AIDS, the battered woman who has run for her life, the divorced woman fighting for custody of her children, the pregnant teenager who feels she has no other option than abortion, the child sitting next to his dying mother in a refugee camp—or do I look away so I can sleep at night? Am I able to extend compassion even when I am hurting and feeling mistreated? How often do I weep over anything but my own pain?

Not often enough. Compassion is not something that can be conjured up by a mere act of the will; it happens in us as we recognize that all people suffer.

> Through compassion it is possible to recognize that the craving for love that men [and women] feel resides also in our own hearts, that the cruelty the world knows all too well is also rooted in our own impulses. Through compassion we also sense our hope for forgiveness in our friends' eyes and our hatred in their bitter mouths. When they kill, we know we could have done it; when they give life, we know we can do the same. For a compassionate man [or woman] nothing human is alien; no joy or sorrow, no way of living and no way of dying.[3]

That is why compassion is revolutionary. When we begin to discover that the weaknesses, sins, and sorrows of others are within us as well, we are changed in relation to them. It is hard to stay angry at someone when you realize that they hurt just like you do (whether they admit it or not), that they cry just like you do (whether they cry in front of you or not), that life is difficult for them, just like it is for you (no matter how troublefree their life appears).

Yes, there is a time for anger in this world, a time to say, "This is wrong and I must stand against it." But there is also a time (perhaps it is the same time) for compassion, for looking at the person on the other side of an argument, the person who has been cruel, the person who has all the power as well as the one who has very little, and seeing that their struggle with the human experience is our own. Their sin is the same sin to which we are prone. Cynicism melts away when hearts are laid bare and we look inside. And condescension seems totally out of place when we realize that "there but for the grace of God go I."

Henri Nouwen makes this observation:

> No one can help anyone without becoming involved, without entering with his whole person into the painful situation, without taking the risk of becoming hurt, wounded, or even destroyed in the process. Who can save a child from a burning house without taking the risk of being hurt by the flames? Who can listen to a story of loneliness without taking the risk of experiencing similar pains in his own heart and even losing his precious peace of mind? In short: who can take away suffering without entering it?[4]

No one. Not even Christ himself.

CHRIST GAVE OF HIMSELF FREELY TO OTHERS

In the midst of rotting chicken pieces and dirty diapers, the poorest of the poor pick through the trash of Guatemala's city dump to find plastic containers to recycle, pieces of cardboard to shade them from the heat, or morsels of food to keep them alive. The dump is their home, and they have little hope of ever leaving it. However, two women, Gladys Acuna and Lisbeth Piedrasanta, are there to offer them hope in Christ.

Gladys and Lisbeth left their comfortable counseling center and founded the Casa del Alfarero ("the potter's house") fifty feet from the edge of the dump. With a team of thirty, they run a medical and dental clinic, offer carpentry and sewing classes, teach Bible lessons, and serve up meals. Gladys serves as spiritual director and Lisbeth as administrative director.

Their dream? In addition to meeting the physical needs of people who live in a place where fresh air is an impossibility and vultures fly overhead, they long to see spiritual revival. Says Lisbeth, "I ask the Lord not to let me die until I see spiritual revival here. We've been planting seeds for several years, and I would like to see kids seek the Lord sincerely. That is my desire: to see spiritual revival here, because I know that's the exit from their pain and suffering."[5]

A life spent serving people who live in a dump? Somehow it seems like something Jesus would do.

Perhaps the most difficult aspect of Christ's life for us to emulate is his passion for serving others. That is why we are surprised when we find people like Lisbeth and Gladys actually doing it. Most of us are more like the disciples who, on the very night when Christ gave an example of servanthood by washing their feet, argued over who would have the most prominent positions in the kingdom. If we are at all honest, many of us would say that we, too, have wasted time and energy striving for positions of prominence at times when we could have been serving. How painful it is to realize that in those moments we are utterly unlike Christ.

The more I study the Scriptures, the clearer it becomes that love (not to be confused with dependency), humility (not to be confused with low self-esteem), and a servant's attitude (not to be equated with being a doormat) are the supreme Christian virtues. Christ modeled them perfectly.[6] Conformity to Christ in these virtues must be top priority *not because I am a woman, but because I am a Christian.*

Answering the Call to Spiritual Transformation

Catherine Booth, cofounder of the Salvation Army, heard and accepted God's call upon her life to preach one Sunday morning as her husband,

William, a Methodist minister, finished his sermon. She later recalled her inner feelings: "It seemed as if a voice said to me, 'Now if you were to go and testify, you know I would bless it to your own soul as well as to the souls of the people.' I gasped and said to my soul,…'I cannot do it.' And then the devil said, 'Besides, you are not prepared to speak. You will look like a fool and have nothing to say.' "

Catherine chose to accept the Holy Spirit's challenge that day rather than the doubts planted by Satan. She stood up in front of a crowd of more than a thousand packed into Bethesda Chapel and said, "I want to say a word." William was as surprised as anyone when she made her sudden announcement, but he quickly recovered, and when she had finished, he announced that she would preach that evening. Catherine's only regret was that she had waited so long.[7]

Women today face the same choice as Catherine Booth did. Our choice is not necessarily whether to preach or not to preach. It is how to answer the challenge that the Holy Spirit is speaking to our soul, whatever that is. For some it is the challenge to begin seeing ourselves as God sees us so we are more able to give of ourselves to others. For others, it is the challenge to pull our heads out of their comfortable position in the sand and stand for what is right. For many in affluent communities around the country, the challenge is to get a grip on our materialism so we can invest in spiritual gain. For all of us, following in Christ's footsteps will involve having a heart that breaks for the pain of those who are still searching for love and meaning because they have yet to find Christ. We, too, face the possibility of regret and the inevitable question, "Why did I wait so long?"

Soon after her pulpit debut, at least one of God's reasons in calling Catherine Booth to preach became clear. William became ill. Because of his slow recovery, Catherine took over his entire preaching circuit, her dynamic and forceful speaking style drawing crowds of thousands. When William recovered they were able to work together again in a revivalistic ministry that involved preaching, rescue-mission work (especially with teenage prostitutes), founding the Salvation Army, and training their own children into the ministry. Many agree that, as important as her work with the Salvation Army was, Catherine's thirty years of preaching ministry was perhaps most significant. "No man of her era exceeded her in popularity or spiritual results, including her husband."[8]

I have heard the question asked, almost tongue in cheek, "Why should women be like Christ in humility and suffering, yet unlike him in authority, power, and exultation?" The answer is: There is no reason at all. Catherine Booth is a flesh-and-blood example of what happens when a woman asks the question "How does Christ want to live his life uniquely through me?" and then follows him with freedom and abandon. Spiritual authority is born of her obedience, power is forged as she speaks the truth, and grace pours from her life as she channels her strength to serve others. The exultation comes when we hear those words, "Well done, good and faithful servant."

⌒ SPIRITUAL EXERCISES ⌒

Alone with God

Silence. As you come to the end of this chapter, take a few moments to sit with God in the silence of your own heart. Allow yourself to simply sit with whatever desire has stirred in you through the reading of this chapter.

- As you read this chapter, what aspect of the life of Christ stirred you most deeply?
- Allow yourself to imagine observing Christ in that particular expression of his character. What do you see? What do you feel?

Prayer and journaling. Review what you have just read, noticing the places of resonance and resistance that you have highlighted. Notice the places where you say, "I really want that" and "I'm not sure I'm up for that!"

What is the one aspect of the life of Christ that you feel called to live into more fully at this time? Tell God what's true about you right now and what you long for. Then listen for his response.

Invitations. *God, how are you inviting me to respond to what I've read today?*

With Your Spiritual Friend(s)

Begin your time together with a moment of silence and a simple prayer of invitation for God to join you.

Listening. Take turns giving each other your undivided attention. Give each other a brief summary of what has happened between you and God this week in the context of your spiritual practices and your reading of this chapter.

- What did God say to you in your times of solitude and silence?
- What were your experiences of resonance and resistance as you read this chapter? How did you process those with God in your journal?
- How do you feel about the possibility of being a unique expression of Christ's life in this world?
- As you observe Christ's way of being in the world, what stirs in your heart in terms of your desire to be transformed into his likeness? What is your intent?

Prayer. At the end of your time together, take time to pray for one another. In preparation for this time of prayer, you might want to review the themes of this book and identify those things that stand out as God's clearest invitations to each of you. Then pray that God would continue to enable each of you to respond faithfully to his invitations to truth, freedom, and spiritual transformation.

STRATEGIES FOR WOMEN AND MEN WORKING TOGETHER

As discussed in chapter 4, God himself decided that the world would be a better place if women and men worked together as a team. But working together has gotten a little complicated lately. At times one wonders if it is possible for men and women to work together in the midst of change and controversy. How can we nourish teamwork today, not only in the church but also in our marriages and our working relationships? Following are some practical steps, which are fleshed out in more detail in my book *Equal to the Task: Men and Women in Partnership at Work, at Church, at Home* (InterVarsity Press, 1998).

MAINTAIN RESPECT AND INTERDEPENDENCE

Respect is a fairly intangible quality, and yet we can all sense when it is there and when it is not. For Christian women and men, mutual respect is rooted in several broad scriptural themes, as we have noted in earlier chapters. The first is that every human being—female and male—is created in the image of God and is responsible for filling, ruling, and subduing the earth (Genesis 1:26-28). Second, the Bible teaches us that every Christian is a priest with responsibility for offering up spiritual sacrifices and proclaiming the excellencies of Christ (1 Peter 2:5,9). Closely related to this concept of the priesthood of all believers is the reality that men and women are interdependent upon one another for our *physical* lives ("In the Lord, neither is woman independent of man, nor is man independent of woman. For as the woman originates from the man, so also the man has his birth through the woman," 1 Corinthians 11:11-12, NASB) and for our *spiritual* lives in the body of Christ ("To each one is given the manifestation [gift] of the Spirit for the common good," so that none of us can say to another " 'I have no need of you,' " 1 Corinthians 12:7,21, NASB).

As we consciously remind ourselves that "this woman or man reflects the image of God to me; he or she is a royal priest just as I am and I need him or her to work alongside me in order to carry out my priestly responsibilities," it will begin to transform our own attitudes and consequently our relationships.

AVOID STEREOTYPES

"All men ever think about is sex." "Women are so emotional you just can't take them seriously." "Real men don't cry." "All women like children." Most stereotypes are either insulting or gross generalizations. Kaye Cook and Lance Lee, in their book *Man and Woman: Alone and Together,* point out that stereotyping is a natural process our mind engages in as it tries to sort out reality.

> Stereotyping (magnifying the differences between the sexes) is harmful and negative, both to women and men. Stereotyping causes us to judge or reject others without getting to know them. This process makes us respond to another based on our expectations, not on the reality of the other person's needs and personality…and to limit our own or another's response to God's calling.[1]

Gender stereotypes are dangerous because they go beyond what the Scriptures have to say about being created male and female. Indeed, they trap us in very small boxes created by our culture rather than freeing us to become all that we are in Christ. The more we believe the stereotypes, the less chance we have of really knowing and understanding one another. True respect takes us beyond stereotypes based on gender (or anything else!) to a place where we recognize the uniqueness, the mystery, and the potential in every human being.

FOSTER EFFECTIVE COMMUNICATION

It is important to realize that conflict is a normal part of any relationship; however, when two people are communicating effectively they will be able to deal with it. If people are *not* communicating effectively they will find themselves in continual conflict. That is why we cannot overstate the importance of effective communication between men and women who are working together. This communication should include frequent, informal conversation ("Say, how did your committee meeting go?" or "You did a great job organizing that social event.") as well as quality time in which more substantial matters are discussed and input is given and received. This happens in several ways.

Acceptance
Effective communication begins with simply recognizing the other person as a worthy individual entitled to his or her own experiences and opinions. Men and women often have very different perceptions of the same situation, and when one or both assume that their thoughts and feelings are the only valid ones, communication is quick to die. It is much better to acknowledge that I might learn something because you have knowledge and perspective that are worth hearing.

Careful Listening

An effective communicator learns how to clarify what the other person is saying. This is the process described in Proverbs 20:5, by which a man or a woman of understanding draws out the true meaning of what is in someone else's heart. Rather than assuming that we have understood the person who is speaking, we check it out to make sure that what we heard is what they really meant: "Are you saying that...?" "I heard you say... Did I understand you right?" "What do you mean when you use that word?" "I'm not quite clear on that. Could you explain it to me again?" The speaker then knows that he or she is being heard accurately or has the opportunity to say, "Well, not exactly. What I really meant was..."

Empathy

This requires us to stand in someone else's shoes, to "rejoice with those who rejoice, and weep with those who weep" (Romans 12:15, NASB). This is an especially important element in relationships between men and women because our experiences within our families, our churches, and our society are so different. Our understanding of each other will be inadequate unless we know, to some degree, what it feels like to be in the other's situation. When a man enters into a woman's experience by asking, "What would it be like for me if I were told I couldn't do things I really wanted to do because I'm a man?" he will respond to her struggle with greater sensitivity. Likewise, when a woman understands how unsettling it would be to have all your rules for relating with the opposite sex turned upside down, she may look for more sensitive ways to approach men with the changes she is looking for.

Empathy requires us to move away from our own experience as the measure of all things and to learn about life and perhaps even ourselves from someone else's vantage point. It takes a very secure person with a lot of self-discipline to set aside her own beliefs and feelings long enough to fully enter into someone else's. It requires listening until you can see how his experience of the situation makes sense. Empathizing doesn't necessarily mean that we agree, but that we are able to say, "In the context of your experience, I can see how you would feel that way or why you have made that choice." Even when we don't agree, to know that we have been heard and understood means a great deal and keeps the relationship growing.

Direct Communication

It is important that men and women deal directly with each other, especially when we start to notice tension. It may be easier to avoid situations that involve conflict or to talk with members of our own sex, because the chances of being understood and agreed with seem higher. While these approaches may keep us within our own comfort zones, we can be assured that by choosing them we will not learn anything new about the person with whom we are dealing. Without direct communication the gulf between men and women struggling to work together will only widen. It is no wonder that the Scriptures are so consistent in telling us that the direct approach is best (Matthew 5:23-24; Ephesians 4:25-27).

Sensitivity to Gender Differences

In *You Just Don't Understand,* linguist Deborah Tannen states that conversation between women and men is very much like cross-cultural communication! Although each style is equally valid, misunderstandings arise because the styles are different. However,

> learning about style differences can banish mutual mystification and blame. Being able to understand why our partners, friends, and even strangers behave the way they do is a comfort, even if we still don't see things the same way.... And having others understand why we talk and act as we do protects us from having the pain of their puzzlement and criticism.[2]

One of the most helpful insights Tannen offers is the importance of learning to distinguish between the *message* and the *metamessage* in conversation. The message is the obvious meaning of an act, such as sharing a problem or giving advice. However, it is the metamessage that really counts. This is the underlying message about the relationships among the people involved and their attitudes about what they are saying and the person to whom they are saying it. And it is at this level that problems usually occur.

For instance, many women complain that when they share a problem with a man, he is too quick to offer a 1-2-3 solution rather than empathy or comfort. According to Tannen, when a woman shares a problem, her underlying message is a bid for an expression of understanding ("I know how you feel" or "That must have been awful for you") or a similar complaint ("I felt the same way when..."). When she doesn't get this kind of reinforcement but gets advice instead, she is likely to hear the underlying message: "We're not the same. You have the problem; I have the solutions."[3] Of course, this isn't the meaningful connection she was looking for.

On the other hand, men tend to be more utilitarian in their approach to conversation. They aren't looking for connection; they are looking to get the job done. Consequently, it is easy for them to feel frustrated when, as one man put it, "women want to wallow in their problems rather than taking our advice and getting on with it." In addition, many men see themselves as problem solvers, so when a woman presents a struggle or a complaint, they offer a solution because they assume that this is what is being asked of them. Most often they offer a solution out of a sincere desire to be helpful. When that help is rejected, it hurts![4]

Once we understand that these two levels of conversation exist and begin being sensitive to them in our conversations, we can tell each other more directly what we want and need. Now that I know about conversational styles, I preface my conversations with my husband about problems by saying, "I need to talk to you about something and I would really like to be able just to 'emote' for a while before we start discussing solutions." Chris is also free to say at any time, "I'm really frustrated because I feel like there is nothing I can do to help." To which I might reply, "I can understand how you would feel that way, but this really *is* helping." In this way we are being much clearer about what we want and need in the conversation, and both of us are getting it more often.

KEEP A BALANCED VIEW OF EMOTIONS

Before going into a meeting with a group of men about a very emotional topic, I remember being told: "Be sure not to cry because then they won't hear you." Well, that was a frightening prospect, so I spent most of my emotional energy that evening making sure I didn't cry. For this group of men, that was probably good advice. But I couldn't help wondering if that was my only option, or if we could have found some sort of middle ground between their discomfort with emotion and my need to express it.

Christians tend to have a deep distrust of emotions, and this puts women at a disadvantage because, in general, women are more emotionally expressive than men. This can result in discomfort for men, as well as in fear about losing respect and credibility on the part of the women. The uneasiness we experience in the face of deep emotion is puzzling to me because it isn't consistent with what we see in the Scriptures. There we learn that you can be angry and not sin (as Jesus did). You can weep over the loss of a friend (as David did). You can be beastly with jealousy and, by admitting it, take the first step to getting free of it (as the psalmist did). You can sing and dance with joy (as Moses and the Israelites did). You can weep with passion for ministry (as Paul did). Rather than reasons for not hearing or respecting an individual, emotions are signs of life and authentic relationships with God and others.

Our uneasiness in the face of deep emotion can result in significant losses to the team. As one writer describes in *Harvard Business Review:*

When an organization [including the church] either denies the validity of emotions or seeks to permit only certain kinds of emotions, two things happen. The first is that managers cut themselves off from their own emotional lives. Even more important, they cut off the ideas, solutions, and new perspectives that other people can contribute.[5]

Because women are traditionally more in touch with feelings and more comfortable expressing them than men, we may well be the ones to lead the way toward a healthier view of emotions. But here, as in many areas, there is a need for balance. In *Getting Together,* Roger Fisher and Scott Brown offer four suggestions for balancing emotion and reason.

Develop an Awareness of Your Emotions

Why do we need to acknowledge our emotions? Because

insecurity, frustration, fear, or anger can take hold and begin to affect our actions without our realizing what is happening. [If we fail to] recognize our own feelings or the feelings of others, it will be difficult indeed to control how we express them. And if we cannot control how we express our emotions, we are unlikely to deal well with substantive issues.[6]

Emotions are experienced in our bodies as physical sensations such as a tightening of the stomach muscles, tension in the jaw, sweaty palms, quicker heartbeat, raised voice, lump in the throat, and tears. By paying attention to my body's signals I have the opportunity to distance myself from my emotions for a moment. Then I can analyze them and think about how I want to respond.

Take Charge of Your Behavior Instead of Merely Reacting

Most women would welcome the opportunity to be more confident in controlling how they express their emotions in pressured or painful situations. We are able to do this once we are more practiced at recognizing our emotions. I realize now that my greatest fear going into the meeting I mentioned earlier had nothing to do with the content of the material I was to present (I was very well prepared) or the quality of my work up to that point (it had been very well received). My greatest fear was that I would not be able to control my responses to the emotions I usually experienced regarding the subject we were discussing. Being out of control was a very frightening prospect indeed. I had not yet learned to create a quiet space within myself from which I could observe my own emotions and then make a conscious choice about what I was going to do or say next. Without that skill, I knew I was at the mercy of some of my strongest emotions. I didn't want to rid myself of them, but wanted to control their influence on my behavior.

One of the great benefits of practicing the disciplines of solitude and silence is that, over time, they help us increase our capacity for internal quietness in the midst of external noise, chaos, and complexity. From that quiet place we can observe external circumstances, notice our emotional reactions, and choose to respond based on truth, our core values, and spiritual insight.

Acknowledge and Talk About Emotions

Fisher and Brown go on to point out that rather than ignoring or suppressing emotion, the third step in achieving a balanced approach is to acknowledge how we feel. While we may try to hide our emotions for fear of the consequences of showing them, denying emotions doesn't make them go away, it only makes them harder to deal with…. Unless we reveal our emotions at least to ourselves, potentially destructive feelings like anger and resentment can fester until they flare into an outburst that causes long-term damage to a relationship. Furthermore when we hide our feelings we may be ignoring underlying substantive problems (in the relationship) that need attention.[7]

One way to deal with emotions is to talk about them. Explaining ("I am starting to feel frustrated because I keep getting interrupted.") rather than displaying or denying the way we feel actually demonstrates self-confidence, honesty, and self-control—all qualities that build trust in a relationship. Our purpose in acknowledging our emotion is not to blame the other person; it is important that we accept responsibility for our emotions and behavior. But we do want to explain them to the other person so that negative feelings will not stand in the way of a good working relationship.

Prepare for Emotions Before They Arrive

Whenever our emotions catch us off guard, we are more likely to react than to make a rational choice about how we want to respond. Any work we can do to anticipate our emotions and plan our response in a given situation will take us a step further toward balance. For instance, a woman who doesn't have children and finds that being asked about it dredges up feelings of pain or frustration can plan her response ahead of time. Choosing a lighthearted response ("That's kind of personal, don't you think?") or a more serious one ("That's something I'm really struggling with right now.") in advance of a situation—say, before she attends a family gathering where it always comes up—puts her more in control than if she were unprepared for the torrent of emotions that may come.

The more we practice recognizing emotions such as anger or disappointment, acknowledging them to ourselves and to those with whom we are working, giving ourselves enough space to analyze them, and choosing a constructive response, the more effective we will be in our team relationships. Every time men and women are able to work through this process with each other, we gain new confidence that we can handle whatever comes up as we partner together. Emotions become less frightening and we're able to view them as important sources of information and guidance. We realize that we really can be angry (or sad or frustrated or disappointed), and yet not sin (Ephesians 4:26).

TOOLS FOR TEAMBUILDING

Chris and I started working as a team in ministry shortly after we started working as a team in marriage, and it didn't take us long to discover that becoming an effective team doesn't happen by accident. What did happen "by accident" is that our egos collided, insecurity and competitiveness surfaced, and communication became more challenging under the pressure of tasks that needed to be accomplished.

In response to these realities, we have identified three sets of questions that help us deal with important issues before we get into the heat of tense moments. By answering these questions together, with equal regard for the other's input, we have formed a stronger foundation for our working relationship.

1. *What are our goals for the area in which we are working together? How can those goals best be accomplished?* Each of us has very personalized expectations as we approach different tasks and opportunities. We can envision what we would like to see happen and what we would like our role in that to be. Taking time to put these longings into words and brainstorming ways that they can become reality gives each of us a greater sense of ownership in

whatever we are doing together. "Being…intent on one purpose" (Philippians 2:2, NASB) is a key to unity.

2. *What are the strengths that each of us brings to this task? How can we fully utilize these strengths in accomplishing our goals?* Sometimes it is easier to feel threatened or competitive regarding the other person's gifts than to plan ways of allowing those gifts to blossom. However, when we begin our working relationships by sharing strengths and weaknesses and planning ways to help each other grow, we level the playing field and pave the way for true teamwork.

3. *What values are important to us as we work together? How will we deal with difficulties that arise?* Every team experiences conflicts and misunderstandings. Rather than being taken by surprise, we can prepare for the inevitable by deciding ahead of time what qualities are important in the relationship and how we will proceed when the going gets tough. We gain a great deal of trust in each other and confidence in the relationship when we have committed ourselves to speaking directly with one another about problems; listening until both of us feel heard; confessing stubbornness, competitiveness, and pride; getting help from an objective third party when necessary. Any team that begins by discussing these issues will greatly enhance their ability to work together.

God's challenge to us is to learn to function as a team for greater results than we could achieve alone. Mutual respect and acknowledging our need for one another will help. So will effective communication, a balanced view of emotions, and an avoidance of stereotypes. But it is Christ among us, who breaks down dividing walls through the power of his blood (Ephesians 2:13-14), who will take us the rest of the way.

A P P E N D I X   B

A LOOK AT 1 TIMOTHY 2:11-12 AND GOD'S VIEW OF WOMEN

As chapter 4 suggests, 1 Timothy 2:11-12 offers an opportunity to wrestle with a complex scripture passage. Addressing the church in Ephesus, Paul wrote, "Let a woman learn in silence with full submission. I permit no woman to teach or to have authority over a man; she is to keep silent." This is the primary passage from which people infer that women are to be limited in the scope of their ministry. While an exhaustive study of this passage and related research is beyond the scope of this book, I would like to provide an overview of important new research that sheds greater light on these difficult verses.

HISTORICAL CONTEXT

At the time Paul wrote this letter to believers, Ephesus stood as a bastion of feminine supremacy in religion. The shrine of the great mother goddess Artemis (or Diana, as the Romans knew her) was located in Ephesus, and there she was worshipped as the mother of gods and men. It was believed that she was the originator of life and her presence or intervention guaranteed economic and political security.

It was in this religious climate that gnosticism, with its radical distortions of biblical stories, began to develop and infiltrate the church. One such distortion twisted the story of Eve to say that she was the one who brought life to Adam. Richard and Catherine Kroeger write: "According to gnostic thought, all matter was evil. The Creator, the God of the Hebrew Bible, was evil because he made the material world. The serpent was beneficent in helping Adam and Eve to shake off the deception perpetrated on them by the Creator, and Eve was the mediator who brought true knowledge to the human race."[1]

The veneration of Eve that grew out of this gnostic distortion dovetailed perfectly with the practice of goddess worship that was already firmly entrenched in the religious psyche of those living in the first century. It was a logical progression to mythologize and deify Eve as the mediator of truth and special hidden knowledge. Gnostics developed an entire belief system that claimed that mystic knowledge resided not only in feminine figures of sacred literature (such as Eve and Mary the mother of Jesus) but also in actual gnostic women who were willing to share their divine secrets. These secrets were often conveyed through the use of repetitious syllables, riddles, and paradoxes that apparently made sense to gnostics themselves but were very difficult for anyone else to understand and refute.

Paul wrote to his young protégé, Timothy, for the express purpose of encouraging him to stay at the church in Ephesus to combat such false teaching: "I urge you…to remain in Ephesus so that you may instruct certain people not to teach any different doctrine, and not to occupy themselves with myths and endless genealogies that promote speculations rather than divine training that is known by faith." (1 Timothy 1:3-4). The church in Ephesus was not a healthy church; it was in crisis due in part to confusion about the woman's role as mediator of religious truth. Rules that were harsher than normal were needed to give these women an opportunity to learn and submit themselves to the true mediator of knowledge—Jesus Christ, as revealed in the Scriptures and the teaching of the apostles.

KEYWORDS

It is important that we understand the meaning of two keywords: *hesuchia* (translated "silent" in many versions of 1 Timothy 2:11-12) and *authentein* (translated "to have authority" in verse 12).

According to widely respected Greek scholar W. E. Vine, the Greek word *hesuchia* denotes "quietness" or "tranquility arising from within."[2] He does not even list "silence" as a possible translation. Consistent with this definition, *hesuchia* is translated "quiet" in 2 Thessalonians 3:12 "Such persons we command and exhort in the Lord Jesus Christ to do their work quietly *[hesuchia]* " and 1 Timothy 2:2 "so that we may lead a quiet *[hesuchia,* adjective form] and peaceable life."

There is a world of difference between the absolute silence implied by the translations to which most of us have had access and the quiet tranquility that a more careful translation describes! We need to ask ourselves, why would the translators make this kind of a word choice? What impact does a more accurate translation have on our understanding of the role of women?

The Greek word *authentein* presents us with a different kind of challenge. Although there are several other Greek words translated "authority" in the New Testament,[3] this is the only time the Greek word *authentein* appears there. In cases like this it is common practice for translators to turn to secular literature of the same time period for further clues as to the meaning of such a rare word. However, in the case of the word *authentein,* it is not that easy. Until this century, it was not found in any other works written around Paul's time! With this keyword being so difficult to pin down, no wonder scholars have found the passage hard to understand.

Fortunately, recent scholarship has uncovered new information about this rarely used word. Greek scholars Richard and Catherine Kroeger offer a fascinating study of *authentein* based on their extensive research of ancient history and literature. By tracing this word through ancient documents, they have found that it had a wide range of meanings as follows:

1. to begin something, to be primarily responsible for a condition or action (especially murder)
2. to rule, to dominate
3. to usurp power or rights from another
4. to claim ownership, sovereignty, or authorship[4]

Furthermore, new sources in classical Greek literature demonstrate that *authentein* is often used to describe religious activity that was characterized by promiscuity and reversal of gender roles, sex and death mingled together in cultic practice, murder, and women claiming a monopoly on religious power (as among the Amazons). In addition they found several older dictionaries in which *authentein* is defined "to represent oneself as the author, originator, or source of something."[5] This definition is particularly interesting in light of the fact that in the ancient world of Asia Minor, many viewed women as the ultimate source of life. These meanings put a whole new spin on 1 Timothy 2:12 as we consider how a more careful translation might clarify Paul's meaning.

Again, why would Paul, a scholarly writer, use such a rare word that carried with it such unpleasant connotations? If he meant to bar women from all legitimate authority, he could have used any of the other words that are much more straightforward in their meaning.

GRAMMATICAL STRUCTURE

The grammatical structure of verse 12 is noteworthy. It contains three infinitives: to teach, *authentein,* and to be. The Kroegers suggest that the separation of "to teach" from the other infinitives (apparent in any Greek New Testament or interlinear) may indicate that one or more of these two infinitives deal with the content of a woman's teaching. They point out that Paul never used the infinitive "to teach" without accompanying clarification as to the content of the teaching. In Pauline writing, the infinitive "to teach" is always accompanied by another verb that serves to sharpen its focus. For instance, in 1 Timothy 1:3-4 Paul said "instruct certain people not to teach any different doctrine, and not to occupy themselves with myths and endless genealogies." And in 1 Timothy 6:3 he spoke of one who "teaches otherwise and does not agree with the sound words of our Lord Jesus Christ." The verb "to teach" *(didaskein),* linked as it is to the verb *authentein* by the negative *oude* (meaning "nor"), gives us the possibility that *authentein* serves to explain what *kind* of teaching is prohibited to women. An alternate translation would then be, "I do not permit a woman to teach nor represent herself as originator (or source) of man, but she is to be peaceable."[6]

As you can see, translation is a complex process that is full of many challenges. When we translate the inspired Word of God from the original language, we face the difficulty of word equivalency and cultural considerations. Translators often have a range of English words to choose from when translating particular Greek words into English. The final word choice is left to their discretion. Also, in Greek sentence structure, the words are not in the order to which we are accustomed. This requires that the translators (again, at their discretion) arrange the words in an order that makes sense to the English reader. This is a process that is subjective, at best, and yet the order of words can have a significant impact on meaning.

It is difficult for a translator to maintain objectivity; the temptation always exists to translate a passage to be consistent with the way one already sees life. When we consider that most translators have been men who have come out of societies that did not appropriately value women and some of their gifts, it is not so difficult to see how some of the more obscure words and passages could be translated with a bias. That's why it is so important for us as women to become students of the Scriptures ourselves rather than merely taking other people's word for it. Then we can do our own hard work of discovering what God is saying to us through his Word.

STUDY GUIDE FOR
INDIVIDUALS OR GROUPS

In addition to thinking through the spiritual exercises found at the end of each chapter, or in their place, you may want to follow a more structured approach to working through this book. The study guide below offers questions for individual reflection and journaling or group discussion.

Chapter 1: The Freedom to Make Life-Giving Choices

1. Tell about a choice you've made that turned out to be a right choice. What helped you make that choice? Or, tell about a choice that turned out to be a wrong choice. What were the consequences of that choice? What could have helped you make a better one?

2. What are some of the main influences in your life right now as you make choices? How do you feel about the direction these influences are encouraging you to take?

3. How do the practices of solitude and silence fit into your life right now? In what ways do you feel drawn to be more intentional in incorporating these into your life?

4. What are some of the choices you are facing right now? What can you do to slow down and listen to God as you contemplate these choices?

Chapter 2: The Freedom of Finding Our Identity in Christ

1. Describe yourself in some way that would give others a good sense of who you are. How do you feel about the person you have just described?

2. As quoted in the chapter, Anne Morrow Lindberg says that a "woman must come of age by herself—she must find her true center alone." Do you agree or disagree with this statement? Why or why not?

3. What early experiences shaped your feelings about yourself? When did you feel that you were significant or insignificant? When did you feel unique and separate from others? When did you feel "part of the group"? When did you first start to realize that you could make an impact on the world?

4. What kind of information were you given about how the world works? What experience did you have in learning to use that information? Did you have a clear idea of what was right and wrong? Do you feel the information you were given was adequate enough that you could take care of yourself, or were you led to believe that someone else would take care of you? What impact has this made on your life choices?

5. Which of the essentials of self-esteem are you deficient in right now? What kinds of experiences could you structure in order to begin acquiring these essentials?

6. Do you feel you are prepared for the time when you may have to journey on with Christ alone? If not, what steps would you like to take to prepare for this eventuality?

Chapter 3: The Freedom to Say Yes to God's Purposes

1. What are some of the gifts, opportunities, burdens, and preparations that God is blending together in your life right now? Do you have a sense that God has brought you to this time and place for a purpose? (If your answer is no, don't force it. God will make it clear in his time.)

2. As you think about what God may be calling you to do, what are the limitations you face? How will you approach these areas?

3. What is your plan of action for accomplishing the purposes that God is impressing upon your heart? What will you need to say yes to and what will you need to say no to?

STUDY GUIDE FOR INDIVIDUALS OR GROUPS

Chapter 4: The Freedom to Serve God in the Way That He Calls

1. All of us begin collecting impressions of what it means to be male or female long before we learn how to evaluate their truthfulness. As a child, what were some of the impressions—both positive and negative—that you collected about what it means to be female? What were you taught about how God viewed you as a woman? What thoughts and feelings did you have about these impressions?

2. Now that you are an adult, do you agree or disagree with what you learned as a child about God's view of women and our place in his plan? Explain.

3. If a woman who was searching for the truth about God expressed her impression that "Christianity is male religion, written by men, for men, with a male God," how would you respond? How would you demonstrate your beliefs from your own experience of God and your understanding of the Scriptures?

4. Has there ever been a time when you felt limited in some way by your gender? How did you respond at the time? How would you respond now?

Chapter 5: The Freedom to Live in Truth

1. Can you think of a situation in which you felt that the only way to get what you wanted was to be manipulative? What was the result of your manipulation?

2. "Men who stand up for themselves are [seen as] competent and assertive; women who do the same are obnoxious and aggressive." Do you agree or disagree with this statement? How comfortable do you feel about your strength at home, at church, at work?

3. Identify a relationship in which you need to do more truth-telling, whether in your everyday communication patterns, regarding your life experiences, or regarding issues that affect your relationship. What fears do you have about taking this step? What steps are you willing to take to achieve authenticity in this relationship?

4. Is there a true question, a lingering doubt, something you know about yourself (but have been hesitant to look at) that you need to explore in order to achieve more "truth in the inward being"? Who or what could help you with this exploration? Are you willing to pursue truth in this area?

Chapter 6: Freedom from the Tyranny of the "Never Enough" World

1. If you had to leave your home as suddenly as Lot's wife did for physical or moral reasons, what would be the hardest thing for you to leave behind?

2. Describe an incident during the past week or two in which a television commercial, magazine ad, or salesman "sold to your hidden needs." Did you succumb to the sales pitch? Why or why not?

3. To which of the dangers of materialism are you most vulnerable?

4. Which of the questions raised in this chapter interests you the most on a personal level? Do you have enough quiet in your life to explore the answers?

Chapter 7: The Freedom of Unity in Marriage

1. Do you feel that your marriage is "big enough for both of you"? Explain.

2. In what areas have you had to stretch or are you now stretching to accommodate growth and change in each other? How do you feel this is going?

3. How do you feel about the way you and your spouse make decisions? What happens when you just can't agree?

4. How easy or difficult is it for you and your spouse to discuss problems (such as outside attractions, disappointments with your spouse) in your marriage? Do you have someone to whom you can go for help when you need it?

5. On a scale of one to ten (ten being the highest) how do you feel your marriage is working? How do you think your spouse would rate it? (Go ahead and ask!) What changes would be meaningful to one or both of you? In what areas is your marriage vulnerable to attack?

Chapter 8: The Freedom to Embrace Our Sexuality

1. What were some of the early messages—positive and negative— you received about sex? How do you think they affected your sexual development? What about early sexual experiences?

2. How comfortable are you with looking at your sexuality in the context of spirituality? Explain your answer. Is this a new concept for you?

3. What sexual stereotypes have you spotted that have affected your sexual functioning? Can you identify other stereotypes not addressed in this chapter?

4. If you are married, do you feel that you have had adequate information about sexuality in preparation for and during your marriage? What kind of information did you need, or what misinformation caused you trouble? Where would you have liked to get this information?

5. Describe your experiences of being a sexual person in a state of singleness. What was (or is) most difficult about it? What were (or are) some ways in which you were (or are) able to be comfortable with your sexuality even though you were (or are) not married?

6. What would you like to communicate to the next generation—your children, grandchildren, nieces and nephews, teenagers in the church—about their sexuality? What would you communi-

cate that was the same or different from what you were told? Brainstorm practical ways in which this could be done.

Chapter 9: Freedom from the Role of Supermom

1. Although the Scriptures tell us that children are a gift from the Lord (Psalm 127:3-5), in today's society they are often viewed as a nuisance or an interruption. Why do you think children seem to be "God's least-wanted blessing"?

2. How does an understanding of God's role in conception and birth affect your view of children? How can we communicate God's view of children to those around us?

3. Practically speaking, what does it mean for you to love your child(ren)? What factors keep us (men and women) from throwing ourselves wholeheartedly into parenting?

4. What are some of the things that only you can give to your child(ren)? What do you need to do to ensure that your children receive these things from you?

Chapter 10: Freedom in the Midst of Difficulty

1. What is causing difficulty or pain in your life right now? What are your current patterns of coping with this difficulty?

2. Which of Abigail's character qualities do you admire most? Which would be most beneficial for you to develop in your life right now—especially as it relates to the situation you described in question one? (Remember, God doesn't expect you to work on everything at once!)

3. Describe a time when someone "let you in" on their pain in a way that was meaningful for you. What impact did that have on you? How difficult is it for you to allow others to see your pain?

4. What do you need to do to keep growing spiritually even though you have this area of difficulty in your life? What good can you see coming from it?

Chapter 11: *The Freedom to Reach Across Generations*

1. Describe a relationship with an older woman that was beneficial to you. What was it about this woman that made you willing to learn from her? What kinds of things did you learn?

2. What are some of the potential pitfalls of such relationships? How can these pitfalls be avoided?

3. In your particular setting and stage of life, how easy or difficult has it been for you to begin and maintain cross-generational relationships? Brainstorm ways that you and others can facilitate these friendships.

Chapter 12: Free to Be Christ in the World

1. What seems most challenging to you about living as Christ in your corner of the world? How do you think Christ wants to live his life uniquely through you at this time?

2. What aspect of the Christ-life is most difficult for you to give yourself to at this time?
   ❑ singleminded focus on doing God's will
   ❑ relaxing into the process of learning and growing
   ❑ speaking the truth and/or standing for what is right
   ❑ moving with compassion
   ❑ serving others

   What would be the next step of obedience for you in this difficult area?

3. Looking back over the themes of this book, what are the areas of truth and freedom that God seems to be inviting you into more deeply? (You may want to pick two or three.)

RESOURCES FOR FURTHER STUDY AND REFLECTION

You may want to look into the following books for further study on the themes discussed in this book. Please note that inclusion of a work on this list does not signify my endorsement of all its content. Rather, its inclusion here is meant to indicate that it is a significant source that warrants serious consideration.

Chapter 1

Barton, Ruth Haley. *Becoming Women of Purpose*. Colorado Springs: Shaw, 2001.

Miley, Jeanie. *The Spiritual Art of Creative Silence*. Wheaton, Ill.: Shaw, 1996.

Tucker, Ruth. *Multiple Choices*. Grand Rapids: Zondervan, 1992.

Willard, Dallas. *Hearing God: Developing a Conversational Relationship with God*. Downers Grove, Ill.: InterVarsity, 1999.

Chapter 2

Hsu, Al. *Singles at the Crossroads: A Fresh Perspective on Christian Single-ness*. Downers Grove, Ill.: InterVarsity, 1997.

Littauer, Florence. *Wake Up, Women! Submission Doesn't Mean Stupidity*. Dallas: Word, 1994.

Malcolm, Kari Torjesen. *Women at the Crossroads.* Downers Grove, Ill.: InterVarsity, 1982.

Miller, Jean Baker. *Toward a New Psychology of Women,* 2nd ed. Boston: Beacon Press, 1976.

Rivers, Caryl, Rosalind Barnett, and Grace Baruch. *Beyond Sugar and Spice: How Women Grow, Learn, and Thrive.* New York: Putnam, 1979.

Tschirhart Sanford, Linda and Mary Ellen Donovan, *Women and Self-Esteem.* New York: Penguin, 1984.

Van Vonderen, Jeff. *Tired of Trying to Measure Up.* Minneapolis: Bethany House, 1989.

Chapter 3

Barton, Ruth Haley. *Becoming Women of Purpose.* Colorado Springs: Shaw, 1992, 2001.

Biehl, Cheryl. *I Can't Do Everything!* Sisters, Oreg.: Questar, 1990.

Covey, Stephen. *The Seven Habits of Highly Effective People.* New York: Simon & Schuster, 1989.

Hersh, Sharon A. *Bravehearts: Unlocking the Courage to Love with Abandon.* Colorado Springs: WaterBrook, 2000.

Chapter 4

Barton, Ruth Haley. *Equal to the Task: Men and Women in Partnership at Work, at Church, at Home.* Downers Grove, Ill.: InterVarsity, 1998.

Bilezikian, Gilbert. *Beyond Sex Roles.* Grand Rapids: Baker, 1985.

Kroeger, Richard and Catherine Clark. *I Suffer Not a Woman.* Grand Rapids: Baker, 1992.

Osiek, Carolyn. *Beyond Anger.* New York: Paulist Press, 1986.

Tucker, Ruth. *Women in the Maze.* Downers Grove, Ill.: InterVarsity, 1992.

Tucker, Ruth and Walter Liefeld. *Daughters of the Church*. Grand Rapids: Zondervan, 1987.

Van Leeuwen, Mary Stewart. *Gender and Grace*. Downers Grove, Ill.: InterVarsity, 1990.

Chapter 5

Backus, William. *Telling Each Other the Truth*. Minneapolis: Bethany House, 1985.

Backus, William and Marie Chapian. *Telling Yourself the Truth*. Minneapolis: Bethany House, 1980.

Hybels, Bill. *Honest to God?* Grand Rapids: Zondervan, 1990.

Lerner, Harriet Goldhor. *The Dance of Deception*. New York: Harper-Collins, 1993.

Schaeff, Anne Wilson. *Women's Reality*. San Francisco: Harper & Row, 1981, 1985.

Chapter 6

Bellah, Mike. *Baby Boom Believers*. Wheaton, Ill.: Tyndale, 1988.

Jones, Landon Y. *Great Expectations: America and the Baby Boom Generation*. New York: Coward, McCann & Geoghegan, 1980.

Packard, Vance. *The Hidden Persuaders*. New York: Simon & Schuster, 1957.

Starkey, Mike. *Born to Shop*. E. Sussex, U.K.: Monarch, 1989.

Chapter 7

Barton, Ruth Haley. *Equal to the Task: Men and Women in Partnership at Work, at Church, at Home*. Downers Grove, Ill.: InterVarsity, 1998.

Bilezikian, Gilbert. *Beyond Sex Roles*. Grand Rapids: Baker, 1985.

Gundry, Patricia. *Heirs Together: Mutual Submission in Marriage*. Grand Rapids: Zondervan, 1980.

Kindig, Eileen Silva. *Goodbye Prince Charming: The Journey Back from Disenchantment.* Colorado Springs: Piñon, 1993.

Olthuis, James. *I Pledge You My Troth.* San Francisco: Harper & Row, 1975.

Van Vonderen, Jeff. *Families Where Grace Is in Place.* Minneapolis: Bethany House, 1992.

Chapter 8

Castleman, Robbie. *True Love in a World of False Hope: Sex, Romance, and Real People.* Downers Grove, Ill.: InterVarsity, 1996.

Crooks, Robert and Karla Bauer. *Our Sexuality,* 5th ed. Redwood City, Calif.: The Benjamin-Cummings Publishing Co., 1993.

Cutrer, William and Sandra Glahn. *Sexual Intimacy in Marriage.* Grand Rapids: Kregel, 1997, 2001.

Dawn, Marva. *Sexual Character: Beyond Technique to Intimacy.* Grand Rapids: Eerdmans, 1993.

Dillow, Linda and Lorraine Pintus. *Intimate Issues: 21 Questions Christian Women Ask About Sex.* Colorado Springs: WaterBrook, 1999.

Hybels, Bill. *Tender Love: God's Gift of Sexual Intimacy.* Chicago: Moody, 1993.

Penner, Clifford and Joyce. *The Gift of Sex.* Waco, Tex.: Word, 1981.

Smedes, Lewis B. *Sex for Christians: The Limits and Liberties of Sexual Living.* Grand Rapids: Eerdmans, 1976, 1994.

Smith, Harold Ivan. *Singles Ask: Answers to Questions about Relationships and Sexual Issues.* Minneapolis: Augsburg, 1988.

Starkey, Mike. *God, Sex, and the Search for Lost Wonder.* Downers Grove, Ill.: InterVarsity, 1998.

Chapter 9

Adeney, Miram. *A Time for Risking.* Portland, Oreg.: Multnomah, 1987.

Clapp, Rodney. *Families at the Crossroads: Beyond Traditional and Modern Options.* Downers Grove, Ill.: InterVarsity, 1993.

Kroeker, Ann. *The Contemplative Mom.* Colorado Springs: Shaw, 2000.

Malcolm, Kari Torjesen. *Women at the Crossroads.* Downers Grove, Ill.: InterVarsity, 1982.

Stonehouse, Catherine. *Joining Children on the Spiritual Journey: Nurturing a Life of Faith.* Grand Rapids: Baker, 1998.

Thompson, Marjorie. *Family the Forming Center.* Nashville: Upper Room Books, 1997.

Van Leeuwen, Mary Stewart. *Gender and Grace.* Downers Grove, Ill.: InterVarsity, 1990.

Van Vonderen, Jeff. *Families Where Grace Is in Place.* Minneapolis: Bethany House, 1992.

Yates, Susan Alexander. *And Then I Had Kids: Encouragement for Mothers of Young Children.* Dallas: Word, 1988.

Chapter 10

Crabb, Larry. *Shattered Dreams.* Colorado Springs: WaterBrook, 2001.

Monk Kidd, Sue. *When the Heart Waits: Spiritual Direction for Life's Sacred Questions.* New York: HarperCollins, 1992.

Nouwen, Henri. *The Wounded Healer.* New York: Doubleday, 1972.

Olsen, Kathy. *Silent Pain.* Colorado Springs: NavPress, 1992.

Tada, Joni Eareckson. *A Step Further.* Grand Rapids: Zondervan, 1990.

Yancey, Phillip. *Disappointment with God.* Grand Rapids: Zondervan, 1988.

Regarding Domestic Violence and Other Abuse:

Alsdurf, James and Phyllis Alsdurf. *Battered into Submission.* Downers Grove, Ill.: InterVarsity, 1989.

Fortune, Marie. *Keeping the Faith: Questions and Answers for the Abused Woman.* San Francisco: HarperSanFrancisco, 1989.

Johnson, David and Jeff Van Vonderen. *The Subtle Power of Spiritual Abuse.* Minneapolis: Bethany House, 1991.

Rinck, Margaret J. *Christian Men Who Hate Women.* Grand Rapids: Zondervan, 1990.

Scott, Catherine. *Breaking the Cycle.* Elgin, Ill.: David C. Cook, 1988.

Streeter, Carole Sanderson. *Finding Your Place after Divorce.* Wheaton, Ill.: Shaw, 1992.

Chapter 11

Barton, Ruth Haley. *Ruth: Relationships That Bring Life.* Colorado Springs: WaterBrook, 2001.

Brestin, Dee. *The Friendships of Women.* Wheaton, Ill.: Victor Books, 1988.

Clinton, J. Robert. *Connecting: The Mentoring Relationship You Need to Succeed in Life.* Colorado Springs: NavPress, 1992.

Kraft, Vicki. *Women Mentoring Women.* Chicago: Moody, 1992.

Weems, Renita. *Just a Sister Away.* San Diego: Luramedia, 1988.

Chapter 12

Groothuis, Rebecca Merrill. *Women Caught in the Conflict: The Culture War Between Traditionalism and Feminism.* Grand Rapids: Baker/Revell, 1993.

Nouwen, Henri. *In the Name of Jesus: Reflections on Christian Leadership.* New York: Crossroad, 1993.

Piper, John. *Desiring God.* Portland, Oreg.: Multnomah, 1986.

Swindoll, Charles R. *Improving Your Serve.* Waco, Tex.: Word, 1981.

Yancey, Philip. *The Jesus I Never Knew.* Grand Rapids: Zondervan, 1995.

Appendix A

Barton, Ruth Haley. *Equal to the Task: Men and Women in Partnership at Work, at Church, at Home.* Downers Grove, Ill.: InterVarsity, 1998.

Cook, Kaye and Lance Lee. *Man and Woman: Alone and Together.* Wheaton, Ill.: Scripture Press, 1992.

Fisher, Roger and Scott Brown. *Getting Together: Building Relationships as We Negotiate.* New York: Penguin Books, 1988.

Tannen, Deborah. *You Just Don't Understand: Women and Men in Conversation.* New York: Ballantine, 1990.

_____. *Talking from 9 to 5.* New York: William Morrow, 1994.

NOTES

Chapter 1

1. William Ecenbarger, "The Bane of Democracy," *Chicago Tribune Magazine,* March 10, 1991, 24.

2. Barbara Walters in *The Quotable Woman* (Philadelphia: Running Press, 1991), 15.

3. Ecenbarger, "The Bane of Democracy," 25.

4. Jaclyn Fierman, "Why Women Still Don't Hit the Top," *Fortune,* July 30, 1990, 58.

5. Linda Tschirhart Sanford and Mary Ellen Donovan, *Women and Self-Esteem* (New York: Penguin, 1984), 219.

6. Kay Ebeling, "The Failure of Feminism," *Newsweek,* November 19, 1990, 9.

7. Alice Slaikeu Lawhead, *The Lie of the Good Life* (Portland, Oreg.: Multnomah, 1989), 54.

8. Fierman, "Why Women Still Don't Hit the Top," 58.

9. Peggy Orenstein, *Flux: Women on Sex, Work, Love, Kids, and Life in a Half-Changed World* (New York: Anchor Books, 2000), 4, 17.

10. Parker Palmer, *To Know As We Are Known* (New York: Harper Collins, 1993), 124.

11. Material on silence and solitude adapted from Ruth Haley Barton, "Beyond Words," *Discipleship Journal*, Sept./Oct., 1999, 34-9.

Chapter 2

1. Anne Morrow Lindberg, *Gift from the Sea* (New York: Pantheon Books, 1955, 1975), 16-7.

2. Lindberg, *Gift from the Sea,* 128.

3. *Chicago Tribune,* quoted in *Marriage Partnership* (Summer 1991), 27.

4. Caryl Rivers, Rosalind Barnett, and Grace Baruch, *Beyond Sugar and Spice: How Women Grow, Learn, and Thrive* (New York: Putnam, 1979), 25.

5. Linda Tschirhart Sanford and Mary Ellen Donovan, *Women and Self-Esteem* (New York: Penguin Books, 1984), 40.

6. Emily MacFarquhar, "The War Against Women," *U.S. News and World Report* (March 28, 1994), 44.

7. Following are some of the realities reported in the MacFarquhar article (pp. 44-56):

   • In the new Russia, women applying for office jobs are often told that their duties include sleeping with the boss. A typical want ad reads, "Not older than 25; bright appearance, long legs compulsory."

   • In China, India, and other nations where sons are still valued more highly than daughters, ultrasound is now being used to determine the sex of babies so that females can be aborted or poison can be administered at birth.

   • In some Islamic countries, rape *victims* are charged and imprisoned for adultery. Those who try to fight such inequities receive death threats, have their passports revoked and their writings banned.

   • In parts of Africa, the Middle East, and Asia, genital mutilation, a custom in which all or part of a girl's outer genitalia is removed, is still practiced. Female circumcision (removal of the hood of the clitoris), clitoridectomy (removal of the clitoris), or genital infibulation (removal of the clitoris and labia, stitching the vulva together, leaving only a small opening for urine and menstrual flow) are procedures performed without anesthesia, causing severe medical problems and removing almost any possibility for sexual pleasure.

   • In India, bride burnings, dowry-murders, "stove burstings" (so-called "domestic accidents" in which a young wife is killed) are common forms of domestic violence that take the lives of many women whose families cannot keep paying for their protection. In countries where dowries can add up to ten times a man's annual income, dowry extortion is very common and there is little protection for the women who are being used as merchandise.

- In industrial nations, women's pay still averages two-thirds that of men's, mainly because women are clustered in low-wage "women's jobs." In the United States, for instance, year-round full-time working women earned 71 percent of the male wage in 1992, and women high-school graduates earned slightly less than did men who dropped out of school before ninth grade.

8. Sanford and Donovan, *Women and Self-Esteem*, 3.

9. Kari Torjesen Malcolm, *Women at the Crossroads* (Downers Grove, Ill.: Inter-Varsity, 1982), 40-1.

10. Lawrence J. Crabb, *Understanding People* (Grand Rapids: Zondervan, 1987), 112.

11. In Jewish culture women were viewed as little more than the "property" of fathers or husbands. In addition, Jews viewed Samaritans as "leftovers" from Israel because they intermarried with foreigners after the chiefs and nobles had been captured during the Babylonian captivity. "Real Jews" despised Samaritans because they felt that the Samaritans had sold their birthright. Consequently, they had forced the Samaritans to build their own place of worship at Mount Gerazim. Most Jews avoided contact with the Samaritans at all costs, choosing to go around Samaria rather than through it.

12. Jesus told her that God was abolishing the old way of worshipping, which was based on outward rituals. In its place, he was ushering in a new kind of worship that was not associated with any outward trappings but involved the spirit of the worshipper (John 4:23). This would be a radical shift!

13. Sanford and Donovan, *Women and Self-Esteem*, 12.

14. Penelope Russianoff, *Why Do I Think I Am Nothing Without a Man?* (New York: Bantam, 1981), 3.

15. Mary Stewart Van Leeuwen, *Gender and Grace* (Downers Grove, Ill.: Inter-Varsity, 1990), 46.

16. Crabb, *Understanding People*, 110.

17. Rivers, Barnett, and Baruch, *Beyond Sugar and Spice*, 18.

18. For an excellent discussion of practical information women need to have, see *Wake Up, Women! Submission Doesn't Mean Stupidity,* by Florence Littauer (Dallas: Word, 1994).

19. Marie Chapian, *Staying Happy in an Unhappy World* (Old Tappan, N.J.: Revell, 1985), 37.

Chapter 3

1. Edgar Lee Masters, "George Grey," *Spoon River Anthology* (1st edition, 1915; New York: Penguin Books, 1992).

2. One commentator notes, "had the king been sober, he would not have considered such a breach of custom, for he knew that Eastern women lived in seclusion and that such a request as he made in this drunken condition amounted to a gross insult. For Vashti to appear in the banquet hall, though dressed in her royal robes and crowned, would be almost as degrading as for a modern woman to go naked into a man's party. What Xerxes demanded was a surrender of womanly honor, and Vashti, who was neither vain nor wanton, was unwilling to comply." Herbert Lockyer, *All the Women of the Bible* (Grand Rapids: Zondervan, 1958), 165-6.

3. Stephen Covey, *The Seven Habits of Highly Effective People* (New York: Simon & Schuster, 1989), 98.

4. Miriam Adeney, *A Time for Risking* (Portland, Oreg.: Multnomah, 1987), 61.

5. Adeney, *A Time for Risking,* 56-7.

6. For a step-by-step workbook on purposeful living, see Ruth Haley Barton, *Becoming Women of Purpose* (Colorado Springs: Shaw, 1992, 2001).

Chapter 4

1. Linda Tschirhart Sanford and Mary Ellen Donovan, *Women and Self-Esteem* (New York: Penguin Books, 1984), 173.

2. You can read about these women in 1 Samuel 25, Judges 4–5, 2 Kings 22:14-20, the book of Esther, and Acts 18:24-26 respectively.

3. This Bible study is now published as *Women Like Us: Wisdom for Today's Issues* (Colorado Springs: Shaw, 1989, 2001).

4. Faith Martin, *Call Me Blessed* (Grand Rapids: Eerdmans, 1988), 123.

5. Ruth A. Tucker, *Women in the Maze* (Downers Grove, Ill.: InterVarsity, 1992), 37-8.

6. L. E. Maxwell, as quoted in Richard Kroeger and Catherine Clark Kroeger, *I Suffer Not a Woman* (Grand Rapids: Baker, 1992), 33.

7. The Kroegers note that the phrase "silence and submission" is a Near Eastern formula implying willingness to heed and obey instruction—in this case that instruction contained in the Word of God. Indeed, the rabbinic scholar himself was required to learn in silence as this was how one gained knowledge of God (*I Suffer Not a Woman*, 75-6).

Chapter 5

1. In Bible times, the blessing from father to son was like an oral will that was legally binding and could not be revoked. Each child usually received a blessing, but the oldest son got a special one that included prosperity, headship over his family, and divine judgment on those who opposed him. In the case of Esau, his father's blessing would also have included the privilege of having God's promise to Abraham fulfilled through him ("I will make you the father of a multitude of nations," Genesis 17:4-5, NASB).

2. It was assumed that Rebekah died during Jacob's long absence and was buried in the cave of Machpelah near Hebron (Genesis 49:31). (From *All the Women of the Bible* by Herbert Lockyer [Grand Rapids: Zondervan], 140).

3. Harriet Goldhor Lerner, *The Dance of Deception* (New York: HarperCollins, 1993), 14.

4. Linda Tschirhart Sanford and Mary Ellen Donovan, *Women and Self-Esteem* (New York: Penguin Books, 1984), 44.

5. Bill Hybels, *Honest to God?* (Grand Rapids: Zondervan, 1990), 51.

6. Lerner, *The Dance of Deception,* 49.

7. Carolyn Stahl Bohler, *When You Need to Take a Stand* (Louisville, Ky.: Westminster/John Knox, 1990), 63.

8. William Backus, *Telling Each Other the Truth* (Minneapolis: Bethany House, 1985), 26. Feminine pronouns mine.

9. Hybels, *Honest to God?* 56.

10. Backus, *Telling Each Other the Truth,* 16-7.

11. Lerner, *The Dance of Deception,* 218.

Chapter 6

1. Materialism is the theory that physical well-being and worldly possessions constitute the greatest good and highest value in life.

2. Vance Packard, *The Hidden Persuaders* (New York: Simon & Schuster, 1957), 14.

3. Packard, *The Hidden Persuaders,* 30.

4. Packard, 16.

5. Landon Y. Jones, "The Baby Boomers," *Money* (March 1983), 300.

6. Mike Bellah, *Baby Boom Believers* (Wheaton, Ill.: Tyndale, 1988), 22.

7. Mike Starkey, *Born to Shop* (E. Sussex, U.K.: Monarch, 1989), 35.

8. John F. Walvoord and Roy Zuck, eds., *The Bible Knowledge Commentary* (Wheaton, Ill.: Victor, 1985), 60.

9. Starkey, *Born to Shop,* 106-7.

10. Starkey, 106-7.

Chapter 7

1. Alice Slaikeu Lawhead, *The Lie of the Good Life* (Portland, Oreg.: Multnomah, 1989), 70-1.

2. James H. Olthuis, *I Pledge You My Troth* (San Francisco: Harper & Row, 1975), 36-7.

3. Girard Kittel, ed., *Theological Dictionary of the New Testament,* vol. 3 (Grand Rapids: Eerdman's, 1965), 673-82.

4. Gilbert Bilezikian, *Beyond Sex Roles* (Grand Rapids: Baker, 1985), 161.

5. Annette LaPlaca, "Teamwork," *Marriage Partnership* (Fall 1993), 87.

6. Julie Connelly, "The CEO's Second Wife," *Fortune,* August 28, 1989, 53.

7. George Barna, *The Frog in the Kettle* (Ventura, Calif.: Regal, 1990), 72.

8. Connelly, "The CEO's Second Wife," 55.

9. Deborah Diamond, "The Affair: Is Betrayal Therapeutic or Merely Common?" *The Chicago Tribune* (WOMANEWS section), Nov. 28, 1993, 11.

10. As quoted in Alice Slaikeu Lawhead, *The Lie of the Good Life* (Portland, Oreg.: Multnomah, 1989), 126-7.

11. As quoted in Harriet Goldhor Lerner, *The Dance of Deception* (New York: HarperCollins, 1993), 164-5.

Chapter 8

1. Ann Landers, *Chicago Tribune* (January 22-23, 1989).

2. Linda Tschirhart Sanford and Mary Ellen Donovan, *Women and Self-Esteem* (New York: Penguin Books, 1984), 389.

3. Marian Liautaud, "What's Amore?" *Marriage Partnership* (Summer 1991), 26.

4. Robert Crooks and Karla Bauer explore this issue in *Our Sexuality* (Redwood City, Calif.: The Benjamin-Cummings Publishing Co., 1993). Child sexual abuse is much more prevalent than many of us realize. It has been only recently that we have begun to lift the shroud of silence that has obscured this painful issue. More and more victims of this abuse of power are finally beginning to speak about their suffering and to grapple with the long-range effect it has had on their lives. As Crooks and Bauer write,

> There is increasing evidence that child sexual abuse can be a severely traumatizing and emotionally damaging experience with long-term negative consequences for the victim. Clinical contact with adult survivors of child sexual abuses often reveals memories of a joyless youth filled with pain. Survivors speak of their loss of childhood innocence, the contamination and interruption of normal sexual development, and

a profound sense of betrayal at the hands of a beloved family [member]
or trusted friend.... Many victims have difficulty forming intimate
adult relationships, particularly with men. When relationships with
men are established, they are frequently devoid of emotional and sexual
fulfillment. Sexual abuse is not uncommon in the histories of women
who seek treatment for sexual difficulties (Crooks and Bauer, 656).

5. Although there are no simple solutions to the pain of sexual abuse, a sexual
    abuse survivor owes it to herself and to those she loves to deal with this difficult
    part of her past. Karen, a survivor of child sexual abuse and rape has this to say:

> Healing is painfully slow and difficult. Both therapists I have worked
> with have suggested a seven-to-ten-year recovery process. I have
> struggled to overcome guilt and shame, finally being able to admit I
> did not invite the experiences of childhood abuse or rape. I am still
> working on remembering parts of my story. I continue to express
> anger and rage, which are essential to my healing. I have learned to
> trust some people. And I still grieve for the losses...I can now cry in a
> limited fashion, and my self-concept and self-esteem are fairly restored.
>
> Incest and rape are not about sex. They are about power and con-
> trol. It's about big people over little people, superior over subordinate.
> To heal requires that I gain a sense of control over my life. I've gained
> enough control to make the transition from victim to survivor. The
> healing process is long, but I've surrendered to the fact that being in
> the process of healing is a respectable and legitimate place to be. I
> deserve to heal. My greatest victory is to break the promise [not to tell]
> and tell my story. I have been able to use the power of writing and
> speech to transform, to change anger, fear, shame and guilt into useful
> tools for cutting away lies and deception. (Quoted in James Newton
> Poling, *The Abuse of Power* [Nashville: Abingdon Press, 1991], 41.)

6. From *SummaTheologica,* 1267–1273. As quoted in David Olive, *Gender Babble: The Dumbest Things Men Ever Said About Women* (New York: Perigee, 1993).

7. "Letters," *Marriage Partnership* (Summer 1994), 9.

8. James B. Nelson, *Body Theology* (Louisville, Ky.: John Knox Press, 1992), 19.

9. As quoted in *The Lie of the Good Life* by Alice Slaikeu Lawhead (Portland, Oreg.: Multnomah, 1989), 114-5.

10. Ann (not her real name) is a friend of the author.

11. Freud was convinced that every woman wished she had a penis and that that is exactly what the clitoris was—a stunted penis. This led him to conclude that erotic sensations, arousal, and orgasm resulting from direct stimulation of the clitoris were all expressions of "masculine" rather than "feminine" sexuality—and therefore were undesirable. At adolescence a woman was supposed to transfer her erotic center from the clitoris to the vagina. If she was not able to do so at this time, psychotherapy was sometimes used to help her attain "vaginal" orgasms. Unfortunately, this theory led many women to believe incorrectly that they were sexually maladjusted. Today we understand that Freud's theory is physiologically inaccurate. (Crooks and Bauer, *Our Sexuality,* 171-2.)

12. Crooks and Bauer, *Our Sexuality,* 68.

13. Clifford and Joyce Penner, *The Gift of Sex* (Waco, Tex.: Word, 1981), 304.

14. Penner, *The Gift of Sex,* 305.

15. Crooks and Bauer, *Our Sexuality,* 79.

16. Elizabeth Haich, as quoted in Gabrielle Brown, *The New Celibacy: Why More Men and Women Are Abstaining from Sex—And Enjoying It* (New York: McGraw-Hill, 1980), 212.

17. As quoted in Dana Kennedy, "The New Monogamy," *The Chicago Daily Herald,* (February 18, 1993), Section 8, 1.

18. Sanford and Donovan, *Women and Self-Esteem,* 401.

19. Crooks and Bauer, *Our Sexuality.*

20. Hurlbert and K. Whittaker, "The role of masturbation in marital and sexual satisfaction: A comparative study of female masturbators and non-masturbators," *Journal of Sex Education and Therapy,* (1991) 17, 272-82.

21. Therapy programs for anorgasmia are based on progressive self-awareness activities such as body exploration, self-examination of the genitals, self-stimulation to learn about pleasure and arousal, and self-stimulation to orgasm. Once a woman has experienced orgasm through self-stimulation, she progresses step-by-step toward experiencing orgasm with her husband by guiding him in stimulating her to orgasm. They can then incorporate what they have learned into their experiences with sexual intercourse. This process takes time and commitment, but can greatly enhance a woman's ability to respond to her husband. Her willingness to take responsibility for learning about herself, for pursuing the pleasure of orgasm and sharing what she has learned with her husband is one of the keys to her sexual fulfillment.

22. The "evils" of masturbation received a great deal of publicity in the name of science during the 1800s and early 1900s, when certain physicians attributed such maladies as blindness, stupidity, consumption, insanity, and idiocy to this practice (Crooks and Bauer, *Our Sexuality,* 252).

    In addition, strongly negative attitudes toward masturbation have been based on the Judeo-Christian view that procreation is the only legitimate purpose for sexual activity. Because masturbation does not result in pregnancy, it has often been condemned. This, added to the sexual/spiritual split we discussed earlier, has made it easy for religious folks to look askance upon this particular way of enjoying one's own body.

    The most obvious negative about masturbation is its capability of controlling us. [There are] many things in this life that are good but have the potential to become enslaving (food, shopping, exercise) or to be used selfishly (sex, money, power). Any habit that causes us to reshape and reschedule the rest of our life has gained undue influence over us. In their book, *The Gift of Sex,* Clifford and Joyce Penner offer three biblical guidelines by which we can evaluate whether masturbation has become a positive or negative activity in our lives. I have adapted them here.

1. *Is it loving?* If our behavior takes something away from our marriage partner, it is not loving. However, if masturbation helps alleviate pressure between two people who have differing degrees of sexual interest or helps a woman learn to be more responsive to her husband, then it could be viewed as a loving choice.

2. *Is it lustful?* Some people feel that you have to lust in order to enjoy self-pleasuring. However, many people report that when they masturbate they think only of their spouse or the physical sensations they are experiencing.

3. *Is it addictive?* If a woman is masturbating excessively as a way of avoiding relationship issues or emotional needs, then this is not healthy. If a woman uses masturbation as a way of becoming more comfortable with her body and her sexuality, then this can be life-enhancing. (For a complete discussion of this topic see Penner, *The Gift of Sex,* 231.)

23. Caryl Rivers, Rosalind Barnett, and Grace Baruch, *Beyond Sugar and Spice: How Women Grow, Learn, and Thrive* (New York: Putnam, 1979), 207.

24. M. Scott Peck, *Further Along the Road Less Traveled* (New York: Simon & Schuster, 1993), 225.

25. As stated in a personal interview with the author. Used by permission.

Chapter 9

1. Linda Tschirhart Sanford and Mary Ellen Donovan, *Women and Self-Esteem* (New York: Penguin Books, 1984), 144.

2. Nancy Gibbs, "Shameful Bequests to the Next Generation," *Time* (October 8, 1990), 43.

3. Philip Elmer-Dewitt, "The Great Experiment," *Time* (Fall 1990, special issue), 72.

4. James Dobson, *Focus on the Family Newsletter* (February 1994), 3.

5. Wendy Wright, *Sacred Dwelling: A Spirituality of Family Life* (Leavenworth, Kan.: Forest of Peace Publishing, 1994), 31.

6. Elmer-Dewitt, "The Great Experiment," 75.

7. Simone Weil, *Waiting for God* (New York: HarperPerennial, 2001).

8. Bill Hybels, *Honest to God?* (Grand Rapids: Zondervan, 1990), 85-8.

9. Hybels, *Honest to God?* 85-8.

10. In Jewish culture the raising of children was a real family affair. Education of the children was the mother's responsibility for the first three years (probably until weaning), but after that, religious education of the sons became the father's responsibility. During this time he also taught them the family trade. In addition, extended families lived together so that grandparents, aunts, uncles, and older children participated in caring for the younger ones.

11. A greater sharing in the joys, frustrations, and hard work of parenting will benefit not only women, but men and their children as well. Mary Stewart Van Leeuwen describes the benefits to children at great length in a chapter on coparenting in her book *Gender and Grace*. As one example she cites a study in which psychologist Michael Yogman found that men and women tend to play with their children in different ways: Fathers were more likely to engage in physical play, tapping or patting younger infants and doing controlled roughhousing with older ones. Mothers made more sounds and played more verbal games with their children, particularly games involving imitation and taking turns. Yogman's conclusion is that "children need both kinds of play for social and intellectual development. The mother-infant dialogues encourage language development and turn-taking, while the father's more physically oriented games help develop spatial and motor skills" (Mary Stewart Van Leeuwen, *Gender and Grace* [Downers Grove, Ill.: InterVarsity, 1990], 158) Other studies indicate that, later on, a father's availability or absence also affects such things as academic achievement (in sons in particular) and career success (in girls in particular). Of course the benefits to the child's self-esteem are incalculable when there are two adults who are highly involved and available (as opposed to the "exclusive mothering and marginal fathering" that is so common).

12.   Personal interview with Rev. Steve Williams. Used by permission.

13.   Van Leeuwen, *Gender and Grace,* 176-7.

Chapter 10

1.   Ruth Tucker, *Multiple Choices* (Grand Rapids: Zondervan, 1992), 111.

2.   Tim Hansel, *You Gotta Keep Dancin'* (Elgin, Ill.: David C. Cook, 1985), 100.

3.   Em Griffin, "What It Takes to Lead People," *Lay Leadership III,* 46.

4.   From a sermon given by Jim Dethmer at Willow Creek Community Church, October, 1990.

5.   My thanks to Bill Hybels for differentiating these categories.

6.   Nancy Gibbs, " 'Til Death Do Us Part," *Time* (January 18, 1993), 41. This article cited the sobering statistic that in 1991 alone, 4 million women were beaten and 1,320 murdered in domestic attacks.

7.   James Alsdurf and Phyllis Alsdurf, *Battered into Submission* (Downers Grove, Ill.: InterVarsity, 1989), 68.

8.   Alsdurf and Alsdurf, *Battered into Submission,* 9-10.

9.   Alsdurf and Alsdurf, 17.

10.   Alsdurf and Alsdurf, 17-8.

11.   Alsdurf and Alsdurf, 18.

12.   Grant L. Martin, *Counseling for Family Violence and Abuse* (Waco, Tex.: Word, 1987), 99-100.

13.   Alsdurf and Alsdurf, *Battered into Submission,* 101.

14.   M. Scott Peck, *The Road Less Traveled* (New York: Simon & Schuster, 1978), 1.

Chapter 11

1.   Gene Getz, *The Measure of a Woman* (Ventura, Calif.: Regal, 1977), 59-61.

2.   Win Couchman, "Cross-Generational Relationships," speaking at Women for Christ conference, 1983.

3.   Alice Slaikeu Lawhead, *The Lie of the Good Life* (Portland, Oreg.: Multnomah, 1989), 144.

Chapter 12

1. "In a real sense, not fully comprehensible, the Incarnation gave the already infinitely wise and perfect Son of God the experiential acquisition of knowledge about the human condition. He had to experience the true meaning of obedience in terms of the suffering it entailed. He was thereby made perfect for the role he would play as His people's Captain and High Priest. Suffering thus became a reality that he tasted and from it he can sympathize deeply with his followers." John F. Walvoord and Roy B. Zuch, eds., *The Bible Knowledge Commentary* (Wheaton, Ill.: Victor, 1983), 792.

2. W. E. Vine, Merril F. Unger, William White, eds., *Vine's Expository Dictionary of Biblical Words* (Nashville: Nelson, 1985), 116-7.

3. Henri Nouwen, *The Wounded Healer* (New York: Doubleday, 1979), 41.

4. Nouwen, *The Wounded Healer,* 41.

5. Ana Gascon Ivey, "Down in the Dumps in Guatemala," *Clarity* (July/August, 1994), 31-5.

6. One of the reasons Christ was able to give so much of himself was because he had a self to give. He knew who he was so he didn't have to prove it, and he replenished himself in the presence of God regularly. On the other hand, a woman who sees herself as one who is "shot full of holes" or "a total blank" doesn't have much self to give. It is hard to lay down your life if you don't have one yet. That's why the issues covered in the early chapters of this book are so important.

7. Ruth Tucker and Walter Liefeld, *Daughters of the Church* (Grand Rapids: Zondervan, 1987), 264.

8. Norman H. Murdoch, "Female Ministry in the Thought and Work of Catherine Booth," *Church History* 53 (September 1984), 354, as quoted in Tucker and Liefeld, *Daughters of the Church,* 269.

Appendix A

1. Kaye Cook and Lance Lee, *Man and Woman: Alone and Together* (Wheaton, Ill.: Scripture Press, 1992), 77.

2. Deborah Tannen, *You Just Don't Understand: Women and Men in Conversation* (New York: Ballantine, 1990), 47-8.

3. Tannen, *You Just Don't Understand,* 32, 50.

4. Tannen, 52.

5. Jeanie Daniel Duck, "Managing Change: The Art of Balancing," *Harvard Business Review* (November/December 1993), 113.

6. Roger Fisher and Scott Brown, *Getting Together: Building Relationships as We Negotiate* (New York: Penguin Books, 1988), 48-9.

7. Fisher and Brown, *Getting Together,* 54-5.

Appendix B

1. Richard Kroeger and Catherine Clark Kroeger, *I Suffer Not a Woman* (Grand Rapids: Baker, 1992), 60.

2. W. E. Vine, Merrill F. Unger, William White Jr., eds., Vine's *Expository Dictionary of Biblical Words* (Nashville: Nelson, 1985), 503.

3. *Huperoche,* meaning "preeminence, superiority, excellency"; *exousia* meaning "the right to exercise power"; *epitage* meaning "command, authority." From Vine's *Expository Dictionary of Biblical Words.*

4. Kroeger and Kroeger, *I Suffer Not a Woman,* 84.

5. Kroeger and Kroeger, 102.

6. Kroeger and Kroeger, 103.

About the Author

Ruth Haley Barton is a spiritual director and retreat leader trained through the Shalem Institute for Spiritual Formation in Washington, D.C., and the Pathways Center for Spiritual Leadership in Nashville, Tennessee. Formerly the associate director of spiritual formation at Willow Creek Community Church, Ruth is now involved in the ministry of spiritual direction, organizational discernment, and teaching and training in the area of spiritual formation.

Ruth is the author of *Equal to the Task: Men and Women in Partnership* and coauthored, with John Ortberg, *An Ordinary Day with Jesus: Experiencing the Reality of God in Your Everyday Life.* A contributor to *The Couples' Devotional Bible* and *Today's Christian Woman Study Bible,* Ruth is also the author of three Fisherman Bible Studyguides, including *Becoming Women of Purpose, Women Like Us: Wisdom for Today's Issues,* and *Ruth: Relationships That Bring Life.*

Raised an evangelical Christian and educated at Wheaton College and Northern Baptist Theological Seminary, in recent years Ruth has been enriched by the contemplative tradition with its emphasis on solitude, silence, and response to the invitations of God in the present moment. In her work as a spiritual director, Ruth's emphasis is on leading individuals, groups, and organizations beyond chaos into the quiet where the still, small voice can be heard.

Ruth lives with her husband, Chris, and their three daughters (ages 11, 16, and 18) in Wheaton, Illinois.